PRAISE FOR *ON THE RUN* BY DANIEL VOLL

"This book can and should be read as a beautifully written memoir. When Daniel Voll ends up in Nick Nolte's pajamas or sharing a bed with a militia leader preparing for civil war, witnessing Nelson Mandela's inauguration, and so much more, you know no one else could have lived this life or rendered it with such captivating prose that it feels more like watching the movie than reading."

—Lawrence O'Donnell, MSNBC

"Voll puts you on the front lines—whether he's hanging with a Bosnian warlord, an Iraqi hunter of terrorists, an 82nd Airborne white supremacist, the father of the H-bomb, or his wife during childbirth. Exciting reading." —Oliver Stone, director

"Shocking and irrefutable reporting . . . a portrait of a world coming apart at the seams." —Mark Warren, 2025 Pulitzer Prize Winner

"Daniel Voll approaches all his subjects—from Malibu movie stars to Serbian war criminals—with a true storyteller's eye. His literary journalism belongs to the best tradition of magazine writing—meticulous, provocative, deeply human, and always compelling. My favorite of this rich collection is an extraordinary piece on a pair of incestuous siblings that is at once compassionate and devastating."

—Patricia Evangelista, author of *Some People Need Killing: A Memoir of Murder in My Country*

"*On The Run* is not a traditional collection of journalism. It is a book of nonfiction short stories, written as if by a recording angel. Daniel Voll may choose ethnic-cleansers, aspiring assassins and eccentric actors as his subjects, but he never treats them as anything but people, and so is able to bring them to dangerous and funny life without the usual insulation of authorial judgement. These are stories stripped of journalistic apparatus, and hence they are the finest kind of journalism; they take care not to offer explanations, and hence they explain everything." —Tom Junod, author of *In the Days of My Youth I Was Told What It Means to Be a Man*

"It is quite a thing to behold a master of his craft at the peak of his powers as Daniel Voll is here in *On The Run*. How does one even describe the stories collected within? Long-form journalism? Gonzo narrative? How about plain old, knock-down, no-shit literature? If you scour the finest magazine writers of the past decades, you'd be blessed to count on one hand those who match Voll's daring, breadth of insight, and ability to break your heart a half dozen ways on a single page. This collection is an astounding display of intuition and raw talent." —Gregg Hurwitz, *New York Times* bestselling author of the *Orphan X* series

"Unblinking dispatches that stand the test of time, and that remain as fresh, compelling, and relevant as when first published. Voll lets the story come to him, without preconception or judgment. The reader is always there, a fly on the wall to his fly on the wall. Be warned that Voll's characters may take up residence in your mind for weeks." —Kevin Sack, *New York Times* bestselling author of *Mother Emanuel: Two Centuries of Race, Resistance, and Forgiveness in One Charleston Church*

"Hold on to your hats . . . these are ripping yarns!" —David Mamet

"Voll is crazy and we're lucky for it. This journalist has a compulsion for putting himself in the most dangerous places, getting a story, and making it out alive—giving readers astonishing tales of life on the fringes with murderous antiabortionists, mass murderers, and nazis within the US military. He even transforms the pro forma "celebrity profile" into what would work as a fictional short story were he not writing about real people. In each of the pieces in *On the Run*, Voll raises journalism to the level of art."
—Michael Ruhlman, *New York Times* bestselling author of *Soul of a Chef*

"Voll was one of the first to see the political danger ahead, and his reporting from inside extremists' bunkers maps in real time how we got here. These stories have a madcap feel, as if we're heading off to see the Wizard of Oz, but somewhere along the way, we take a detour and end up at the gates of hell."
—Jervey Tervalon, author of *Understand This*

"Daniel Voll sees the unhinged as our brothers and sisters. He dives into their water—lives in it, breathes it, swallows it whole. And, back on shore, gulps it back out here for us to see the insanity of our moment, the horror of our time. It's all here, spilled on the living room rug. It's also funny as hell."
—Terry McDermott, *New York Times* bestselling author of *The Hunt for KSM: Inside the Pursuit and Takedown of the Real 9/11 Mastermind, Khalid Sheikh Mohammed*

"As a reporter, Daniel Voll has the gift to gain the confidence and trust of the most reluctant, seemingly unapproachable subjects. Unafraid of the darkness, Voll guides us through mysterious parts of the human experience with an unceasing desire to see things as they are. Which is always more than first appears. There is an undeniable moral core that informs each of these stories."
—Alex Belth, editor of *What Makes Sammy Jr. Run? Classic Celebrity Journalism Volume 1*

MORE FROM
THE SAGER GROUP

The Stacks Reader Series
The Cheerleaders: A True Story by E. Jean Carroll
An American Family: A True Story by Daniel Voll
Flesh and Blood: A True Story by Peter Richmond
An Accidental Martyr: A True Story by Chip Brown
Death of a Playmate: A True Story by Teresa Carpenter
The Detective: And Other True Stories by Walt Harrington
Soldiers in the Army of God: A True Story by Daniel Voll
Original Gangster: A True Story by Paul Solotaroff
The Dreamer Deceiver: A True Story by Ivan Solotaroff
Mary in the Lavender Pumps: A True Story by Joyce Wadler
The Strange and Mysterious Death of Mrs. Jerry Lee Lewis
by Richard Ben Cramer

General Interest
The Stories We Tell: Classic True Tales
by America's Greatest Women Journalists
New Stories We Tell: True Tales
by America's New Generation of Great Women Journalists
Newswomen: Twenty-five Years of Front-Page Journalism
The Devil & John Holmes: And Other True Stories by Mike Sager
Lifeboat No. 8: Surviving the Titanic by Elizabeth Kaye
Stopping the Road: The Campaign Against a Trans-Sierra Highway
by Jack Fisher
Notes from the Road: A Filmmaker's Journey through American Music
by Robert Mugge
What Makes Sammy Jr. Run?: Classic Celebrity Journalism Volume 1,
edited by Alex Belth
Into the River of Angels: A Novel by George Wolfe

See our entire library at TheSagerGroup.net

ON THE RUN WITH MAD BOMBERS, OUTLAW LOVERS & MOVIE STARS

TRUE STORIES

DANIEL VOLL

**On the Run with Mad Bombers, Outlaw Lovers &
Movie Stars: True Stories**

Cover and interior design by Siori Kitajima, PatternBased.com

Cataloging-in-Publication data for this book
is available from the Library of Congress.
ISBN-13:
eBook: 978-1-958861-41-7
Paperback: 978-1-958861-42-4
Hardcover: 978-1-958861-43-1

Published by The Sager Group LLC
(TheSagerGroup.net)

ON THE RUN WITH

MAD BOMBERS, OUTLAW LOVERS & MOVIE STARS

DANIEL VOLL

For Cecilia, who brought me home

CONTENTS

In the laboratory with the mad scientist of Malibu. How the Oscar-nominated actor ended up with a drawer full of syringes and the brain scan of someone who has "experienced the equivalent of blunt trauma." Our journalist becomes his guinea pig.

There comes a time in a man's life when he has to take up with a desperate former New York gangster, a retired Serb-sympathizing Special Forces commando, and a Croat stripper or two and go off to war-ravaged Bosnia in search of Radovan Karadzic, the world's most wanted man.

Patty and Allen are in love. Patty and Allen have four beautiful children. But there's something illegal about that. On the run with the first brother and sister sent to prison for incest in the United States.

Who is killing our doctors? The Army of God believes violence is the only means to end legal abortions. A former dope dealer, a convicted killer, and a mixed-up kid come together to make a hit list. The kid buys a gun.

For years, Private Jim Burmeister and his buddies proudly displayed swastikas in their barracks at Fort Bragg, North Carolina. So why did it take the murder of a Black couple for the US Army to notice its white supremacist problem? A special report from inside the bunker.

You don't know his name, and you've never seen his face. But as America leaves Iraq for good after eight years of war, we also leave behind a man believed by our military and intelligence agencies to be the best terrorist hunter alive. He's still there, hunting. And so are the terrorists.

In the wake of the Rodney King verdicts, American society ruptured in South Central, L.A., resulting in the worst riots in our nation's modern history. This is the life story of ten-year-old Jelani Stewart, who came into this world as his city burned.

A month on the run in South Africa, during the election of Nelson Mandela, with the mad bombers of the ultra-right wing Afrikaner resistance.

Like many Americans, Bobby Crabtree felt that only a gun could protect his family. Then, one night, he shot his daughter. A journey through the nation's gun culture.

When the bomb hit, John Trochmann's Militia of Montana went on red alert, called up the FBI, and headed for a strip joint. An intimate week in the bunker with the most dangerous patriots in America.

Billy Bob Thornton is writing, directing, or starring in six movies in the next year—and recording an album with Johnny Cash. He's newly married but hasn't seen his movie-star wife in months. He can't sleep in his own house. Billy Bob has trouble sleeping at all.

In the delivery room—drinking Guinness, listening to The Rolling Stones, and battling a doctor.

Why get married when we're having so much fun? To marry or not to marry.

Bosnia's Muslim prime minister longs to be in Hollywood development hell.

Edward Teller helped build the hydrogen bomb—the most powerful bomb ever invented. He believes he saved the world. Interviewed at 93, in Palo Alto, California.

With filming just wrapped on a Hollywood version of *The Crucible*, Arthur Miller, at eighty, talks witches and Marilyn Monroe.

The Nobel Prize winner wants to open your brain, literally. Francis Crick on free will, artificial intelligence, and his hunt for the human soul.

Novelist Nadine Gordimer and poet Jeremy Cronin were born into South Africa's "big white country club." Cronin spent seven years inside maximum-security prisons for his underground work with the ANC. Gordimer wrote to him in prison, and a friendship formed. In a country now under emergency rule, both writers keep fighting to dismantle the apartheid regime.

FOREWORD

At about 10 p.m. on October 23, 1998, in a suburb of Buffalo, New York, Dr. Barnett Slepian had just returned from Friday evening services at his synagogue and was in his kitchen making soup. As he talked with his kids, a round from a high-powered rifle shattered the window of the kitchen, slamming into Slepian's spine, and shredding his aorta. His wife and kids tried desperately to save him, but he was already gone. Dr. Slepian was an OB/GYN, and as part of his practice he also performed abortions. He was the third abortion provider in America to be murdered by militant anti-abortion activists in the 1990s, and the first to be murdered at home, his assailant having set up his rifle and scope in the woods near the doctor's house, laying in wait.

The next day Daniel Voll and I met at the *Esquire* offices to talk about Slepian's murder, and the growing armed anti-abortion movement. It was a gruesome and frightening story, the sort that would be covered exhaustively but superficially in the churn of the news. To do it right and make it distinctive would require the sort of immersion that Daniel did better than anyone. The challenge, as ever, was finding a way into the story. I had by then been at *Esquire* for ten years—for the first couple of years as a fact checker before starting to assign stories and work with writers. Daniel had come to the magazine several years earlier with a letter of introduction from John Sack, one of the greatest magazine writers ever. They had met skiing in Idaho, or they had met fighting over the same girl in Idaho—I never quite got it straight. (It was John who had written the longest piece to be published in *Esquire*—33,000 words—the October 1966 cover story on M Company, from basic training at Fort Dix, New Jersey to combat in Vietnam, with its stark white type on a black background: "Oh my God—we hit a little girl.") I was looking for writers to call my own, and the recommendation of a legend carries a lot of weight. John Sack's letter of introduction landed on my desk, and in early 1994 Daniel and I met and began a conversation that I hope will never end.

By the day of Dr. Slepian's murder in the fall of 1998, Daniel and I had worked on several stories together—in August 1994, his first story for the magazine had had him embedding with the right-wing bombers who were determined to disrupt South Africa's first multi-racial democratic elections ever, the next year he had embedded with right-wing state militias in Florida, Michigan, and Montana, before the Oklahoma City bombing, and before anyone had ever even heard of the "militia movement," and the year after that, he had gone to Ft. Bragg, North Carolina and embedded with active duty members of the 82nd Airborne Division who also happened to be avowed nazis, and were openly wearing swastikas on their flight jackets on base. An airman from the 82nd named Jimmy Burmeister had murdered a Black couple as they strolled home one evening in nearby Fayetteville, a sick initiation ritual into a white supremacist order. It was that shocking crime that had sent Daniel to Ft. Bragg, where he discovered and documented the fact that Burmeister had not been alone, but was rather just one in a vibrant subculture of active-duty nazis in the United States military. That story got the magazine into a brawl with the Pentagon before Daniel's piece was even published, with the Secretary of the Army attacking the magazine as liars—until Daniel's shocking and irrefutable reporting (which included photos of active-duty paratroopers in their barracks, saluting the flag of the German Reich) caused the secretary to get very quiet very fast.

You may have noticed that a pattern was emerging. Daniel didn't report. Daniel *embedded*. And that is how he became a master of long-form narrative journalism, producing classic after classic during the very lucky fifteen years or so that I got to work with him most intimately. When he showed up for a story, he would simply stay, and never leave, as he was convinced that if he left—to go back to the hotel, or grab dinner, or even just relax for a moment like most mortals would require—then the most important parts of the story would be happening without him. While he was at the bar, the truth would be revealed. So the bar could wait. Even assign-ments that seemed comparatively easy would become all-or-nothing propositions for Daniel. Once we sent him to profile the actor Nick Nolte, figuring that a clash of eccentrics would stand a chance of yielding something people might need to read. We didn't realize that Nolte had embarked on a mission to repair all of the damage he'd done to himself over the years with drug and drink, and that he'd make Daniel his guinea pig for all of his homemade potions, elixirs, injections, and inhalation therapies. By the time that Daniel staggered out of Nolte's Malibu encampment, he wasn't sure how long he'd been there. Probably days, but who could really be sure?

The more difficult the subject, the longer Daniel would camp out. He had inexhaustible energy and a lovely and exceedingly rare quality for a journalist—there was no question that he wouldn't ask. He was incapable of embarrassment. Some journalists want to show a subject how much they know, and engage in a test of wills. They'll prove themselves to be so smart that they might miss the story that is right in front of them, entirely. Daniel would take the opposite approach—he would empty himself out and say, *Tell me everything.* Like a child he would ask questions—probing, pushing, humanizing, figuring it out, hoovering every last detail and turning the material into the astonishing tableaus of deeply human literary journalism in this book. Taken together, these pieces make up a portrait of a world coming apart at the seams.

Something at once awful and extremely interesting was happening in America in the 1990s. Since the fall of the wall, with the world having lost the also awful but certainly stabilizing effect of the Cold War, the United States—newly bereft of any sort of grand strategy for organizing the world—seemed to no longer know how to behave. Almost out of boredom it seemed that we as a country decided to turn on ourselves. And there were suddenly a thousand flashpoints for anyone paying attention. The somnolent stability of the old world order had given way, and amid the new chaos, there were important stories everywhere. What may have been terrible for the American civilization was a lightning rod for a free agent like Daniel Voll, who had no attachments, a reporter's sharp eye, a poet's ear, and a crazy sense of story. I was amazed by his willingness to just throw himself into even the most complex settings, with the most difficult or even dangerous subjects.

Speaking of danger: It wasn't just the United States that was coming apart. When Yugoslavia broke into ethno-states and genocide again erupted in the heart of Europe, led by a maniacal Serb psychiatrist named Radovan Karadzic, Daniel packed thousands of dollars in cash and went to Bosnia, which was then regarded as the most dangerous spot on this dirty globe, to pursue the war criminal. For months he would stay, in only sporadic touch, immersing himself in the conflict, surrounded by killers, black marketeers, Serb nationalist fanatics, and assorted other lovers of death, returning home twenty-five pounds lighter and with as deep an understanding of that conflict as any journalist working. I remember thinking to myself during that time that just because he is so talented and willing, that's no reason to get Daniel killed.

After lunch on the day following Barnett Slepian's assassination—as news spread about a website called "The Nuremberg Files" that kept dossiers on abortion doctors and clinic employees and escorts, and had apparently given the killer the information he needed to find Slepian and murder him in his kitchen—we planned our approach. A wire story mentioned that the zealot who ran the website was named Neal Horsley, an IT guy who lived in Marietta, Georgia. He fashioned his website as a hit list. Horsley had drawn lines through the names of the dead doctors and clinic personnel and changed the font color of the wounded from black to gray, as if to say, *Better luck next time.*

Horsley was a nut, possibly an accessory to an extraordinarily high-profile murder, and he seemed proud of this fact. This was an important story. And Horsley was a perfect subject for Daniel. That is, of course, easy for me to say, from the safety of my midtown high rise. We were young, had some very presumptuous notions of pushing the form, and thought we knew what we were doing. We didn't. But when you don't know what you're doing, you also don't know what you're not allowed to do. By this time, Daniel had taken to saying that he was "Mark Warren's hunting dog," and that he was good for retrieving any bird in any swamp anywhere. He was extraordinarily good at that, and never failed to find a story that he went looking for. But that formulation is totally wrong, and annoyingly humble. It's more accurate to say that I was Daniel Voll's case officer, or maybe travel agent. I would manage the logistics, and he would take all the risks. I'll leave it to you to figure out who had the more important job. He inspired me, utterly, and I pushed him. As he was about to leave for Georgia, I said, "Daniel, help us understand how you get to be a human being like Neal Horsley. Sleep on his couch. Watch him brush his teeth."

I didn't think he'd actually do exactly that.

He did exactly that.

By October 30—one week after Dr. Slepian's brutal murder in upstate New York—Daniel sent me a picture on what must have been the very first email server. As I sat in my office in that midtown high rise, I opened the file to see a photo of Neal Horsley and Daniel Voll sitting on Horsley's front porch, carving pumpkins for Halloween.

Daniel would tag and bag Horsley, writing a story of such dimension and danger—documenting his extremism and active recruitment of young like-minded people to his violent cause—that Horsley would be a watched figure for the rest of his life, his danger blunted, his extremism impaired. And that's not even counting the artistry of the story's writing. All for the price of a magazine.

I worry that with the fortunes of magazine publishing not what they once were, work that requires this degree of commitment and love isn't being done anymore, or at least not as much as it once was. All the more reason to celebrate the miracle of these stories. I hope you enjoy them. They are the work of a great reporter, a true artist, and a damn fine man.

—Mark Warren, 2025 Pulitzer Prize Winner;
Editor, *Esquire* 1988–2016

AUTHOR'S NOTE

I'd never done a celebrity interview. I wasn't even sure I knew how. I'd recently returned from an assignment chasing a war criminal in post-war Bosnia; but with a baby at home in New York, I'd promised my wife I'd take fewer risks, at least for a while. The interview was in Malibu with the actor, Nick Nolte. He'd just made two movies and was up for an Oscar. I could do the interview and be home in a day. What could go wrong?

I dove into the research, boned up on Nolte's films, wrote a list of questions. Got out my microcassette recorder, packed my duffle, and flew to LA. I was driving to Malibu when my phone rang. It was my wife. I'd left my tape recorder on the kitchen counter. *Shit.* My appointment with Nolte was in 30 minutes. My wife told me there was a RadioShack in Malibu. At the store, the clerk sold me a new tape recorder. He asked what I was up to. I told him I was interviewing Nick Nolte. *Cool,* he said, and told me Nolte came in here all the time hunting parts for his microscope. *Science is his thing. He's got a big microscope.*

You saw this, right? The clerk pulled the latest issue of *Playboy* from under the counter. Nolte was on the cover, and inside was one of those wide-ranging, comprehensive interviews that *Playboy* was famous for. Flipping through the pages confirmed my fear: all my planned questions had been answered by Nolte. My interview would just be a rehash. I felt stricken and stupid. How could I not have known? I drove to Nolte's house feeling dread. I called my wife from the car. *What do I do?* She said, *Just stay in the moment. Let go of everything. When you meet him, say whatever comes to your mind.*

When I arrived, Nolte was barefoot, wearing striped pajamas. I shook his hand and blurted the first thing that came to my mind: *Congratulations on the Nobel Prize. Can we talk about your latest science project?* His eyes brightened. Nolte rubbed his hands with glee. *Let's go upstairs!* I followed him up to his laboratory, where I spent the next twenty-four hours. By the time the interview was over, I was wearing Nolte's pajamas.

In most of the stories collected here, I never knew what would happen next. The story was going to take me where it wanted. My job was to stay alive and take notes.

I was just out of college in 1984 when I pitched my first freelance story to *Vanity Fair*. That assignment sent me to South Africa to cover the anti-apartheid resistance; a decade later I returned for *Esquire* to follow Nelson Mandela as he ran for President. My days were spent with Mandela, and my nights with right wing bombers who vowed to kill him and disrupt the nation's first democratic elections.

Many of these stories are about political violence and killers, subjects that preoccupied my reporting from the '90s onward. What I was hearing among extremists at home and abroad was jolting, terrifying. The lone wolves, it ended up, weren't so alone.

I also chased love stories, including one about a brother and sister who had kids together. I traveled to Wisconsin to meet Patty and Allen. Both were in maximum-security prisons—the first brother and sister ever imprisoned for felony incest. In Milwaukee, I watched them in the back hallway of the courthouse, each in hand-cuffs and waist chains. I saw their hands touch, and a stolen kiss. I wanted to understand Patty and Allen's emotional hunger. I realized they were outlaw lovers—and that this was a love story, which would allow me to interrogate the taboo itself and the very nature of love as a reckless, consequential act.

I've included a few personal pieces (on the birth of my son for Esquire; on my marriage for *The New York Times*). "Riot Baby" remains one of my favorites, because I met young Jelani Stewart, who was ten years old at the time; Jelani had been born during the 1992 Los Angeles riots. That he and his mother trusted me to come into their lives for the nine months I reported the story is still a miracle to me. That Jelani remains in the life of my family is an ongoing blessing.

I spend a lot of time in these stories in the company of violent extremists, here and abroad—some were mass murderers. While reporting on these groups, I wore an old leather holster on my belt. I kept my microcassette recorder visible in the holster. The holster was from my grandfather, who'd been a Wisconsin sheriff during Prohibition. I needed my subjects to understand that my presence wasn't an endorsement. My listening was not affirmation. I wanted no confusion—I needed them to always know I was the journalist, and they were on the record.

This is that record.

—Daniel Voll, 2025

NICK NOLTE IS RACING THE CLOCK TO REPAIR THE DAMAGE

In the laboratory with the mad scientist of Malibu. How the Oscar-nominated actor ended up with a drawer full of syringes and the brain scan of someone who has "experienced the equivalent of blunt trauma." Our journalist becomes his guinea pig.

There's a strip mall in Malibu. The surf crashes right across the highway. At the RadioShack, Eric the audio geek helps me select a new microcassette recorder. He asks what I'm up to. I tell him I'm interviewing a guy.

"Who?" he asks. "I don't want to be pushy."

"It's okay," I shrug. "It's Nick Nolte."

"Cool—why didn't you say so? He comes in here all the time hunting for parts for his microscope. Science is his thing. He's got a *big* microscope."

Nolte's rural six-acre compound is a few miles north of RadioShack, back in the hills, away from the ocean. I push a buzzer, the gate opens, and I drive in. Lush grounds, a canopy of trees. A couple houses on the property. Gardeners everywhere. A big yellow Lab with a plastic megaphone around its neck bounds out of the main house. The doors to the house are open. I follow the dog inside.

Nolte is standing in the center of a large room, wearing a black long-sleeved T-shirt and wide-striped Calvin Klein pajama bottoms. He's barefoot. Face tanned and lined, eyes sunk in. Strong neck. Lean as a bull rider. His hair is the same tawny color as the Labrador's and flies back over his ears and floats above his forehead and down into his eyes. He peers through his hair at me, and there is an energy to those eyes, a crazy vitality. He is mixing a little something in a small cup, a brown potion, looks earthy. There's a dropper and a spoon and he's stirring and then he drinks it down. I wait for him to say something. But he just looks at me. Finally, I shake his hand and say, "Congratulations on the Nobel Prize. Can we talk about your latest science project?"

"Great!" Nolte says, sort of rubbing his hands together. "I've evolved deep into dark-field blood work. Let's go upstairs."

Up the stairs we tramp, through a construction zone of plastic walls with zippers, sawhorses, and power saws, into a massive, high-ceilinged upper room that looks over a garden. This is his bedroom and laboratory. A schoolboy's dream of a room. A Buddha watches over the large, book-strewn bed. Naked women with trumpets adorn lamps. Another dog comes in and sniffs us out. And then there it is, in an alcove where he does his work: a vintage, professional-grade Ortholux microscope.

Nolte stands in front of the microscope, eyes wide, a sideways look, mouth cocked open. "My blood?" he asks. "Or yours?"

I tell him I'm squeamish about needles.

He looks at me and growls, voice deep as a lion's. "You'll have to get over that if you want to do blood work."

He pricks his finger, squeezes a drop of his blood. "We don't want the first drop. We want to get down a little deeper." He squeezes again, a second perfect drop onto a glass slide, which he slips under the microscope. "Our blood tells us everything. By watching your blood, you become connected to yourself in a way that you have never before been connected." He's flipping switches. Light passes through the iris, illuminating the blood cells. The picture is projected on a nearby monitor.

"Yes, *yes*, that's it!" He's pointing to cells moving on the screen. "Here's a real good cell structure, perfectly round. When you're young, the red cells are plump and shimmering—that's what you want." He points out a dying cell. "I've watched my blood degenerate over twenty-four hours. You'll actually see long strings of bacteria coming out of them as they decay." He lingers on the word *decay*, giving it a couple more syllables.

The blood cells are quite beautiful, but all of a sudden the microscope is smoking. It's like a magnifying glass that has been left in the sun and now there's fire inside. "Whoa," he says, surprised, blowing at the smoke. "*Whoa!* Who's been messing with this?"

He tries to close the iris, but it's too hot. "We're screwed," he says. "Oh, shit!" He might have burned himself a little. "Oh, Aidan, *Aidan*, what have you *done*?" he moans. The smoke starts up again. Small puffs of it, like smoke signals.

"Brawley!" Nolte bellows, calling his twelve-year-old son.

Brawley is in a room across the hall, and I'm sent to hunt him down. I unzip the plastic sheeting and walk into the space that Brawley calls his cave. He and his best friend, Aidan, are hunched over separate computers playing *EverQuest*. The game takes nine hours to cross a virtual landscape. The room is pitch-black except for the glowing monitors, and it's throbbing, incredibly loud. I have to shout to get their attention.

The microscope is still smoldering as the boys shuffle into the lab, wanting to know what happened. They crowd around Nolte's shoulders, looking at it.

"Somebody's been on this while I was out of the house," Nolte says. "*That* is my paranoid conclusion." He looks at Aidan, a chubby kid with acne, a real whiz kid, who says, "I get blamed for everything around here. I could be fifty miles away and you'd still blame me."

Aidan is the son of Brawley's shrink. They met when Aidan's dad was trying to help Brawley cope with Nick's divorce from Brawley's mom six years ago. Then the shrink himself got divorced, and now the two boys are best friends. Sometimes Aidan sleeps on the floor next to Brawley's bed.

The boys want to check out the iris of the microscope, and Nolte cuts a flashlight on. "Maybe it's an aging problem," Aidan says. They all peer through the smoke at the inner workings. Even though Nolte is fifty-eight, and Brawley and Aidan are twelve and thirteen, the three confer like colleagues, and that is, in truth, the relationship. They hang out here, for weeks sometimes, without visitors, plotting new science projects, along with Nolte's girlfriend, the comedic actress Vicki Lewis. The compound is tricked out with ten computers, each with a large color monitor, and Nolte has his own internet server. To Brawley and Aidan, he's just Nick. No big deal. He's a grown-up kid with a credit card and the best toys.

But his blood work has been interrupted, and his frustration is beginning to show. He doesn't want to scold, doesn't want to accuse, because Brawley's a good kid, and he's still working out this post-divorce relationship. Anyway, you can't yell at them, because if you yell, they'll just sneak around and do bad-boy things. Aw, hell. "Maybe I shouldn't let the two of you in here for a while," Nolte says. "Let's shut it down for now, let it cool down."

"We should test his blood type!" Brawley suggests.

Yes! Let's test his blood type! Nolte is immediately back in motion. Suddenly, all three of them are looking at me hungrily.

Aidan swabs my fingertip with alcohol. "This will hardly hurt at all," he says. "Wanna hear a joke? Something to get your mind off it? Okay, how many blonds can you fit into a van? I mean—oh, shit, that's not it. I mean, four blonds die in a minivan—what's the tragedy?"

He pricks my finger, and Nick squeezes a drop of blood onto the test strip.

"The van could've held eight!" Aidan cries.

Nolte says, "Brawley, Aidan, read this to me. What's the protocol?"

"Um, protocol," Aidan says. "Step one, okay, mix in for thirty seconds, rub it across the thing for thirty seconds."

Brawley studies how the blood instantly starts breaking up, like red paint left in the rain. "I betcha it's A negative," he says. "Me and Aidan are the same type. A negative."

As he waits for the results, Nolte looks over at the wreckage of the microscope, flipping switches again, and says, "It's absolutely *broken*. *Now* I'm frustrated." He breathes. *Maintain*. He's not going to yell. He knows it can get fixed, damage can be repaired—that's one of the things he's learned. You just have to go to the expert.

He knows a guy who can fix it, but still, he's feeling a little jangled. Meanwhile, Brawley was right. I'm A negative.

Nolte pushes away from the microscope. "Who wants a shot of B-12?" he asks.

No, thank you, I say. My needle problem. Maybe coffee? Or a drink?

"*No, no!*" he says. "This is better."

There is a small, gray medical cabinet on his desk. One drawer labeled SYRINGES. Another drawer TOURNIQUETS. He takes out a narrow-gauge needle.

"Don't worry," Brawley says. "He does this all the time."

Every night, for instance, before he goes to bed, Nolte fills a syringe with .5cc of human growth hormone, which is generally illegal unless you are a dwarf, and shoots it into his stomach. Someday, he figures, we'll all just take a pill, encoded with all the testosterone and hormones our body needs, guided toward specific tissues, to retard aging. Until then, he'll keep buying on the underground market. "All the old hippies are doing it now," he says. A lot of corporate executives. "If Charlie Rose and Larry King aren't on human growth hormones," he says, laughing, "they're thinking about it. I guarantee you, they all want to keep a step ahead of the competition.

"And if I'm feeling a little stressed," Nolte says, "I'll come in and shoot a little B with a little pull of folic acid, which is good for the heart, and a little B-12."

In *North Dallas Forty*, he played an over-the-hill football player who shoots painkillers into his knee. "I like needles," the broken-down ballplayer declared. "Anything to keep me in the game."

"Nothing to it," Nolte says. When he's *really* stressed or feeling depleted, he fills an IV bag with thirteen different vitamins and minerals, puts a tourniquet around his arm, and drips them through a needle into his bloodstream. The procedure takes more than an hour, and he figures he does it several times a week, often while in bed.

Well, I guess a little B-12 never hurt anyone. I offer my right arm, but he waves it off. "Need your right butt cheek, just off the hip." He swabs me with alcohol. The needle doesn't go in readily, and he's got to jab it in a second time. Right into muscle. The boys are watching me, and I try not to wince, but the damn needle stings, and immediately I feel the stuff hit my bloodstream. My forehead warms. My feet tingle. An incredible humming rush for about a minute. I'm feeling a little light-headed, I tell Nolte.

"Man, he doesn't look good," Brawley says.

You sure you only put B-12 in there? I ask.

The room has begun to spin, and the boys ease me down onto the floor, where I rest on a round Feldenkrais mat, which feels like a soft, white buoy. I am quite woozy and sweating, and I hear something strange emanating from somewhere—I'm not sure where—a sing-songy, possibly computer-generated voice. A very pleasant, clipped voice. Sad Man, a life-sized papier-mâché figure, is seated near the bed, his head bowed in a posture of sadness. Nolte pats Sad Man on the head as he passes. Books are strewn about—scientific journals, Philip Roth's *American Pastoral*, *Better Sex Through Chemistry*. From this angle I also see Nolte is filling up another syringe for himself, mixing a vitamin cocktail, holding it above his head, thumping it, squinting. Nolte pulls down his pajamas a bit on one side, exposing a few inches of skin, from his waist to his right cheek, a lean flank for a guy almost sixty.

After shooting up, he's feeling a bit strange himself. He's looking a little worried now, too. You sure you didn't mix the wrong thing? I ask. "No," he says, "I think I'm picking up your vibe. A kind of placebo effect."

When the room stops spinning, the boys help me up, each taking an arm.

"I could give you some ozone," Nolte says. "It will make you feel better."

Ozone? Like the hole?

"This works. I can prove it to you. Bad things can't live in it. Viruses can't live in it, bacteria can't. Cancer can't. Gets more oxygen into your plasma. It's all about getting oxygen into your brain. Everything I do is about getting more oxygen. Need oxygen."

He sits me down. There's a cylinder the size of a standard fire extinguisher bolted to the wall, next to the microscope. He hands me a tube with a nosepiece at the end. "Here, take this." I stick the two soft tubes up my nostrils and breathe deeply, holding this stuff in and, man, is it a buzz. Buzz.

"Have a cigarette," he says, handing me a Marlboro. "The ozone'll scrub the nicotine before it gets into your system."

It's illegal, he tells me, to claim that ozone has medical benefits, but he's convinced it's changed his life, and he's got tanks of it bolted to walls in rooms all over the property. Next to the toilet, in the gym, in his office, in the greenhouse. "If you write 'Nolte uses ozone for medical use,' they may come asking," he says. "They may not. But I'm telling you it works."

He turns to Brawley. "Anybody else need some B-12?"

"Nah, I'll have some raspberries," says Brawley.

"Raspberries! Strawberries! *Great idea!*" Nick yelps. "C! We need vitamin C!" Sometimes he'll just stand out there in his berry patch and eat until he's full, a whole meal. It is late in the afternoon, the golden hour, and this will be Nolte's first meal of the day. And so there he goes, enraptured, the energy of a child, all action, pushing down the hall and out the door and into the garden to pick some plump, juicy organic fruit.

***

To kill a neuron, Nolte says, you really have to go at it. A night out with amphetamines just won't do it. "You've gotta do amphetamines and maybe some heroin and then a couple of gallons of vodka and then Drāno."

And then you pay a doctor to take a nuclear brain scan so that you can see what you have done. Before us is Nolte's brain. Floating in the glowing yellows and reds are islands of neurons that are dead or misfiring. This is the brain of an actor.

When Nolte's doctor first saw this scan, he wanted to know if he'd ever been knocked out. "Well, doc," Nolte said, "I was an alcoholic; there was drug use." The doctor said, "Well, you've experienced the equivalent of blunt trauma."

There has been quite a lot of damage, he says. Nolte honors the damage, and he considers it a gift, a special knowledge. There's a black binder on the table. It's a three-ring binder labeled CONFIDENTIAL, and it contains the story of Nick Nolte's life. It's a rather clinical story, in black and white and X-ray and MRI and brain scan and full-body nuclear PET scan in living color. It is sort of the scrapbook of this whole Nolte reclamation project, which is what his life in the last decade or so has become. This black binder is one of many such binders in Nolte's house. He analyzes and thinks and collects the effects of every character that he plays. To build a real character, it pays to understand his damage. This particular binder, the confidential one, is really just the dossier on another character. Most people don't have such a detailed accounting of their own dysfunctions, their failures, their fuckups, their rate of decay, and their halting human efforts in the face of such. Most people would just rather not know how they stack up against the inevitable. But of course, most people have not had as much of a god's hand in willfully accelerating their own demise as Nick Nolte has, and if a man has the power to find the violence inside to harm himself and bring on the end, then he must surely, Nolte feels, be able to find the grace to reverse the process.

It is, at the very least, an interesting hobby.

"Here's the blunt trauma," he says, pointing to dark areas on the brain scan, which is otherwise a gorgeous swirl of color. His fingers are stained from the strawberries.

To increase Nolte's brain function, his doctor prescribed the same treatment that Edward Teller, the father of the H-bomb, used to jump-start his own brain after he had a stroke: sessions in a hyperbaric chamber, the kind they stick divers into when they have the bends. Nolte spent ten hours in one. The goal was to push oxygen into his plasma so that it would be picked up by the brain and metabolized, and where once had been darkness and stupor and death would be bright colors and vitality and life. A new brain.

Like a schoolboy who's just won the prize, he hands me another brain scan taken after these sessions. "See how these yellow streaks don't shoot clear out to the sides anymore? That means the surface is metabolizing." The dark areas are now blue and yellow. Neurons, he says. Neurons that are *firing*.

"I've had some success." He flips to a chart. "It means my body is almost daily repairing everything that's damaged. And you never can get to zero, because life itself means a certain amount of destruction. You have to use things up in order to live."

Flipping through the black binder, we stop on a recent psychiatric workup, and I read the following aloud:

> Results suggest that the patient possesses traits associated with histrionic, narcissistic, and antisocial qualities, which indicate that the patient may seek reassurance or approval from others or may be uncomfortable in situations where he or she is not the center of attention. He may react to criticism with feelings of humiliation. His personality requires attention from others, and he may have a sense of self-importance. His personality type also tends to be a rule-breaker.
>
> The patient's attention as assessed was found to be abnormal. Results indicate anxiety-induced attention deficit, which he committed several times, in the second, third, and fourth quarters of the test. This is also indicative of anxiety or impulsivity.
>
> Notable: He has very rapid brain speed. Approximately at age forty, with a voltage of 5.03, which may cause him to be prone to addiction. His memory is in the very superior range—no doubt this aids him as an actor.

"All true," he says.

Nick Nolte is indeed an actor. And he says that in those years when he was working away at destroying himself with the drugs and the alcohol, he was taking some roles that in their way were destroying him, too.

You see, big movies are toxic. Of course, just because movies are small doesn't make them good. But Nolte is a constant; he is ever present. Whatever role he undertakes, there he'll be, digging, digging, going deep, trying to find something, trying to talk to ghosts. These movies, he says—whether last year's *Affliction*, for which he was nominated for an Oscar, or *Mother Night*, or a pair of new ones, *Simpatico*, from the Sam Shepard play, and *Breakfast of Champions*—they are having the same effect as the ozone. If he chooses them, breathes them in, lives them, they will restore him, cleanse him, clear out the bad stuff, all those movies he shot for $7 million apiece—*I Love Trouble, Mulholland Falls, Blue Chips*—that led him to a heart murmur in the early nineties. And so he's sucking them in, these little movies, because they are like a drug, and if he had to make *Yet Another 48 Hours*, it just might take him around the bend. Eddie Murphy told him that he wanted to do what Nolte was doing, those artistically satisfying, small, gritty movies. Nolte told him he'd have to cut his salary. "Oh, man, I can't do that," Murphy said. "I have my needs."

Now Nolte beckons me into the bathroom. "You want some tea?" he says, waving me in. "This is the best tea. Made in China." We troop into the bathroom, Brawley and Aidan following. The computers have crashed, the server's down, and the boys are at loose ends. Nolte brews the tea on a bureau across from the shower. A tank of ozone is bolted to the wall next to the toilet. He hands me a framed mug shot of himself. Nabbed by the Feds at twenty for selling draft cards. Got a forty-five-year sentence, suspended. A felon, he's never voted.

It's a large bathroom, with a huge tub in one corner, a deep, splendid tub with a Jacuzzi. Laminated script pages from his upcoming film are stacked next to the tub. Every morning, he comes in here, turns on the Jacuzzi, and reads his pages. When he was preparing for *The Thin Red Line*, he'd soak in here and yell, *Move those damn troops! Take that goddamn hill!* Pajamas are scattered on the floor. All over the room—in fact, all over this house—are quotes that serve as affirmations, trying to buck Nolte up. One on the bathroom wall reads: "Why are you frightened of being alone? Because you are faced with yourself as you are, and you find that you are empty, dull, stupid, ugly, guilty, and anxious." Nolte thinks it's from Krishnamurti, but he's not sure. The twelve steps of AA are taped to the wall, at his left elbow when he's in the tub. The page is mottled and water-stained. He used to go to meetings regularly, but it wasn't quite enough. Then he discovered science. Now Scotch-taped floor to ceiling on the shower door are pages and pages of large-type definitions from a book on brain chemistry — *addiction* and *craving brain* and *inescapable stress* and so on.

It's dark outside now. The room is illuminated only by a small penlight that Nolte is holding. There is a window above the tub. A large gray-and-white cat with white-socked feet is on the roof, staring into the window. "Coyotes have been trying to ambush him for years," Brawley says. "So he lives on the roof." Nolte opens the window and calls out, "Kitty, kitty, kitty, come in, man, come in." The cat rubs up against Nolte's hand. It's very big. Nolte steps into the empty bathtub, picks the cat up off the roof, and hands it to me. "He's real affectionate," Nolte says.

Brawley and Aidan vanish into their cave, hoping to get back online. I follow Nick down the wide, wooden stairs, carrying the cat, its claws sinking deep into my arm. I am hearing water trickling. I look to the ceiling. The Labrador, its tail banging the wall, comes around the corner. The cat is holding on to my forearm for dear life. Now the floor is wet all around our feet, and we're slipping our way down the stairs. I feel wetness running down my pants. The cat has been pissing straight out into the air. Nolte now looks down for the first time and sees the puddle he's standing in.

"Oh, *Jesus,* who pissed all over the place?"

"It wasn't me," says Aidan, sticking his head out of the cave. "I need your credit card number. Brawley and I found plans for an ultralight on the internet."

"You know where the card is," Nolte says.

The cat leaps from my arms and runs. Nolte crouches down with a towel and is sopping up the mess. He looks up at my pee-stained khakis. "Looks like you're going to need some pajamas," he says.

He bounds up the stairs and tosses some down. They are like his, soft, with white piping. I put them on and wait for him to come back. A few minutes later, he slowly descends the stairs, rubbing his butt and screwing up his face a little.

"Had to give myself another hit of B-12."

***

Eating slips his mind sometimes. It is midnight and, save for a handful of berries, he hasn't eaten. I am faint from hunger.

"You hungry?" he asks.

He pulls on a flimsy pair of canvas shoes, gets us each a small flashlight, picks up a basket. "To the garden!" he says. "I'll cook you some dinner."

The garden is ringed with garlic plants to keep rabbits and gophers out. Only one gopher has gotten past the garlic, but it's driving Nolte crazy. The holes he and the gardeners have dug on their hunt for the gopher are wide and deep enough to fit a body in, tunneling in one direction and another. "We throw poison in," he says, "and the gopher throws it back out."

Tall corn is in our faces as we hunt for tomatoes, which are flourishing between the cornstalks. Vines all around our feet. And we're looking for squash. And we keep coming upon watermelon. Nolte is on his knees, rooting around in his pajamas. "*Oooooo*, squash, squash, squash," he mutters to himself. "Oh, these are nice. I'll have some of these. I'll take some of those. These are butternuts. I'm gonna slice 'em and steam 'em a little bit in olive oil with some of the Vidalias."

As he's scooting down the rows, sizing up the butternuts, he's talking about this year's Academy Awards. "Everybody gets devastated," Nolte says, "or everybody gets elated, a little bit. But usually everybody gets devastated. It's horrible, it's rejection. No matter that you're one of only a few actors that have been nominated, or you're one of just a few directors—in the final analysis you're a loser. How can you be happy in that situation?

"Listen, I was glad for Roberto Benigni, you know?" Nick says. "But it's not fun. It's never fun to lose." During the commercial break, after the Best Actor award was presented, Nolte saw that Edward Norton and Ian McKellen, his fellow nominees, were no longer in their seats.

"I knew those fuckin' guys were at the bar. So I excuse myself and I find 'em, and I say, 'Motherfuckers!' And Ian says to me right off the bat, deadpan, 'You know, Nick, I don't really see why you expected to get the award. You do nothing but play yourself.' I look at Ian, who played a homosexual artist in *Gods and Monsters*, and I say,

'Look who's calling the kettle fuckin' black,' and then we both turn to Ed, who played a skinhead in *American History X*, and say, 'What'd you think? Bald head and tattoos were gonna win?' And we all just started laughing."

Nolte sat on his hands when they honored Elia Kazan. Sean Penn is Nick's friend. Penn's dad was blacklisted. Kazan, of course, named names. "He was a great director," he says. "No question. So we would have had to do without *On the Waterfront*. So what?"

In another decade of his life, he'd be having this conversation on a barstool. But we're inside now, back in the kitchen, and he's slicing up squash and Kentucky wonder beans and sautéing onions in olive oil, mixing it all with brown rice.

Not that he's an AA purist. He drank on Oscar night. "My soul needed that one," he says. "If I have that occasional drink, I can, you know, end up drinking for a day or so, but I no longer have that illusion that drinking is the only way to deal with life. And invariably, after a coupla days, the body is just aching and hurting, and the soul is in pain 'cause you're destroying it."

The food is all gone and it's 1:00 a.m. and Aidan is worrying about his pimples. "I have the next experiment!" Nolte yells, charging in from another room. He has a jar in his hands. Brawley and Aidan watch him as if he were a magician and a white rabbit might pop out of his hat at any moment. He opens the jar and begins to goop an organic mud mask on Aidan's face. Aidan recoils. "Hey, what's that?" he hollers.

Nick answers, almost tenderly. "Here, you put it on like this." He shows him by applying it to his own face. "It's good for you."

The phone rings. It's Vicki, calling from her office thirty feet away. She's been in there scissoring apart the dresses she wore on her recently canceled TV show, *NewsRadio*—miniskirts, pink taffeta bridesmaid's gowns. Making them into a quilt. "Come on out, baby," Nolte says. "Yeah, he's still here. It's an interview, but it evolved. You gotta come out; it's my big hurrah."

Brawley asks if it's true that there are benefits to playing video games. "Dad, since I play so many video games, I have more of those little roots. . . . What are they?"

"Dendrites," Nolte says. "The more challenged the brain is, the more dendrites it builds. They help make more connections."

Aidan pipes up. "How many do you think I have? 'Cause I do, like, problem solving every day in school. And complicated math." The mask is drying on Aidan's face, pulling his eyes apart. With the paste smeared high into his hairline, Nick looks like the fool from *King Lear*.

Brawley has clear skin, looks very much like his father, and has actually played Nolte as a boy in two films. He was also the kid in *Ransom*. "After doing *Ransom*," he says, "it was confusing. All of a sudden I understood who all those people were who kept stopping my dad on the street. I thought he had a lot of friends. Now I understood—you get in the movies, you get a lot of friends you don't know." He pulls me aside. "Is it true my dad won the Nobel Prize?" he asks quietly.

***

Nolte is at the computer, a cigarette in his mouth, typing with one finger. It's the middle of the night. Aidan is right next to him at another terminal, his complexion much improved, and a panel of blinking red lights means that Brawley is in the next room, playing *EverQuest*. Aidan has found a medical-surplus store online. He's clicking through the screens, yelling out prices of used electron microscopes.

Nolte says, "We don't want to get too complicated. There are setup protocols that would take us all day."

"The way an electron microscope works," Aidan says, "is they incinerate the stuff you're sampling, and it searches for higher electrons it might give off."

"Wow, would that be fun!" Nolte says, his voice pitched high with excitement.

Nolte is working on his lines for his next movie, *Trixie*, with Emily Watson, in which he plays a senator falsely accused of murder. On the screen, he highlights a speech from the script, then he leans back and waits for the computer to recite it to him.

"I-could-even-have-you-arrested," says the clipped, high-pitched computer voice. "I-am-guilty-of-absolutely-no-wrongdoing-anywhere."

"See how she sounds?" he says. He's rubbing his forehead with a fist, eyes closed, just listening as his right hand, fingers spread wide, tilts outward, dipping and rising in concert with the voice. The voice is amplified throughout the upper room.

He used to ask friends to speak random passages from scripts into tape recorders, just to learn the words in a new way. "I'll have him punched," he repeats along with the computer, which answers, "May-I-say-I-find-you-attractive? You're-so-fresh-and-unspoiled. Is-it-okay-that-I-say-that? Does-that-scare-you-hon?"

The phone rings. It's Alan Rudolph calling from Canada, where he'll be directing *Trixie*, starting in a few weeks. There's the matter of a little S&M to discuss. Nolte sits and listens, pushing his hair off his forehead. He'll be shorn as the senator, hair white. "Do I literally beat her up?" he asks Rudolph. He listens for a few moments, nodding his head. "Well, that's something she and I can figure out."

The computer murmurs in the background. "I'm-single. Are-you-married? A-woman's-sexual-temperature-is-never-lost-on-me. Even-nice-guys-have-nasty-ideas. What-color-underpants-are-you-wearing-right-now?"

Nolte is pacing in his pajamas, intense on the phone. "I think I'll have prepared well enough to be—like we did with Julie in *Afterglow* with that restaurant scene—I want to be able to be that free with it so we can go anywhere we want to go. I've got the second scene, the big, long one, pretty much that free . . . and that's the one I've been really concentrating on. The other one, it's me and her, you know. It's tricky." He hangs up the phone.

He finds that as time goes by, the roles stay with him more and more. They become sort of encoded. He figures it's the way he prepares in the first place, but he can't help continuing to sort of live them after they're done. After *Jefferson in Paris*, he had to have his windows redone and a gazebo built to match Monticello's. After *U Turn*, the raven that had perched atop the shoulder of his sadistic, incestuous character stayed on here with Nick. The bird died not long ago and is buried in the yard.

In the new adaptation of Kurt Vonnegut's *Breakfast of Champions*, Nolte steals the movie as a cross-dressing car-lot manager.

"I designed my own dress," he says. "I told the costumer, 'It has to feel sensual. It has to be what the men don't get to wear, you know, the silk and this kind of thing.' So I took this one little dress, a sheer red dress, and I had it on and said, 'This would be good, but he'd probably like the silk to flow down here.' And then I took the dress and I spun it around backward, so the top was cut down here and the straps crossed here. Now I was bare-breasted—a Phoenician woman. That was key to the character."

He wants the dress this second. "I loved shaving my chest!" he says. He gets up off his chair to leave the lab. The computer voice croons to him, "A-woman's-sexual-temperature-is-never-lost-on-me." Dark-field photos of his sperm are on the table near the scans of his brain. He is pulling open drawers. One is filled with bottles, another with Scotch tape. He throws open the doors of a large armoire. He's saying he thinks he's found the undergarments, sheer and red. "I know it's here somewhere. I swear it! I'll find the dress!"

Esquire, 1999
National Magazine Award Finalist
Selected, *Esquire's Big Book of Great Writing*

A DEEPLY MISUNDERSTOOD MASS MURDERER

There comes a time in a man's life when he has to take up with a desperate former New York gangster, a retired Serb-sympathizing Special Forces commando, and a Croat stripper or two and go off to war-ravaged Bosnia in search of Radovan Karadzic, the world's most wanted man.

Radovan Karadzic is on the phone.

He is wounded and in search of a little understanding.

"Why does America hate me?" he pleads. "What did I do wrong?"

The fugitive Bosnian Serb leader, indicted by the International Criminal Tribunal at The Hague in 1995 for genocide in the war that killed two hundred thousand people, sounds tired, with just a touch of whine, some manufactured outrage, and real fear in his toastmaster's voice. His English is pretty good.

"How can they call me the worst war criminal in the world?" Things have gotten way out of hand. It's all a terrible misunderstanding. Others are to blame.

"I was a moderate!" he cries. "We didn't kill any prisoners of war!"

He never imagined that this day would come, and now he wants to meet somewhere and set things straight.

"I'm not in charge. I wasn't in charge then. I'm not a magician; I can't make more than a million people follow me. I can't stop them from committing acts of violence," he says.

"Uugghh!" he groans, exasperated. "Where can I get a fair trial? They are spitting on me in America."

***

"He's got smoker's foot," Bosko's young wife says as her husband, a former New York City gangster, spurs our puny car around a dark mountain curve. We're on a road somewhere in Yugoslavia, slewing on thin tires downward toward an isolated border crossing into Bosnia, toward the town of Pale and Radovan Karadzic, whose thugs in the secret police are waiting for us on the other side.

Smoker's foot?

"His feet are numb. The doctor says if Bosko doesn't stop smoking, they'll have to cut them off." She turns toward me in the backseat, her blond hair cascading onto my hand. "Promise me you'll keep him from smoking."

Our driver, Bosko Radonjich, fifty-four, a squat bear of a man with thick black hair and a mad, triumphant smile, is a fugitive from American justice.

He is wanted by the FBI for fixing the jury in the 1987 racketeering and murder trial of his close friend John Gotti, head of the Gambino crime family. Bosko, though a Serb, was also a boss of the Westies, the murderous Irish gang that served as enforcers for the Gambino family and controlled a good chunk of New York's West Side in the 1980s. Bosko fled the United States in 1990, just weeks before Gotti and several associates were indicted again.

The Serbian mafia that Bosko currently runs out of Belgrade has won him certain privileges and some very powerful friends. During the Bosnian war, he provided Karadzic and the deadly Serb paramilitary with millions of dollars in cash and weaponry and became one of Karadzic's close advisers. Now Bosko has a secret plan to save Karadzic, the man he describes as "my angel, my saint," but time is running out. He's afraid that it might be too late already.

Tim Buckholz, an ex-US Army Special Forces soldier, is squeezed in beside me on the backseat. Seventeen years on covert missions for your government. Now he's a freelancer and considers Bosko his friend.

Buckholz doesn't look military. His hair is sandy, his face kind, almost innocent. In 1978, when he was eighteen, he was an army medic assigned to bag bodies in Guyana after the Jonestown mass suicide. The Special Forces sent him to school to knock the military out of his gait and speech. He specializes in counterterrorism, hostage rescue, and close-quarters combat.

I am here to talk to Karadzic, who, until very recently, was the least sought, most wanted war criminal in the world. Why does a psychiatrist wake up one morning and decide it's time to kill his neighbors? And how has he managed to keep the world at bay? Two weeks ago, NATO came calling, and a British team killed indicted war criminal and Karadzic crony Simo Drljaca, the police chief of Prijedor, in a botched snatch attempt. The White House had given the green light, and another indicted war criminal was successfully captured the same day. Just days before, Karadzic was breezing through NATO checkpoints in his Mercedes.

I am also here because I happened to meet Tim a couple of years ago at the Pub, a netherlounge of military spooks, conspiracists, and soldiers for hire, just outside Fort Bragg, North Carolina. Tim invited me to Belgrade to meet Bosko, who wants to broker a meeting with Karadzic. The last time Bosko escorted an American to visit Karadzic was when Jimmy Carter came to negotiate a cease-fire during the Bosnian war. This time, Bosko wants to prove again that he's an international fixer, and he seems to think that my story will give Karadzic a new reputation.

At the border, the three of us get out of Bosko's Honda. It is 3:30 a.m., pitch-black, and the early August air is damp and chilly. Bosko's wife, Sabrina, turns around and heads back into Yugoslavia. Their car has Florida license plates. "I could have FUCK USA on my license plate, but I don't, because I love America," Bosko growls in his gravelly Serbo-New Yorker accent. "Even though the cocksuckers betrayed me."

Bosko steps gingerly. "Damn, my feet hurt." His hand is on my elbow, steering me toward the crossing. Up ahead is a guard shack illuminated by a milky, fluorescent light. Tim walks behind us, covering our backs.

Two armed Yugoslav guards step toward us. They each, in turn, hug Bosko and kiss him on both cheeks. Tim and I produce our American passports. Bosko, wearing tennis shoes with no socks, shiny sweatpants, and a jacket with BOSS emblazoned across the front, never bothers to show his papers.

We walk across the border toward a Volkswagen Golf idling in the darkness. We are now inside the self-declared Republika Srpska, an "ethnically cleansed" area the size of Vermont that is home to nine hundred thousand Serbs. To a nationalist like Bosko, this land, blood-soaked by war, is Palestine. He has dreamed his whole life of a Serbian state independent of Yugoslavia.

Tim has stood on this border before. In 1994, when the Serbs were winning the Bosnian war and when Yugoslavia was trying to convince the world that it wasn't helping them do it, the United Nations Security Council hired independent contractors like Tim to monitor this very crossing. Only medical supplies, food, and used clothing were allowed through. Unless, of course, you were a VIP or a smuggler.

That's when Tim and Bosko first came to an understanding. Along with a handful of other ex-Special Forces soldiers on the same detail, Tim became sort of an honorary Serb nationalist. As an unpaid favor to Bosko, in his spare time he helped train several bodyguards for Karadzic, who was just being isolated by the West as the Maximum Villain of the war. "It was standard executive-protection training," Tim says. "Route planning, countersurveillance, that kind of thing."

Did they follow your advice?

Tim raises an eyebrow. "He hasn't been caught yet."

At the end of his last stay here, in July 1995, Tim was asked to leave Yugoslavia, having been informed by the US State Department that his safety could no longer be guaranteed.

Why not?

"Because of my association with Bosko. The chief of the mission asked, 'Do you know who you're dealing with? This is the man who fixed the Gotti trial. He's been convicted of blowing up embassies in America. He was involved in Jimmy Hoffa's murder.'"

Tim's response: *Cool.*

***

As we head down a winding mountain road into the strange new country of Srpska, we are being tailed.

"Friend or foe?" Tim asks, checking the headlights behind us.

"Friend," Bosko affirms.

Earlier that night, at Club Boss, his mountain casino an hour from the border, Bosko told me that we'd be escorted by a "war criminal" into the Serb enclave. "They hate Americans down there," Bosko said. "Nobody is safe. I'll need to go with you."

When I asked Bosko the name of our escort, he traced a finger down the middle of his face and across his lips—the mob sign meaning *silence.*

In the aftermath of a war with mass murderers on all sides, men who committed unspeakable atrocities, that any one man's name could inspire such caution, even in someone like Bosko, chilled the room.

In the escort car behind us now is that faceless, nameless war criminal. He is providing us safe passage into the darkness of Srpska.

***

Dogs, yelping wildly, race our car into the sleeping town of Visegrad, where we see in the beam of our headlights the face of Karadzic. Blown up poster-size, it is pasted on every shopwindow. His silver hair, usually an unruly bouffant, has been combed; the cleft in his chin looks the size of a bullet hole. In red, under each of these color portraits, are the words DON'T TOUCH HIM!

Karadzic is hiding out somewhere in this country, protected by his most trusted soldiers, surrounded by mines and anti-aircraft weapons. Bosko says that Karadzic has ten different hideouts. Eight thousand American soldiers are currently in Bosnia, the largest contingent in a NATO force of thirty-one thousand. Even though Washington denies it, Tim believes that an American snatch team has been training secretly since the spring to bring him in. Karadzic has instructed his guards to shoot him rather than allow him to be captured.

Visegrad, a garrison of hard-line Serbs, was one of the first towns to be cleansed of its Muslims. Fourteen thousand just vanished, deported or executed in the summer of 1992. A laboratory of killing, Bosko calls it. My homework, he calls it. He doesn't say what he means by that, but he knows this town. Visegrad is where he went to school as a boy.

Our driver turns down an alley and stops at a bar called Cafe 10. A half dozen men, mostly former soldiers and paramilitary men, step out of the darkness. Each one greets Bosko with an embrace and a kiss.

It is 4:00 a.m., but they have kept the lights burning for us. Inside, we crowd into a corner booth. Our driver pulls out his wallet. I see the flicker of his secret-police badge. No one uses names, and it is understood that we are not to ask. The bartender opens a bottle of slivovitz, the local homemade plum brandy. Tim, who is not much of a drinker, figures it's 400 proof. Even Bosko must hammer his chest with every swallow.

After three shots, Bosko throws a heavy arm around me. "You'll put in a good word for me with our friends in Virginia when you return," he says.

"You know, Bosko," I answer carefully, "the CIA no longer recruits journalists or priests."

Still, he slides the bottle of slivovitz over to me to consecrate the moment. "You are the voice of America," he says, pulling me closer. "You can help the Doctor. My angel is getting bad advice. It's my advice he needs. I know the double game. America is after him, but these fuckers here are ready to kill Americans if they try it. We need to convince America that Radovan Karadzic is the only hope for stability in this whole fucking godforsaken country. We need to show the world the good man he is."

Bosko raises his glass. "Somebody put dirt on the Doctor," he says. "We've got to make the Doctor clean. You put in a good word for me and make me clean, too."

It's almost dawn, and Bosko Radonjich, John Gotti's fixer, wants to mediate this grave international crisis. He wants to save Karadzic. He wants to save American lives. But most of all, he wants to save himself. He wants to go home to New York, where he lived in a $5 million townhouse on the East Side and drove a Rolls-Royce Corniche. He misses his "work" for the CIA, and he surely doesn't want to be here if the war breaks out again.

The Serbs at the table seem not to comprehend Bosko's agenda. They are soldiers in a lost war, unready to concede defeat, willing to kill again, expecting to kill again. They sit now with their arms draped easily over one another's shoulders, their young faces spent and teeth broken.

"If they try to snatch Karadzic, that is war," says a young Serb quietly, not a hint of bravado in his voice. "We will kill every soldier we see. We will pile American bodies to the sky. We'll start with you if we have to."

***

At daybreak, having killed only two bottles of slivovitz, we leave the bar. Mist is rising off the Drina River, which runs through the heart of Visegrad. A massive stone bridge, built in 1510 by Turks during the days of the Ottoman Empire, spans the river's jade water. At one end of the bridge is Bosko's old school.

"Don't let the beauty fool you," Bosko says as we drive over the bridge. So many Muslims—he calls them Turks—were executed on this stone bridge during the war that the Drina turned red. And I now see in the hills beyond the bridge what had been hidden from view in the night.

"Them is all the houses of Turks," Bosko says sleepily. Each charred house is a tombstone. We pass hundreds in the hills above the Drina.

Tim, seated again beside me in the backseat, checks for the tail car, but the faceless war criminal is no longer behind us. Bosko snores in the front seat as our driver races at drunken speeds toward our rendezvous with Karadzic.

***

In the mountain village of Pale, the seat of Karadzic's power, the Minister of Fear plants three kisses on Bosko, Serbian style, one on each cheek and then back to the first. As head of the Republic of Srpska secret police, Dragan Kijac is one of the most feared men in the country.

Bosko introduces Tim and then me. "This is Daniel. He was with me and the Irish in New York," he says, lying.

"So you want to see Dr. Karadzic? If only you had come a few days earlier," the minister says, stiffing us fast. "Now even I cannot know where he is."

The minister, who looks a bit like Bobby Kennedy, is saying something else to me in Serbo-Croatian.

"He wants to know," Bosko translates, "how big is the circulation of your magazine?" His final words to me before this meeting had been "Lie, lie, lie—everything is a double game."

"Seven million," I answer.

The Minister of Fear, who I suspect speaks perfect English, raises his eyebrows, impressed. But then I falter. "Well, uh, actually, it's a couple million, if you count, like, people who, you know, pick it up in a bus . . ."

I don't dare look up. I can feel Bosko's glare, his disappointment. "And he'll appear on TV," he says confidently, stepping in. "CNN, CBS, all the networks. He's the greatest writer about postwar countries. He is the voice of America."

The Minister of Fear shakes his head. A period of awkward silence follows. Tim, who has been sitting quietly nearby, playing the role of my bodyguard, reaches for his business card. In America, Tim is a partner in Spartan Security out of Mamers, North Carolina. Recently, his firm, made up of a couple of other ex-Special Forces buddies, bought a $45,000 copier and added "International" to its name. Now Tim is after high-stakes contracts. The first proposal Spartan printed on the new copier is titled "Current Training Programs Available to the Serb People."

"Right now, America is arming your enemies," he tells the Minister of Fear. "Hell, former associates of mine are training the Muslims and Croats with $100 million from the United States.

When the American troops leave here next summer, you're going to be slaughtered. It'll be Serb season." For Tim, it's an avalanche of words. It's his Hail Mary pass, a way to save me and sign up a client. Tim's prospectus offers "cutting-edge hostage-rescue and surgical-strike operations" and proposes training for "worst-case scenarios."

With forty thousand police on his payroll, the largest armed force in the Republic of Srpska, the minister perks up.

"I live one step away from treason," Tim winks.

***

The Minister of Fear directs us to a ruin of a hotel at the top of the mountain, Hotel Paranoia, where we are to await further instructions.

At twilight, we settle into a room. Tim opens a window. Outside, NATO helicopters are flying patterns over Pale. And higher up, Tim figures, there are at least four satellites watching this area.

Bosko hunches down in front of me. I've been kicking myself since we left the Minister of Fear. "So you fuck up," he says. "Forget about it."

The phone rings and Bosko answers, switching between Serbo-Croatian and English. "That was Karadzic," Bosko says, hanging up. Former US assistant secretary of state Richard Holbrooke is touring Bosnia, trying to salvage his Dayton Peace Accord, and he is making Karadzic's life hell. Our meeting has been postponed. "But he's got a package for you," Bosko says. "Something he wants you to advise him on. He'll call you next week at the casino."

***

Bosko is in pain. "You have to help me," he says. There is fear in his eyes. He's very worried about his feet. He wants to be healthy for our meeting with Karadzic. We are now in Zlatibor, a spa on the Yugoslavian side of the mountains. He's been getting therapy for his feet here all summer.

"The capillaries have all collapsed," his doctor tells him as Bosko pulls off his shoes and stretches out on the bed, his feet naked. A nurse hooks Bosko up to a machine that sends electric pulses into his feet. "He's only fifty-four years old," says the doctor, shaking her head. "We don't amputate the feet here. They do that in Belgrade."

Bosko's feet are numb, swollen, and blue. But he is in good cheer, and the staff of women, all wearing white, brighten when they see him. He introduces me. "This is Danny. He's writing the screenplay about my life. He knows things about me I forgot."

After these treatments, we wrap ourselves in towels and head into the Truth Sauna, where no lies can be told. He's talking not of Bosnia, but of New York and the mob. "When Eddie came back from Attica," Bosko says, "he put a cock on the bar. Somebody's fucking cock he had cut off. 'Anybody who be a stool pigeon,'" he says, affecting an Irish brogue, "will be like this.' That's what Eddie says. Shit, the Irish were good killers."

Bosko believes that if we understand New York mobs, we'll understand Bosnia. Maybe even the world. It's his Hell's Kitchen school of diplomacy. "America is the Boss of Bosses," Bosko says. "The Serbs, Croats, and Muslims are three rival gangs—no matter who started the damn thing, everyone has spilled blood. When you have a turf war like this, you separate the gangs. That's why Dayton won't work. You *don't* ask them to live together. Not after boundaries have been set in fresh blood."

Bosko is not one to offer up his own history easily, but in these Truth Saunas, I hear of his relationship with death, a relationship that started early, with the killing of his father, who was shot by communist police when Bosko was a toddler. Soon after, his brother was imprisoned for his anti-communist beliefs, and then one day came a knock at the door. Bosko and his older sister were home when the secret police entered. The two agents wore black trench coats; they had pistols. They were in the basement, scraping the walls. "They were looking for a radio transmitter, a channel to America. I was just a kid. I didn't know what they meant. I thought maybe behind our wall there was a long tunnel across the ocean." Finding nothing, the police pistol-whipped Bosko's sister. Two days later, she died from a blood clot. Whenever he needs fuel to fight, Bosko remembers that scene.

When he was twenty-seven, he fled to America. "Without America, the world is shit, do you understand?" he says. "Without that dream, without that beautiful fucking Constitution." Granted political asylum, he arrived in Manhattan, Hell's Kitchen, in 1970 and joined New York's Serbian underground, becoming an explosives expert.

In 1979, Bosko pleaded guilty to bombing the Yugoslav consulate in Chicago and served three years in Allenwood Federal Prison in Pennsylvania. He got out of jail in 1982 and soon after took over the Westies. "If you're a freedom fighter," he says, "you have to love the Irish."

After the sauna, Bosko cannonballs into the swimming pool. Suddenly, out of nowhere, his former high school teacher arrives poolside with two glasses and a guitar, pours us slivovitz, and, in honor of Bosko's American patriotism, strums "When the Saints Go Marching In."

***

At his casino the next evening, Bosko sits near the piano and plays host to a constant parade of customs officials, Serbian film stars, military judges, basketball stars, cops, and war criminals. All come to pay homage and to seek favors of the man they call Boss. A young Serb, returning from South Africa, unfurls the gift of a zebra skin.

Tonight, Bosko cooks spaghetti for twenty. Before dinner, he makes everyone watch *Getting Gotti*, a video that tells the story of how Bosko's jury tampering kept the crime boss from going to prison in 1987. "The actor playing me looks like Boris Fucking Yeltsin," he complains.

Three weeks after Bosko left America in 1990, Gotti was arrested again. Sammy "the Bull" Gravano, the number-two man in the organization, later turned state's evidence. Gotti was eventually convicted of ordering the murder of Paul Castellano, his former boss in the Gambino family, and was sent away for life without parole.

Gravano also testified that Bosko had paid $60,000 to a member of Gotti's first jury, a man named George Pape. Pape had been an usher at Bosko's wedding, had testified on Bosko's behalf in his Chicago trial, and had visited him in prison. "There were people in high places who knew that he was my best friend," Bosko says. "Somebody wanted Pape on that jury, just like somebody wants Karadzic in power. One man does not hold off the superpowers of the world unless someone wants him to remain in power."

Belmondo, one of Bosko's self-named errand boys, joins us for dinner. He has a pistol in his waistband and the swagger of a young thug on the make. Also slurping spaghetti at our table is a man with a pronounced underbite who is known as Mr. Fun. A former police chief and bamboo-furniture executive, Mr. Fun always wears a suit and will cross a room to light a lady's cigarette. For laughs, he slaps his face like Curly and stuffs his necktie into his mouth. On the Hague list of indictments, he is murderer number seventy-four. I have a copy of the list. Mr. Fun circles his name for me.

When Karadzic finally phones, a waiter whispers the news into Bosko's ear. Bosko waves me through swinging doors into the casino's back room.

"I knew Daniel back in New York," Bosko lies into the receiver. "He was with Mr. Gotti. He's a journalist now—on TV, in the magazines. You must tell them you're a friend of America, that you are anti-communist your whole life. It's only in America that you could get a fair trial."

He hands me the phone: "Say hello to Dr. Karadzic."

This is strange. Somewhere, the most wanted man in the world has found the comfort to chat on the phone. I look at the receiver for a moment. "Hello?"

"I was sorry I didn't have the pleasure of seeing you in Pale," he tells me. No satellites could scramble the energy out of that voice. "I've been having a few security problems."

He asks about the package he sent: "You read my blue book. What did you think?"

His gift had been an advance copy of *The Case of Dr. Radovan Karadzic*, a defense written on his behalf. In the literature of shifting responsibility, it is a masterpiece. Truly the thinking of a psychiatrist, a man whose specialties were depression and paranoia, a man who once hypnotized the entire Sarajevo soccer team.

"Dr. Karadzic, I wonder what's *not* in the book. In order to indict you, The Hague must have strong evidence."

"They arrested two Serbs, took them to The Hague, and then had to send them home," he says. "They had the wrong men. And another one they sent home for lack of evidence. The Hague is a political institution. They respond to pressure. They make mistakes."

A number of legal scholars had told me that the second indictment against Karadzic, for the massacre at Srebrenica in July 1995, in which as many as eight thousand Muslim civilian men were executed, will be very difficult to prove. In his book, Karadzic is eager to implicate Slobodan Milosevic, the president of Yugoslavia, for devising and carrying out the military plan that led to the genocide. No wonder he is afraid for his life. The threat he poses to Milosevic, or any of the other leaders America has kept off the Hague list, could earn him a bullet from anyone. Even his own people.

He says he wants to meet but explains that he can't appear to grant an interview.

"He says I can't talk."

Who says?

"Richard Holbrooke."

"Is he promising you something if you stay quiet?"

There is silence on the other end.

"Do you trust him?"

Bosko is whispering into my other ear. *Tell him you're a psychiatrist, too.* Tim has told me that every syllable of this conversation is being sifted somewhere, analyzed. Somewhere, an analyst can hear the fear in Karadzic's voice. Even on the phone, I can feel it in his breath. This is a man counting his days.

Recalling that he likes chess, I suggest a game. "The loser goes to The Hague," I say.

He laughs. "I'm very good at chess."

Finally, he says, "If you wanted to do a fact-finding mission . . ."

Yes, I say, yes, a fact-finding mission sounds perfect.

"That wouldn't be regarded as an interview."

Absolutely not. There's a real distinction.

"When we meet, you can ask me anything. You, of course, can't say that you were here."

This is Bosnia, and everything is a double game. It was all a matter of language, of finally detecting the nuance of what he was driving toward.

I pass the phone back to Bosko. Karadzic tells him, "We will have to blindfold Daniel, and he'll have to walk deep into the mountains."

"He'll go naked if that's what it takes," Bosko tells him as he hangs up.

We can't tell the Minister of Fear about this, Bosko says, turning to me. "It would make trouble." This means we have no guarantee of safe passage across the territory. In fact, now we have to evade the secret police.

Tim opts to stay behind. "By now, they'll have checked up on me," he says. "My background is just too suspicious. If they think we're a snatch team, we're all dead."

He kindly instructs me on what to expect from Karadzic's security detail. "They'll most likely put a hood on you. They'll remove your watch, electronics, anything where a transmitter can be squirreled away. And they'll make you change clothes. They'll be worried about magic dust. The KGB used to use a kind of radioactive dust when they were trailing people in Washington."

I'm a little worried and don't quite know what to say. I have gotten used to having Tim watch my back. "It's in their best interest for you to come out alive," he says, punching my arm. "Just don't do anything stupid."

***

Bosko and I hit the road again that night, leaving the casino at 2:00 a.m. Karadzic's voice compels us forward. Belmondo, the wiry thug who during the war was in the deadliest Serb paramilitary, is riding shotgun. We're in a black Jeep, heading back into Srpska. "This is a black operation," Bosko says. "Nobody can know we're going in."

Again we arrive at Hotel Paranoia, following Karadzic's instructions. I am trapped with Bosko and Belmondo in a room with orange bedspreads. Karadzic will contact us with the next move. From our window, I watch refugees picking mushrooms on the ski slope.

The next day, we don't venture from our room, wary of alerting the Minister of Fear that we are here. Bosko is lying supine, with his feet up on a pillow. An arm covers his eyes, and he is moaning from pain as he drifts in and out of sleep. It is more than either Belmondo or I can bear. Something must be done. We flip a coin. I lose.

"I'm going to try to put some life back in these dogs," I tell Bosko. Back at the casino, during off-hours, I had seen a Serb bartender take out a bottle of slivovitz, the good stuff, and pour it over Bosko's feet before he began to massage them. My technique is not nearly so inventive. I drape a white towel over Bosko's feet. He winces at first as I dig my thumbs into the ball of his foot, but then he begins to relax. "When I was a boy, I had a dog named Jack," he says. "One day, a cop asks me the dog's name. I tell him, you know, 'It's Jack.' The cop says, 'That's a fucking capitalist name.' He takes out his pistol. He shoots Jack."

And with that, Bosko's eyes roll back and he is snoring. Belmondo and I wait a few minutes, and then, despite Bosko's warning to stay out of sight, we head to the hotel bar, dying for a drink. We order and look up to see that seated not twenty feet away, with a blond at his side, is the Minister of Fear. He has a wary smile and lifts his hand slightly. Belmondo orders a drink for the minister, who, leaving his date behind, walks over and joins us. He speaks smugly in Serbo-Croatian. "He is sorry that your interview with the Doctor is not possible," Belmondo translates. "Please call again in a year." The minister sniffs, downs his drink, and returns to his table.

Belmondo and I finish our drinks. It's over. Upstairs, we lie in the dark, listening to Bosko snore. Neither of us wants to wake him and deliver the awful news.

***

So you fuck up. Those are Bosko's first words in the morning, said with a devil's smile. *Forget about it.* No one knows about our meeting except us and Karadzic. Bosko says he's sure. "I hear his voice. Only me. And you."

At the gates of Karadzic's compound later that day, Bosko and I are surrounded by soldiers, all heavily armed and wearing bulletproof vests. A guard asks for identification. "My *cock* is the only identification you'll *ever* need!" Bosko thunders.

The guard retreats into his shack and dials the rotary phone. When he comes out again, his hands are up in apology. And now a hand is gently on each of our backs, ushering us in. Karadzic's compound is the Famos truck factory. Inside, everyone is on high alert. But no one has taken away my backpack yet. No naked trek through the mountains. No magic dust. We're walking in. We're escorted past another guard station and then upstairs and down a hall to the end office. Karadzic's office. A very familiar photo of him is on the wall. His secretary hands me a document. She says it was drafted last night by Dr. Karadzic himself. Reading it, I am at first puzzled:

COMMITMENT

I, Daniel Scott Voll, herein confirm that I have made a commitment concerning my visit to the Republic of Srpska, as follows:

I have been on a "fact-finding mission" in the Republic of Srpska.

During the visit, I have met Dr. Radovan Karadzic under strict conditions that he give me only some knowledge useful for my mission, and that under no conditions can I quote him, or publish any kind of interview, because he forbids to be interviewed, or considered to be interviewed.

I have made this commitment with my full moral and material responsibility.

This was the double game at its best. Even I had to wonder, upon signing it, if I had perhaps already met Karadzic. "Do we get to see him now?" I ask, looking into Karadzic's office. "Come back next Tuesday,"

I am told. Bosko takes a copy of the letter from Karadzic's secretary, rolls it up, and walks out, holding it as if he were the Statue of Liberty. He's one step closer to his dream. Brokering peace. Winning a get-out-of-jail-free card. Me, I want this business over with.

***

Sick with a hacking cough and a fever a few nights later, I fear I am becoming as toxic as this place. "I know just what you need," Bosko says, and off we go, driving hours through the rainy night to Belgrade for the after-midnight floor show at Club Lotus, a red-velvet den of iniquity on the Danube. The place was an SS bordello during World War II. Bosko owns it now.

The Exhibitionist is dancing in the cage, doing her striptease. In an effort to cure my fever, Bosko orders snifters of warm cognac, and after I've had a couple, he offers his apartment upstairs for the night. He'll sleep elsewhere, he says.

At 4:00 a.m., sleeping fitfully, I hear a key turn in the door. Footfalls cross the floor. And then a hand on my shoulder, touching me lightly. Now a hand on my face.

I turn over, disoriented, and then I see these legs, beautiful, long legs, dancer's legs, sheathed in black silk. The Exhibitionist. A finger against my lips. In this light, away from the stage, I see the circles, like bruises, under her eyes. She kisses my cheeks, kneels beside me.

"I'm your bodyguard."

"I don't need a bodyguard."

"Bosko says you do."

"Did Bosko send you?"

"I told him I wanted to come and see you."

"But he gave you the key."

"Yes. And he told me not to fall in love or he would kill me." Now both her hands are touching my face. I close my eyes and take a deep breath. She lies on top of me.

"I had a boyfriend before the war," she says quietly. Her mouth is on my lips, my neck. And then her head is resting on my chest. Her mother, she tells me, is a Serb, her father a Croat. Her Serb boyfriend was killed during the war. Her brother fought for the Croats. She'd worked as an interpreter for the UN before she started dancing for Bosko. "He is my protector, my daddy." And then she adds softly, "Be careful of Bosko."

***

"Do not underestimate how dangerous this world is," Bosko says the next day as we stroll through downtown Belgrade, trailed by his male bodyguard. "We are surrounded by killers."

Bosko is waiting for the details of last night. I can see it in his sly smile. He likes to get folks dirty. He once got a rival gangster in New York addicted to cocaine, took him right out of the picture. He likes to control his world. But when I remain silent, he takes a different tack. "You're a good boy," he says. "I taught you well."

I stop walking. He wanted to set me up. "Fuck you, Bosko. I'm not going to play your game anymore. I'll go to Karadzic myself. Or I'll go home."

He shrugs. Lights a cigarette. Squints. "Bosko, what did you mean that Visegrad was your homework?"

"It's a joke. Like when I say, 'I want a donkey to fuck you.' It's a joke."

I'm sick of jokes. This morning, my editor in New York faxed me a newspaper article about a killer named Lukic from Visegrad. According to the article, Lukic is responsible for killing more Muslims with his bare hands than any other individual in the war. Lukic has been so well protected that no journalist has ever seen him.

"Bosko, do you know Milan Lukic?" He stops, waves his bodyguard away. For a moment, he's off-balance.

"It's no good to say his name out loud. Them's killers."

"Do you know him?"

"Sure, I know him. So do you. Lukic arranged for your safety the first night we crossed into Bosnia."

"What?" Now I am off-balance.

"He is the one I called to make sure you would be safe. He was in the tail car," Bosko says. "You sat with him on our last trip across the border. At the café in Visegrad. He bought you coffee. You liked him." Bosko grits his teeth; a cloud passes over his eyes. "Don't fuck up, Daniel. You are here for Karadzic, not Milan."

He pauses, lights another cigarette. He is shaking his head, watching me. "I do things wrong, yes. Maybe I killed. Maybe I did other things. But Karadzic is honest. I know devil. He is inside me. But Karadzic is angel to my people."

"But he was president during the entire war," I say. "His own blue book shows that he had command control. And what about Srebrenica? If a mob boss orders a hit, he's still guilty of murder, even if he didn't pull the trigger."

"He didn't know all the killings would happen."

"How do you know?"

"I *know*, goddammit!"

***

On the night before we are to meet Karadzic, American troops storm the Minister of Fear's police barracks in several towns along the Bosnian border. Crowds are retaliating with stones and firebombs. Tim calls from America, worried. Don't go back to Srpska, he warns.

Bosko composes a fax to Karadzic, telling him that we have information vital to his safety and that he must still meet with us. The double game. "It's the only way to get his attention," Bosko says.

An hour later, at Bosko's apartment above Club Lotus, the phone rings. It's Karadzic.

"It's a very bad time," Karadzic says before hanging up. "This is not a safe phone. Be in Pale tomorrow. My office will make the arrangement."

"We're going to need some protection down there," Bosko says to me. "They're handing out long guns."

I am Bosko's hostage. For the first time, I feel like I am in trouble.

***

The Jeep has been making a clanking sound since we left Belgrade. I have ignored it, but now, on a dangerous mountain road, Bosko makes me pull over. Almost all the lug nuts have been sheared off our wheels. "Sabotage," Bosko says. "Because of you. I saved your life."

***

As we approach Pale, Bosko's sources report that Italian troops, who control this NATO sector, have a snatch team on the ground, ready to move on Karadzic. Everyone is on snatch alert. We turn a corner and face the cannon of a tank. Armored personnel carriers and UN trucks with whip antennae are parked on overlooks.

We are invited inside Karadzic's compound for dinner, which is served in a private salon by waiters in black tie. Brandy is poured. Our hosts for the evening are Karadzic's Ministers of Rationalization and Denial. "If they storm the compound, we'll give you a gun," one says, smiling. "You'll have to shoot the Italians."

"Dr. Karadzic sends his apologies," says the Minister of Denial. "He is unavailable and has asked me to provide you whatever help you need." The rumor is that Karadzic has fled to another country, at least temporarily.

Bosko lectures the ministers in English. Their strategy is all wrong. "He's charged with genocide—you can't rationalize genocide! You can't hide from that charge!" he yells. "He's got to show his face to America! Show his heart! It can make him clean!"

The Ministers of Rationalization and Denial trade nervous glances.

***

The Yugoslav border guard asks me to step away from the Jeep. My visa has expired. I cannot leave Srpska. Bosko shrugs. It's dark. "It's Friday night. It might take me a couple days to get you out. I'll start making some calls in the morning. Belmondo will stay behind with you."

As we get into a border guard's car for the complimentary ride back into Visegrad, Belmondo turns to me: "You're chief, I'm security."

Milan Lukic sits on the terrace of his café, which commands a view of downtown. He is surrounded by cops. "Milan trusts no one," Belmondo says as we climb the stairs. "We must let him know we're here."

The last time they met, Lukic kissed Belmondo on both cheeks. Now he gives him only a slight nod. Wearing shirtsleeves, jeans, and tennis shoes, the Butcher of Visegrad doesn't look remarkable. He is in his thirties, tall, with an athletic build, just a little fleshy under the chin. He runs his hand through his hair. The cops talk in whispers.

Belmondo is very nervous. Without Bosko, the rules have changed. Whatever his own killing tally, he is no match for this crowd. During the cleansing, Lukic walked these streets with a megaphone, exhorting, "Rise up, Serb brothers. Kill the Muslims." He killed thousands. Most of his work was done on the bridge. Daily, he would herd groups of Muslims there, garrote or shoot them, and laugh maniacally. So many bodies were swept downriver that the dam clogged. He incinerated hundreds more inside their houses. Lukic is not on the published Hague list; investigators may never even reach Visegrad. His terror was not limited to this town. At Srebrenica, survivors remember Lukic requesting refugee Muslims from Visegrad.

Now Lukic walks over, taps Belmondo on the shoulder, directs him inside, where they sit alone. I hear anger in Lukic's voice. He wants to know why Belmondo has brought this American back here. When Belmondo comes out, he puts a hand on my shoulder and says quietly, "We must go, Friendo." I risk a last look at Lukic. He nods his head, smiles, and shows his teeth. They are discolored, pushed slightly inward, shark's teeth.

We take a room at a hotel in the hills above the town. Filled with amputees, mostly war veterans here for therapy in natural sulfur pools, this is Hotel Sorrow. On a terrace a few hundred yards downhill, accompanied by an accordion, an aging blond sings Serb nationalist songs. We join them, and Belmondo begins downing drinks. "I am not a quisling," he keeps repeating. "I was in the underground. I spent seven years fighting for this country. What the fuck do I have to show for it?" The blond singer comes to our table, and Belmondo gives her a hundred deutsche marks to keep her singing.

A circle of veterans joins us. All seems lost to them but the words to these melancholy war songs. A man with bushy red hair tilts his head back like a hungry bird and sings, his voice barely audible. Another man puts his hand on my shoulder before we leave and says, "Please give my heart to Dr. Karadzic."

Belmondo is smashed and tries to pick up the hotel receptionist. He tells her that during the war, he once killed four Muslims upriver and then returned to this hotel to sleep.

A few hours later, he knocks on my door, appearing sober. He tells me he is afraid Lukic will come in the night and kill us. "Much paranoia," Belmondo says. "Milan much paranoia." Neither of us has slept. "We can walk across the border," he offers. "You and me. I know a secret route along the river. I know it from the war." Yes, I say. I want to leave. I don't want to die in Hotel Sorrow.

***

Back at Bosko's casino in the mountains of Yugoslavia, I am packing to leave. "Always he has been in the company of killers," his wife, Sabrina, says. "In New York, forget about it, they were all killers. When I met Bosko, he thought I was a spy." Sabrina was born in Zagreb. "Isn't it strange, Super Serb marries a Croat?"

They met at the Women's National Republican Club across from Rockefeller Center in New York, where Bosko had an office. She was a concert pianist, spoke six languages, and modeled on the side. After Bosko fled America, she sold their townhouse and followed him here. "I felt sorry for him," she says.

I apologize for keeping Bosko away on the night of their tenth anniversary. "During the war," she said, "he would be gone for weeks."

Doing what?

"Operations. He was training. I had my own work." Sabrina points to a hotel up on the hill. "During the war, I ran the casino up there. Some nights, I had $250,000 in my pocket, and I'd carry three pistols. The town was full of soldiers then." She pauses. She is struggling with something. "Daniel, the night before Srebrenica, Bosko and I had two hundred soldiers locked in the casino, all of them wearing black masks. Nobody in town could know they were here. They left in the night. There were buses and bulldozers." She gets quiet, looks away. "It was awful."

Then she hands me a photo of a magnificent Rottweiler. "The dog is a trophy from Srebrenica. I got her as a gift." I am just beginning to comprehend what she has told me: This place had been a staging area for the worst massacre in Europe since World War II. "Only five living creatures were left when it was over. The dog was one of them." She looks at the picture, and her face brightens. "Isn't she beautiful?"

****

My bus to the airport departs from Uzice, the town where Bosko was born and spent his childhood and where his family was killed. As we stand at the station, he looks at me grimly. His grand plan has failed in every respect. When I last spoke to Karadzic, Bosko's angel sounded to me like an unsaved man, a man trying desperately to compose some contemporary version of the Nuremberg defense, a man signing off as the world closed in.

Bosko stands facing me now and looks himself to be unsaved. He couldn't save Gotti, can't save Karadzic, won't be able to save himself. As we were escaping Visegrad, Belmondo told me a few things. He said that Bosko is furious that I came to know of his familiarity and ease with such a prolific killer as Milan Lukic. Bosko meant to show me one thing, but instead he showed me another.

By introducing me to this world of killers, he knows that he has made Karadzic frighteningly comprehensible. And he fears that I'm actually not CIA, as he had continued to believe, and that there's a chance my handlers at Langley won't come through with that new, clean passport that shows how much the United States of America appreciates his work and his devotion and that all of that mob unpleasantness in New York City is a thing of the past. Come on home, Bosko.

For such an intimidating, exuberant, even winning figure, Bosko seems, like his country, to be completely lost. He knows that when the war breaks out again, it will be Serb season, just as Tim said. And they will never be able to kill enough to keep that from happening. The look in his eyes says, *Get me out of here.* He has a request before I board my bus. He reaches into his pocket, and as he does, he says, "You'll put in a good word. Tell them I'm ready to go to work again." He hands me six unsmiling passport photos of himself, taken this morning. And six copies of his signature on a neatly folded sheet of white paper.

As always, his feet are hurting him, as if just standing on this ground is killing him. "You can make me clean," he says. "Make me clean."

Esquire, 1997

AN AMERICAN FAMILY—A TRUE STORY OF SIB-LINGS WHO FELL IN LOVE

Patty and Allen are in love. Patty and Allen have four beautiful children. But there's something illegal about that. On the run with the first brother and sister sent to prison for incest in the United States.

In the holding pen at the Milwaukee County Jail, Patty and Allen Muth are waiting for the deputy sheriff to turn his back. They are both handcuffed and wearing prison-issue jumpsuits with white socks and flip-flops. She has hazel eyes and dark-blond hair and weighs ninety-five pounds. He is taller by a foot, a lanky redhead. The deputy is distracted by another inmate. Patty and Allen finally do what they've been plotting for months. It is the moment they have been living for, and it is over in one second. They kiss.

Ten minutes later, they are escorted into a hearing to get the results of a court-ordered test to determine the paternity of their fourth child. As Allen is taken by the sheriff's deputy to the other side of the room, Patty's gaze never leaves him. She's worried that he's losing weight. All she ever sees is his quiet tenderness, his kindness. How he would say he was going out for cigarettes and return with a bouquet of her favorite flowers. He's the only man she's ever loved, and she whispered that in his ear before they entered the courtroom; she wanted to make sure he knew. Allen rakes his fingers

through his red muttonchops and buries his face in his hands. He can't even look at her, his despair is so great. If he is the father, the state will take away their child forever.

Large shamrocks are taped to the wall behind the judge, who is wearing a green tie under his black robe. It is Saint Patrick's Day. The judge announces that a DNA test shows a 99.98 percent certainty that Allen is the father. Patty and Allen request a photo of their child. Their request is denied.

Downstairs, Patty is shackled around the ankles, and a chain is locked around her waist. It makes her feel like a dog. The metal links are cold, like they've been refrigerated. The deputy shackles Allen's ankles. A chain is also locked around his waist. When he submits his wrists for the handcuffs, her eyes search his face. She sees that he wants to cry. She strains toward him, but the guard tightens his grip.

They need to touch once more. Allen reaches for her, but the deputy yanks him toward the door. They are marched outside to different vans. She presses her face to the window and watches him being driven away, tears streaming down her face. They are returning to separate maximum-security prisons, where they are each four months into felony sentences—five years for Patty, eight years for Allen. Their crime: Allen is Patty's brother, and Patty is Allen's sister.

***

Most people think incest laws are to keep fathers from having sex with their daughters, not to punish someone whose only sorry crime is to have found as one's mate the single most inappropriate person in the world, and to have started a loving family, well, a family anyway, with that person.

Most people manage to get through life without sharing a conjugal bed with a sibling, and most people are socialized in such a way that they cannot even fathom such a need, and if that isn't the case, then most people certainly don't make a blood knot the one lasting relationship of their lives, thirteen years and counting, up until the moment that they are mug-shot and shackled and led away to prison—to prison!—to keep them from sleeping with a big brother or little sister. But then, most people don't ever feel that intensity of need about anything. The kind of need where you'll get an offer to stay out of jail, and maybe even get your babies back, if you'll just stay away from him or her, and you instead offer the state your bare wrists for handcuffing and say, *Take me away.* No, most people are not the Muths, proud parents of Jennifer, eleven, Crystal, seven, Paul, two, and Lisa, five months.

Although they didn't meet until Patty was eighteen years old, she and Allen have the same biological parents. Patty was the youngest of Dorothy and Ernest Muth's nine children. She was born in Milwaukee in 1967. Four years earlier, Dorothy Muth had been convicted of child neglect and spent six months in the same prison where Patty is now serving her time. On Patty's birth certificate, her father's job is listed as union truck driver; in truth, he was also a shiftless alcoholic with a mean streak. He would use the family money for liquor and leave Patty's mother with a few dollars a month for diapers and food. They moved often, leaving behind filthy houses, to evade the Milwaukee County Department of Public Welfare, which made more than fifty visits to the Muths' homes. As far as her father was concerned, the social workers could all go to hell, and he threatened to kill those he found on his property.

Patty's older siblings had already been removed by social workers before she was born, and they were scattered across Wisconsin. Some were in foster care, and a few, like her oldest brother, Allen, were in a county orphanage. Three months after Patty was born, the state also placed her in foster care.

Patty's foster home, where she had her own bedroom and pet rabbits, was on a Wisconsin farm. There were a half dozen other foster children. Growing up, she thought this was her real family. Her foster parents taught her to milk cows and ride horses, and she has mostly good memories of those years. But when Patty was six, her foster mother packed a suitcase for her, and the little girl was brought before a judge. She was being adopted out. Patty screamed, clinging to the leg of her foster mother. The patriarch of her new family, a bearded Dutchman, stood in the courtroom, his arms open.

After running away from the Milwaukee County Children's Home, Allen was returned to his father. The oldest and quietest of the Muth children, Allen bore the brunt of his father's abuse. To pay room and board at home, he was contracted out to paint houses. Allen got through those years by dreaming of one day driving a big-rig truck. In the back of his Bible, he drew a picture of a truck, and in the picture he was behind the wheel, escaping his father. He quit school after the eleventh grade and went to work at a Big Boy restaurant, making cakes and pies. For two years, he operated a machine at a bindery, shrink-wrapping magazines—*Playboy*, *Hustler*, and *Better Homes and Gardens*. He saved his money, and by 1979 he had the $1,800 tuition to attend the Sun Prairie Diesel Truck Driver Training School.

In her first few years with the Dutch family, Patty had a temper and was defiant. She missed the farm and the only family she had ever known. Her new family lived in Milwaukee, above their craft store, the Dutch Connection. She grew into a pretty girl with a wild streak. She often skipped school, but she loved reading, especially novels, and she played violin in the orchestra. She kissed a few boys in high school, and in her junior year she had sex with her boyfriend, a Black classmate. She got pregnant. When she delivered the child, her adoptive family insisted that she put the newborn in a foster home. She was told that if she kept the baby, she would no longer be welcome in their house. Three months later, in June 1985, Patty graduated from high school.

Standing against the back wall at her commencement that June night were members of an extended family that she had never met and did not even know existed. They watched her cross the stage and accept her diploma from the principal, who wished her good luck and a good future.

Late that night, a strange woman's voice on Patty's phone announced, "This is your biological sister Barbara." For the first time, Patty learned that she had brothers and sisters, that she came from a family of nine. They had hunted her down. It was the end of a long search to reunite the Muth children, and Patty, the little sister, had been the missing piece of the puzzle. Barbara was up from Texas;

most of the rest lived in Milwaukee. The family met two days later at a Dunkin' Donuts downtown.

The only one missing from that gathering was Allen. The others told Patty about him, that his job was long-distance trucking and that he was on the road. He had gotten married, but that was in trouble, they said. She liked this new family. They felt familiar. Within days, Patty moved out of the Dutch Connection and in with her sister Ruth, who was a registered nurse. Ruth wanted to help her get into nursing school.

Patty met Allen a few days after her graduation. He showed up unannounced. Patty came downstairs, and he was outside, smoking a cigarette. He had red hair and was tall, which surprised her. He was wearing cowboy boots, blue jeans, and a T-shirt, and she thought he looked nice. His voice was gentle, and she liked his shy, polite ways immediately.

He showed her his car, a '69 Olds Cutlass 442 with fur seat covers. He was proud of the car, and he kept it clean and polished, the wheels chromed. She told him she was a neat person, too. Neither of them could abide a mess. He invited her to breakfast at Big Boy, and he opened her car door. He was a careful driver, and when they got to the restaurant, he told her to order whatever she wanted, which she did, and he ordered the same thing.

They sat in silence and looked at each other across the table. Finally, she asked, "So you drive trucks?" She didn't know what else to say.

He told her he'd driven all forty-eight states. And about "reefer" units, short for refrigerated produce trucks. And that his rig had twenty-one gears. She'd never thought much about trucks before, but she was fascinated by this stranger who looked so much like her, and so she paid attention.

Allen drove Patty out to the airport after breakfast and parked in a grassy spot near one of the runways, and the two sat in the Cutlass and watched the planes take off and land.

Patty asked Allen to tell her about their mother. "She was pretty when she was young," Allen said. "You look just like her."

"I appreciate the compliment," Patty said.

They talked all afternoon, sitting in the car with the windows open. She told him about her foster family and her rabbits and how she'd learned to milk cows. How afraid she'd been at age six, when she was adopted and had to leave the farm. She kept studying his face, looking for signs of herself in him. He didn't say much. When he did talk, it was quietly. She asked him what the good things were about his childhood, but he couldn't think of any. She reached over and traced the long scar on his face, and he said it was from a car accident.

As the sun set, they watched the lights of planes taking off, the vapor of contrails lingering in the violet sky. Elvis was playing on his eight-track. She said she wished she were on a plane going to someplace with a beach, like Hawaii. Allen said his truck could take him anywhere he wanted to go.

The next time she saw Allen, he was underneath his car, putting on new shock absorbers. She'd just had a fight with her boyfriend, and she wanted to talk. Allen took her for a walk down by Lake Michigan. She liked the way he listened, and it felt as if there was nothing she couldn't tell him. She trusted him. She liked that he was tall and had red hair, strawberry-blond, really, and she liked his mustache and his sideburns, which he said were a tribute to Elvis.

When the whole Muth family went out on a boat to watch Fourth of July fireworks, Allen was the only one Patty wanted to talk to. She wanted to make up for lost time. He gave her a kiss on the cheek that evening. He told her that he was leaving in his truck in a few days, and she wanted to be around him as much as possible. She spent the next few nights at his house, sharing a bedroom with his two kids. Allen and his wife slept in the other bedroom. Patty lay awake at night, listening to them argue.

One morning, after Allen's wife went to work and the children were off to school, Patty read the newspaper aloud to Allen, and he drew silly mustaches on the photos. She told him that reading without her glasses was giving her a headache, and Allen gently massaged her temples. She was sitting beside him on the couch. His fingers were taking away the pain. That feels good, she said, closing her eyes. Even when her headache was gone, she didn't tell him to stop. He held her face in his hands and stroked her hair. She felt safe with him, and this was a feeling she'd never had before. She reached toward him, and they kissed for the first time.

She was lying in her bed later, when he came in and sat next to her. He had just taken a shower and was wearing a blue terry-cloth robe. He held her hand and then kissed her again. She moved over to give him more room, and he stretched out beside her. He kissed her neck and then her shoulders. "If you don't want to, it's okay," he whispered. "I can just leave."

"No, don't leave."

"Okay. I promise I won't. We'll take this slow. We've got all the time in the world."

She took off her nightgown, and he put his arms around her and held her close. He asked if she was on birth control. She said yes and showed him the pills. "I won't hurt you," he said. "I promise." She liked his weight on her body.

Afterward, she put her head on his chest. I love my kids, he told her, but I don't get along with my wife. I get along with you. They knew they had to keep this a secret.

***

Patty didn't want him to go on the road yet, but driving trucks was his calling. He'd once driven a flatbed with a tarped load of lumber from Madison to Los Angeles in twenty-four hours when the boss said it had to be there the next day. Nothing, he told her, compares to the feeling of sitting up there high on the seat, knowing that you're leaving everything behind. He told her about the time he drove across the Canadian border and pulled to the side of the road for a nap and saw a giant moose coming out of the woods. How it had just looked at him.

Allen drove his truck to Patty's house to say goodbye. He was hauling dry goods to a store in New Jersey. Patty had never seen a truck so big. It took up the whole street. The huge diesel cab was polished to a deep black shine. Patty climbed up the ladder on the side and looked in the window and announced that she was going with him. He shook his head no.

"Don't make me beg," Patty said.

Social workers would later tell Patty that since Allen was thirty-two and she was only eighteen when they met, she had been manipulated by him. But Patty never agreed with this version of events. She knew she wanted to go on that first trip with Allen, and nothing could have stopped her. She didn't think about the consequences; she just felt that a long-lost person had come back into her life for a reason, and she wasn't going to let him go.

Patty rode shotgun, her feet up on the dashboard. She enjoyed sitting up so high, trying to figure out all the instruments. It was like being in the cockpit of an airplane, and she liked watching the scenery go by. She liked watching Allen downshift, working the gears. Under her seat was a photo album full of his safe-driving awards. In back, behind a curtain, was a set of bunk beds, a small TV with a VCR, and shelves for his personal gear. It was all very clean and tidy. He looked over at her and smiled. "You've got pretty eyes," she said. "Sky-blue. Really pretty."

After dropping the load in New Jersey, Allen turned south to Florida, where he took Patty swimming in the ocean. She couldn't get him to wear shorts at the beach. He said he'd spent half his life in a short-pants uniform at the orphanage. He went swimming in his jeans, which made him look very funny when he walked out of the surf.

They crisscrossed the country in that 18-wheeler, hauling loads, feeling as if they were on a honeymoon. In Reno, they played the slots, and in Memphis they pulled the rig into Graceland and joined a tour. Allen bought an Elvis doll and a toy pink Cadillac. Sometimes, at night in the truck, before going to sleep side by side on their bunk, they watched Elvis's *Blue Hawaii* or *Kissin' Cousins*. When his hair got too long, past his collar, she'd cut it for him on the side of the road. At truck stops, they would shower together and roller-skate in the wide parking lots for exercise. Everyone they met just figured they were married.

***

If they could get used to the idea, learn to love it, where's the damage? Isn't that feeling what you're supposed to look for in life? Trust and compatibility and a smile just for you? And they hadn't even known each other until just now, so their being brother and sister didn't matter, really, they told themselves. Hell, it was almost a coincidence. Allen had made the break with his wife, and that hadn't been pretty, draining the water bed and leaving on the sly, but who on God's green earth or the interstate highway system would stand in judgment of them now?

The prosecutor in Milwaukee would later say that she wouldn't have cared if Patty and Allen screwed naked on Wisconsin Avenue, as long as they didn't have children.

In April 1986, Patty noticed that she was getting sick a lot. The choice to have the first child was hers. "I fell in love with Allen, and he was in love with me," she says. "I wanted to have one of his children. I wanted to have a daughter by him that would have red hair, blue eyes, and his caring, his heart."

She didn't know how Allen would take the news. But he said, "I'll stick by you."

The child was born in Abilene, Texas, where they tried to start a life far away from Allen's wife, who had refused to grant him a divorce. When Jennifer was born, just after Thanksgiving, Allen was in the delivery room. (*All children's names have been changed.*) A healthy baby, the doctor proclaimed, but small, like her mother. The Muths spent the first Christmas around a tree decorated with baby ornaments. Allen bought an antique cradle, which he stripped, sanded, and revarnished. There were baby clothes and blankets and a nice recliner for Patty. It was scary having the child those first weeks. "She looked so fragile," Patty says. "Like if you held her too tight, she might break."

Allen had taken a leave from driving to be with Patty during the end of her pregnancy, but now he had to get back to work. He called every night, but Patty was lonely, and she struggled with Jennifer, who was twice admitted to the hospital for pneumonia.

Soon after the birth, the Abilene Child Protective Services office began to get calls claiming that Patty and Allen were siblings and that the child was being neglected. Their sister Barbara, who lived nearby, made the calls. "Barbara wants to get Patty and Allen separated," a Texas social worker wrote down. "She wants us to have them split up. She feels that their relationship (incest) is wrong!! Barbara wants the baby."

Now Allen and Patty were about to learn the power of the taboo, the energy and sanction it gave others to end their relationship, to restore order, to put the apple back on the tree. Somebody was starting to make a fuss, and it was dawning on Allen and Patty that sheriff's deputies can drive up and take your baby away. Steal your baby and give it to the rich, Allen said. Social services can order you into parenting classes and counseling, and even if you do that, let some headshrinker give you tests for hours, they can still take away your baby. Take her from her crib. Because now it's on the record, the official record. Not *Allen loves Patty, will give his life for her.* But other words, like *consanguinity.* Words like *sibling relationship.* Words like *terminate parental rights.* Sure, it's only one municipality in Texas, but these records are connected to other places on highways too cryptic for Allen's mind. Highways of information. And these people have power, the keepers of the records, the social workers, the prosecutors. His father used to rail against these selfsame. Now Allen understood. *You're not going to take away my family. Not my little girl.* He'd bottle-fed her the first evenings, up at night, walking her around, cooing her stories. She was a love child, their start toward the future. And it made him angry. Angry enough to say, *I'll shoot you in the face if you touch my child.* The social worker wrote that down, too.

Two months after sister Barbara's first call, Jennifer was taken from them—permanently, as it would end up. They were stripped of their parental rights. The court issued a no-contact order. If the Muths tried to see their child, they would be arrested.

***

Now would be a good time to reconcile yourself to exactly what incest means. All sorts of warnings echo through time of the dire consequences of spilling your seed carelessly, of lying with the wrong one, of tasting forbidden fruit. Forbidden, which means against the laws of God and man. Now would have been a good time for Allen and Patty to reconcile themselves to that reality. They had been warned. Incest is incest. The law is the law. And, Lord, did they have to have babies? That's when things really started to go wrong. But after the loss of their daughter, they were grief-stricken. And, perhaps strangely, they were more hopelessly in love than ever. *We are staying together*, they began saying to each other, repeating it like a mantra. *We can't let them do this to us.*

Patty and Allen left Texas and spent the next three years on the road. Allen's company didn't allow riders in the winter, for fear that the truck might jackknife, but Patty moved into the truck anyway. Allen often cried at the wheel and would stop along his routes from time to time and buy stuffed animals for his lost daughter. That truck became their home, where they loved and fought. Patty once threw an ashtray at Allen, cutting his head; he slapped her hard. Allen got a heart-shaped tattoo with his and Patty's names inside, and when she admired a black-pearl ring, he put it on layaway and later wrapped it in a velvet jewelry box and surprised her with it.

They both loved sex, and they never lost that desire, and even during the time of grief, it brought them closer, gave them a place to forget, but these days it seemed that sex was the only thing they thought about. Patty joked that maybe it was the vibrations from the truck.

After losing their baby, Allen and Patty were certainly more than aware of the taboo. And maybe the taboo exaggerates actual probability. Jennifer, after all, had been healthy, and in fact a court-approved geneticist would later say that other children of theirs he tested had no genetic defects. But of course, Allen and Patty couldn't have really *known* that that's the way everything would turn out.

They conceived their second child in the truck, or on a blanket next to a stream in Yellowstone when they pulled off for a picnic—they could never tell for sure. They were on a night run to Chicago, delivering fresh lettuce, carrots, and tomatoes to the Windy City Farmer's Market, when Patty's water broke. Blaring his air horn,

Allen pulled the truck right up to the hospital door. He carried Patty down in his arms, yelling, "My wife's about to have a baby!"

For her first two weeks, the newborn, named Crystal, would sleep only on Allen's chest. "I never laid on my back before to sleep," he says.

Allen vowed they'd stay one step ahead of the law. They had learned their lesson. Don't put down roots. No fixed address. Stay on the road. They would keep Crystal with them on the truck. Patty knitted scarves and mittens and packed the cooler with baby formula. On quiet stretches of the freeway, Allen taught her to drive so they could trade off watching their new daughter.

At Christmas, Allen decorated the cab with tiny blinking lights and a miniature tree. There was a Santa Claus hood ornament and a wreath wired through the grille. For three years, the child slept to the hum of the tires, the sound of their voices. The sense of flight, of evasion, that they both felt actually helped make these years the happiest of Patty and Allen's lives. But given the world they were running from, a world of rules, where you have to drive between the lines, pay your taxes, and not sleep with your sister, a terminus was inevitable. On a surprise inspection, the trucking firm discovered that Crystal was a permanent passenger, and, for liability reasons, barred Allen from having the child with him. *But you're breaking up our family*, Allen pleaded. Patty took a room with the baby at a motel in Milwaukee, where relatives and friends could help baby-sit, and she divided her time between being with her daughter and being with Allen on the road.

***

In March 1994, while on a run through Texas to Arizona, Patty and Allen committed a series of stupid blunders. At a truck stop in El Paso, they got caught stealing a radar detector. Eleven days in jail, and Allen was fired from his trucking job. Returning by bus to Milwaukee, the Muths faced even worse news. When they hadn't returned as scheduled and failed even to call, the babysitter reported them to county authorities. They had been gone six weeks, and during that time Crystal had been placed in protective custody.

Nancy Ettenheim, a Milwaukee County prosecutor specializing in difficult family court cases, was handed the Muth file. Immediately, a social worker told Patty that she would never get her daughter back as long as she was with Allen. You're a young, attractive woman, Patty. There are lots of men! And Patty took the advice to heart, at least for a little while. She and Allen had moved into a little room at the Skyway Motel just south of Milwaukee. Allen had taken a job working the graveyard shift at Kmart, buffing floors, and sometimes Patty worked there, too, beside him. But mostly Allen worked alone, locked in the store from midnight to 7:00 a.m., and during this time Patty had an affair. Allen went crazy with jealousy, howling in his motel room, begging for her return. Patty came back, and within months, even as Ettenheim prepared to terminate their parental rights to Crystal, Patty got pregnant again.

She went into labor at Wisconsin State Fair Park, and Allen drove her at seventy-five miles an hour to a Waukegan, Illinois, hospital, in the misplaced hope that crossing the state line might allow them to keep their child, a healthy seven-pound boy. But three weeks later, two cops and a social-service worker, authorized by a judge to use "whatever force necessary," took the newborn. Paul was in his crib, asleep. "We haven't done anything wrong!" Patty screamed. The cops told Allen to step back. Seven months later, the court "terminated forever" Patty and Allen's parental rights to Paul.

For Ettenheim, the Muths became a personal crusade. It wasn't even the sex so much as the resulting children. Paul's birth outraged her. She had hoped to separate the couple, but nothing worked. She was even sympathetic to their desperate, pathetic love. She had studied the family history, and she saw the pathology repeating itself. Their parents had spent their lives having children, only to lose them all to the state. Ettenheim was determined to stop what she called the baby-making machinery.

She dusted off an 1849 Wisconsin statute that criminalized incest. The law, which recommended a maximum penalty of ten years in prison, was used to kneecap the occasional father who had abused his daughter. But as far as Ettenheim was concerned, this was abuse. Those poor children were victims. What would they call their mother? Their father? That last one really sealed it for the prosecutor, really got to her. How the hell was a child supposed to be able to explain this out in the world? Her strategy was to arrest the Muths and, perhaps with the help of a reasonable judge, convict them both of felony incest before they could have any more children.

Patty and Allen were booked in February 1997 at the Milwaukee County Jail and released on a personal-recognizance bond, pending their felony trial. Even while being fingerprinted and mug-shot, Patty and Allen had a secret, which they told no one, not even their lawyer. She was pregnant again.

***

They were not going to lose a fourth baby to the state, even if it meant jumping bond and becoming outlaws. They hatched a plan to flee Wisconsin. The court date was set for July, four months away. If they stayed, prison time seemed a real possibility. The presiding judge had once sentenced a man to eight years for breaking into a Pepsi machine.

They once again set their sights on Texas, where their favorite sister, Ruth, offered them refuge in a little town outside Houston. Her husband once worked for the feds, she said, and he might help them create new identities.

A month before their court date, they began quietly selling off their belongings at a flea market, and to earn more money for their trip, they found work through a temporary-job service, getting up at 4:00 a.m. to bring in $5.50 an hour picking up trash with a poker at a landfill. Just after lunch every day, they would report to a factory where, for twelve hours, they would stack magazines onto pallets for $6.50 an hour. They kept up this schedule for a few weeks, until they got so tired that they requested a new assignment, at a linen factory, where they ironed the cloth napkins that were used at local country clubs.

To aid their flight, they bought a midnight-blue 1986 Ford LTD. It was an old squad car, and the used-car dealer who ran the junkyard promised them it would do 140 miles an hour. Allen found a magazine ad that sold identity kits, complete with new birth certificates, new Social Security numbers, the works. Patty dyed her hair brown in the sink, and Allen liked it. He decided to shave his sideburns and mustache. They cut out a magazine article entitled "How to Live in Mexico on $14 a Day." Neither one spoke Spanish, but that didn't matter.

Allen put his .22 pistol under the car seat in a metal gun box. He had never fired it before. They talked about snatching their kids from the foster parents. "I don't want kidnapping charges," Allen said. "But I can dream about it." They would come back and find the kids when they were eighteen. They'd explain what happened. "We'll tell them we thought of them every day," Patty said. "And that their birthdays were the hardest." They packed up the crib, teddy bears, and boxes of clothes for their new baby into a rented U-Haul.

Goodbye, Wisconsin. Allen drove straight through to Abilene, where they unloaded the U-Haul into a storage shed. He had rented the unit since their last stay in Texas, and stored inside was his classic '69 Cutlass, the car he'd driven on their first date. Its engine was blown, but Allen wouldn't part with it.

They headed on down to Shepherd, in the Piney Woods of East Texas, where Ruth took them in. She told them they could stay as long as they needed. The trial date in Wisconsin came and went. Milwaukee seemed a million miles away.

One day in late July, Patty and Allen pulled up to Labor Ready, a temporary-employment office on the outskirts of Houston. They wanted to work so they could chip in for groceries and living expenses at Ruth's. Pushing open the door, Patty said, "I have a bad feeling about this." They filled out applications, and after the manager entered their vitals into his computer, he looked up. Without saying a word, he turned and walked into the back office. A minute later, a uniformed police officer walked through the front door. "Do you know there's a felony warrant for your arrest?" he asked. Patty could feel the baby kick in her stomach. She was six months pregnant. She turned to Allen: "We're going to lose the baby."

It was as simple as that, and the rest just hit like a bad dream, starting with ten days in a Houston jail and the extradition back to Wisconsin in a van with twelve male prisoners, twelve convicts. Handcuffed and shackled at the ankles. Allen told the driver he was Patty's husband, and he requested to sit next to his pregnant wife. Patty rode with her head on his shoulder and their fingers intertwined. Along the way, they named the child. The trip took a week. Patty and Allen blamed each other for being caught. The van stopped rarely, and Patty developed a painful urinary infection. Allen watched the clock to ensure that Patty took her prenatal vitamins on time. They ate breakfast and lunch at McDonald's. At night, they slept in the detox units at county jails.

Back in Milwaukee, the judge was not going to risk losing Patty and Allen again. Locked up on separate floors at the county jail, they began to write letters back and forth. Allen mailed Patty a copy of his mug shot with a note: "Put some toothpaste on the back of it and paste it inside the cover of your Bible so you don't lose it. We'll get out of here," he wrote. "Everything will be all right."

On October 9, in a quick trial, the Muths were convicted of felony incest. One month later, Patty gave birth. The male deputy who guarded her wanted to shackle her feet to the hospital bed. The doctor said no. Patty was scared and in pain. She cried out for her brother. Their newborn daughter weighed six pounds nine ounces. Patty phoned the chaplain and asked him to call Allen at the jail. "Tell him she's got his red hair and blue eyes."

Eight hours later, Patty returned to the operating room for a tubal ligation. A female deputy stood by during the procedure and nearly fainted from the blood. Patty was scheduled for sentencing in two days, and she had been led to believe that voluntary sterilization might be viewed favorably by the court. She believed it was the only way to keep her baby and avoid going to prison.

Patty got to stay with her baby in the hospital for twenty-four hours. She could take two Polaroids. When she returned to the county jail, she was given ice packs to put on her breasts to keep her from producing milk.

In court for sentencing, Allen saw Patty for the first time since the birth. Her eyes were swollen, and he wanted to put his arms around her. He did not yet know that Patty had been sterilized. He had refused to let them cut him. He'd written to Patty from his cell: "Don't do it. They can't sterilize us." But the judge spoke up, and he was complimenting Patty about her decision to submit to sterilization, and how that registered as a good-faith gesture on her part, and Patty nodded her head and kept looking over at Allen because, bless him, he didn't know anything about it, and Allen looked like he might just crumple to the floor, might just die. Patty was pleading to him with her eyes: *Baby, I did it for us.* But Allen felt like it was over. They could do just about anything to him now. He didn't care anymore.

"I believe severe punishment is required in this case," the judge said. "I think they have to be separated. It's the only way to prevent them from having intercourse in the future, and I believe prison is called for." The judge asked if the age difference didn't prove that Allen had dominated Patty in the same way that a father might victimize his daughter. Allen's lawyer shrugged, saying that he knew couples of even greater age difference who are happily married, including his own daughter and her husband. Give them probation, the attorney argued. They've been punished enough. They can never again see or hold their children.

***

Patty was sent to the maximum-security unit at Taycheedah Correctional Institution in Fond du Lac, Wisconsin. Among her fellow inmates are two women who microwaved their babies. Allen was sent to Dodge Correctional Institution, another maximum-security prison, twenty-five miles across cornfields from Patty, where every day he hears the taunts: "Hey, did you fuck your sister today?" "Hey, maybe I can take a whack at your sister."

Allen writes to Patty every night. He illustrates his letters with pale-blue tulips and red roses. On one envelope, he draws with colored pencils a pair of swans, their necks bowed toward each other, the empty space between them forming a heart. When she receives the letters, she holds them to her face and breathes them in, and she rubs her fingers over his drawings. In their Bibles, they both keep photographs of all their children, including the Polaroid of their last child, Lisa, taken moments after her birth. One afternoon, watching *Jerry Springer* on TV, Patty saw a father who'd had a child with his daughter. Patty called her attorney. "Why are they on TV, and I'm in here?"

Allen is scheduled to remain in his maximum-security prison until 2005. Patty will get out first. She says that she will wait for him. Like in a movie, she will have the car parked outside the prison gate. They will drive out of Wisconsin. They will start again.

Esquire, 1998

SOLDIERS IN THE ARMY OF GOD: THE FUTURE OF THE ARMED ABORTION CONFLICT

Who is killing our doctors? The Army of God believes violence is the only means to end legal abortions. A former dope dealer, a convicted killer, and a mixed-up kid come together to make a hit list. The kid buys a gun.

Jonathan O'Toole is nineteen years old. He is from Kansas City. For the last couple of months, he's been sleeping, oversleeping rather, in the spare bedroom of Neal's white-porched house on its sylvan cul-de-sac in Carrollton, Georgia. God sent Jonathan here to help Neal save the babies. But for the moment, he snoozes.

Jonathan always knows that he's almost awake when he feels a little morning twinge in his right arm where the Akita at the animal shelter where he worked sunk its teeth in and wouldn't let go. For half an hour that damn dog held on, tightened its vise grip, as Jonathan punched it in the face as hard as he could. Blood was pooled everywhere, Jonathan was covered in it, and he was about passed out by the time his rescuers arrived. He could hear them whispering: *My God, never seen anything like this kid's arm.* That was a year ago, and now

Jonathan knows what pain is. And his pain makes him identify with the babies even more. The pain increases his grief. Jonathan thanks God for the pain. He feels it has liberated him.

He swings his legs over the side of the bed, sits there for a second, coming to, and then he runs his fingers lightly over the twisted Frankenstein graft that is his reconstructed arm, taps the mottled skin softly to get feeling. Time to get up.

As he pads in his plaid pajamas down the hall and around the corner into the living room, he sees the master of the house, Neal Horsley, sitting at the computer workstation in his glass-enclosed office off the dining room. "Come look at what I did," Neal says, motioning to him, excited.

Neal has executed some commands on his website, which is called The Nuremberg Files: Visualize the Abortionists on Trial. On the website, he collects the names, addresses, and photos of hundreds of doctors across America who perform abortions. Also supplied are pictures of the doctors' houses and cars, license-plate numbers, names and dates of birth of their children, churches and pastors and rabbis, social-activity information, and career profiles, as in: "Has been butchering babies for sixteen years." Neal smiles broadly and bellows, "I would not want to be in the business of abortin' babies in the United States of America today!"

Neal wears reading glasses, green sweatpants stained with paint, a red sweatshirt, and bedroom slippers. A little earlier, he had typed in "Barnett Slepian," the name of the doctor killed last night in Buffalo by a sniper while standing in his kitchen with his wife and two young sons. He then tapped the STRIKE command on his keyboard, which drew a black line through Slepian's name.

When Neal tells him that an abortionist was shot in his own home, Jonathan knows what that means. Despite hundreds of bombings, acid attacks, and killings at clinics over the past two decades, never before in America has somebody killed a doctor at home. This changes everything. For Jonathan, it's the next logical step. It's exciting.

Not every day you get a kill. Neal hums along with "Tangled Up in Blue" and leans back, admiring the color monitor. Animated blood flows down the screen. Big piles of fetuses and aborted body parts. Links to dozens of like-minded sites, all gathered in Neal's internet domain, christiangallery.com. "Good mornin'!" Neal booms, cracking Jonathan on the back. He's in a celebrating mood. "Welcome back to the living!"

When Jonathan showed up at Neal's doorstep two months ago, he was so overwhelmed with grief for the babies that he felt he was on the verge of committing a violent act. He found Neal by searching for the words *murder* and *abortion* on the internet in his parents' basement, and now here he is. Make me an instrument of the movement, he told Neal. Put me on the front lines; teach me. Neal said fine. Gonna show this boy how to turn the internet into a weapon. Since then, Jonathan has become a sort of aide-de-camp to Neal, processing new doctor information: receiving it from all over, confirming it, inputting it, and uploading it onto the website. He's a classic good boy—apple-cheeked, real eager, real serious about his Bible, and reliable. Eats like a horse and is still growing. He was the kind kid in school, the one who befriended the special needs boy when no one else would, always identified with the underdog. *Whatsoever you do to the least of my brothers, that you do unto me.* Jonathan's not perfect by any means. He does have a little trouble getting out of bed. Last night, he was up late composing a love letter to Holly, a college girl from California he met online recently. "Dear Holly," the letter began, "I have come to the realization that my life, and all that I am, is in God's hands." Some nights, he stays up maintaining the abortionist roll call, studying the faces over and over, feeling anger and pity for the butchers.

Jonathan stares at the screen, at the former Barnett Slepian, OB/GYN. Seven other names have also been crossed out; these are the doctors, nurses, and escorts who have been killed in bombings and ambushes in the past few years. Fifteen more names are shaded gray—they have been seriously wounded. Neal reaches to the keyboard to show Jonathan something. It's just a simple command to go from wounded to dead. Jonathan has added lots of names to this list, but this is the first positive result he's actually gotten to participate in. *Seeya, Barnett.*

This is exactly what the Scriptures promised would happen to those who sow bloodshed. "Nowhere to run," Jonathan says, congratulating Neal. "Nowhere to hide."

***

Six hours pass. Gloria Feldt, the president of Planned Parenthood, is holding a press conference, accusing Neal of inciting the murder of Dr. Slepian. She produces a copy of Neal's list with the crossed-out name. She then says that Dr. Slepian's name was marked out *before* he was killed.

"We'll sue her ass!" Neal tells Jonathan. "That's slander!" But Neal has already calculated that the more people think he was involved in the murder, the more they'll visit his website.

The accusation, in truth, is the best publicity Neal could get. You can't *buy* that kind of publicity. It's very good for the movement, of course. The public has got to know, if it doesn't already, that there will be more killings. No more pussyfooting around. But it's also very good for Neal. He's never dreamed of this kind of attention. "Yes, sir, we'll sue her ass!" Neal says again, this time cackling. Neal's cackle rings with utter delight.

***

Every weekday, Neal drives into Atlanta, where he works on computer databases for the Centers for Disease Control and Prevention. He doesn't want anyone to know that, and at work he goes by his first name, Otis. So when the press calls start coming in, Neal tells Jonathan, "Just say I'm a computer programmer, nothing more." Neal wants to maintain a real separation between his daily bread and his anti-abortion activities. He's good at what he does, and he likes his house, with its white porch and the Bradford pear trees, and he wants to keep paying the mortgage and supporting his family. He calls it paradise here.

Dr. Slepian probably liked his family a lot, too, and wanted to support them, as did the security guard who died in Birmingham,

Alabama, and the nurse who had shrapnel and nails from a pipe bomb driven into her legs and eye. But these folks were in the baby-slaughter business, and, as Neal keeps telling the reporters, this is a war, and there will be casualties.

In the three years since he started his website, Neal hasn't ever gotten television producers even to return his calls, except once when he heard from the *Jerry Springer Show*. Now the *networks* are calling, along with dozens of print and radio reporters. Tomorrow, he'll be mentioned on the front page of the *New York Times*.

Jonathan picks up the phone, which has been ringing incessantly in the two days since the killing. It's NBC, wanting a satellite feed with Neal. How long before he can be ready?

On Monday evening, seventy-two hours after Slepian's murder, the names begin to come in. By email and snail mail. Envelopes stuffed with photographs, addresses, and names of more abortion doctors are stacked all over the office. Sent from cities and small towns across America, they also include the names of nurses, clinic escorts, and politicians. One letter, written in long hand, has a dozen new names and includes this postscript: "I got the nurses' names at night from a dumpster behind the clinic."

The emails are running thirty-to-one condemning the website. But even the negative emails make Neal giddy. He has struck a nerve. Jonathan sorts the hate emails into "death threats" and "curses." One begins, "Die, Neal Horsley, Die."

"File that with the curses," Neal says.

"It's not a death threat?" Jonathan asks.

Neal shakes his head. "That's a seriously developed curse." Another reads, "You are an idiot of the highest degree." Neal is delighted. "That's good!" he yells. "Better than being an idiot of the lowest degree."

Just as Neal had promised, Jonathan is right on the front lines. He can hardly keep up with all the new names and all the emails. Neal tells him not to worry about the threats. "We got us a good Jesus," he says. "He holds our enemies' hearts in his hand."

October 28

Mr. Neal Horsley,

I am pleased to tell you that after I finish this letter, my partner and I will catch the first flight to your town. We have a bullet with your name written on it. Hope to see you smile after we've shot you through the spine.

October 28

Watch your back, son . . . you will be shot. Be forewarned . . . this is not an idle threat. To add insult to injury, you will be killed on December 25, 1998. Jesus Christ's birthday. Watch your back. I'm deadly serious.

***

When Neal goes to work, he finds pictures from his website taped inside the elevators. All week long, he feels his coworkers watching him. Most did not know his political views before, and his exposure on national television has alarmed them. They fear his work gives him access to confidential information about doctors, including home addresses and Social Security numbers.

By the end of the week, he gets a call from his supervisor. There will be a meeting to discuss this, and Neal's attendance is required. Several of the top brass at CDC will be there.

"Shall I bring my lawyer?" Neal asks.

***

On Halloween, Barnett Slepian has been dead for eight days, Neal has had a million new hits to his website, and an FBI task force is sniffing around. The Justice Department is promising a separate investigation. Neal jokes that the new neighbors might just be from the government. There is an echo on the phone, and he reminds everybody to say hi to the FBI when making calls. He's never been happier in his life.

Jonathan is at the kitchen counter, carving the jack-o'-lantern, reaching in to pull out the wet orange pulp and seeds. He saws a jagged smile into the face, handling the knife with the surety of a young man who spent his childhood skinning rabbits. He cuts wide slits for the eyes and a triangle nose.

Neal is only a few feet away at the workstation. He is singing along to Bob Dylan's "We Live in a Political World." A love for Dylan is one of the things he and Jonathan share. The first song Jonathan ever heard as a kid was when his father would play Dylan's "Man Gave Names to All the Animals." Neal is particularly happy tonight. The boys at CDC didn't know they were dealing with someone who knew his rights. His job performance is excellent, and he conducts himself in a professional manner, so how can they touch him? The most they could do was move him to a remote facility away from everybody else. A clear victory for free speech, Neal believes. Of course, he's not supposed to tell anybody about the arrangement.

As Neal taps away, joyously answering emails, Jonathan can hear the machine beeping steadily as new mail comes in. One message is from Bob Lokey, a long-haul trucker who wants to pay a visit in the morning. He's got urgent matters to discuss with Neal. Before spending twenty years in San Quentin on a first-degree murder conviction, Lokey was trained by the US Army to infiltrate enemy lines as an intelligence operative. Now, in addition to hauling freight, he's working full-time inspiring people to kill doctors. Any word from Lokey is always exciting to Neal. The man's love for the babies is inspiring.

Neal's wife, Carol, is upstairs working on a research paper for her graduate work in speech and language pathology. Yesterday at school, someone asked her if she was related to Neal. It made her proud to say yes, but she is concerned that Neal isn't choosing his words carefully right now, and she's a little afraid of how it will change their lives. Carol is used to plenty of change with Neal. When they met, he was selling pot, had hair down to his waist, and was known to all as Cowboy Neal. At one point, Cowboy Neal's big dream had been to seed America with marijuana. He wanted everyone high. He spent a little time locked up instead. That's where Neal found Jesus.

A few years out of prison, he enrolled at Westminster Theological Seminary, outside Philadelphia. Neal's father had died from a mysterious infection four months before he was born. Neal says that just days before he passed, knowing that he would never see his child, his father talked deliriously to his unborn son from his deathbed, telling him that everything was going to be okay. In seminary, Neal felt called to speak for unborn babies and to reassure them that they were going to be okay, too. In a talk delivered before he graduated, in 1985, Neal predicted that someday Christians would be aiming rifles at abortionists.

Five months before Carol and Neal met, she had an abortion. She was only sixteen at the time. Years later, when they wanted to start a family, Carol couldn't get pregnant. Neal told her that she never would conceive unless she truly asked God's forgiveness. She resented Neal bitterly for saying it, and she reminded him that he had once begged a girlfriend to have an abortion and that after she had refused, he had never even seen his child. No, Neal had said, I haven't been perfect, but if you want to start a family, you've got to get right with God. After Carol got on her knees and begged forgiveness, she got pregnant.

Neal and Carol's seventeen-year-old daughter, Kathy, bounces down the stairs from her bedroom, where she's been holed up on the phone with her girlfriend, and announces that she's going out to a Halloween party.

"Have you fed Negro?" Neal asks. "Don't let that cat in." As she leaves, he looks after her admiringly. "Lordy, Lordy, is she beautiful," he sighs. Kathy is the youngest of the Horsleys' three children. She has two older brothers. One is an army sergeant stationed in Germany, and the other is on the debate team at Georgia State. A talker and a shooter, Neal likes to say.

As Jonathan lights the candle in the pumpkin, the kids begin to arrive, and Neal calls an end to the day's work. He gets into the Halloween spirit, sitting in his rocking chair as the night darkens, greeting his neighbors as they cross his porch. He tries to guess who is under each mask. One kid carries a bloodied plastic chain saw; there are several Spice Girls; others are dressed as hunters. "Our local militia," Neal says. Locked in a room off the porch, Jesse, the family's schnauzer, is yipping. Negro, crouched in the bushes, watches with his glowing green eyes.

"Neato frito!" Neal exclaims at one kid's outfit. The kid lifts up his mask and glares at Neal. "Hey, don't call me names," he says. Neal practically falls out of his chair laughing.

Tonight, Carrollton, Georgia, feels like the Halloween capital of America. Kids, lots of them, keep coming, dressed as butterflies, in pink tutus, as Bill Clinton. Some trick-or-treaters look to be in their twenties. "Country people," Neal says affectionately. "They think we're rich."

Jonathan sits on the porch swing. He has rolled up the cuffs of his blue jeans and is smoking a corncob pipe. He's been thinking about all the publicity he and Neal have been getting. It's been great, a real charge, and if this is what the Lord wants of him, so be it, but Jonathan wants to *do* something; that's why he came here. He knows that Neal is living in the sniper's reflected glory; without the killing, they wouldn't have had so many more hits to their website. But it's so much more important to remember, he believes, that without the threat of death, doctors will never stop killing the babies. What's the next move? Somewhere out there is a sniper who hasn't been caught. Now is no time to let up. He's been thinking a lot about Paul Hill and how that good man on death row didn't sit idle on a comfortable cul-de-sac. He did something. He shot Dr. Britton. Butcher Britton. Jonathan is in a quiet mood and doesn't feel much like playing.

Finally, the kids stop coming, and Neal turns out the porch light. At about 11:00, as he does every night, he falls asleep in his chair. After a few minutes of snoring, he wakes himself up. "Carol," he calls out to his wife softly, in the voice of a child. "Carol. *Caaaa-rooool.* Need my snuggy buggy. Sleepy-pie time. Need my sleepy pally. Need my snuggy buggy. Carol!"

***

At 4:00 a.m., Jonathan is still awake, anticipating the arrival of Bob Lokey. He's never met a killer before.

He's got such a sense of destiny about this, and always has. Sometimes his level of intensity has scared people. When Jonathan asks his email friend Holly to take a look at The Nuremberg Files to get an idea of what he's about, she goes south on him. You believe this stuff? she writes, signing her email "Your sister in Christ."

Jonathan figures any man who holds a baby in his arms or who watches a child being born could never tolerate abortion. When he was seven, he watched his sister being born. He has since swaddled each of his newborn siblings in his arms, cut their umbilical cords, seen the mystery and beauty of birth.

He took part in his first abortion protest when he was eight. His father was the pastor of a tiny charismatic church in Salt Lake City; the congregation met in a rented restaurant on Sunday mornings. When church elders voted to picket the local abortion clinic, Jonathan's mother took him along, joining about twenty-five kids, most from his home-school group. The church elders locked arms in front of the clinic's glass doors. Jonathan and the other children each wore a sandwich-board protest sign. Some were decorated with a photo of a fetus in a trash can.

The police arrived, and Jonathan watched as his Sunday-school teacher was handcuffed. He wished he could have done more. When he was ten, his family moved to a rented farm outside Kansas City, where Jonathan was home-schooled by his mother and grandmother. In the eighth grade, he was enrolled in a small Christian school. He loved reading Tolkien and C. S. Lewis, but the Bible was his favorite book.

Jonathan was not prepared for public high school. "I'd never been exposed to anything vaguely resembling the world before," he says. "I wanted desperately to live somewhere where the law of God was the law of the land. I lacked the social skills to relate to people who hadn't grown up in a church environment. I went between being withdrawn to having an air of superiority."

Gym class was particularly painful. He had never played team sports and could barely throw a ball. He began to lift weights to fill out his six-foot frame. One night during his sophomore year, he had a dream in which he stalked into gym class with an automatic rifle and slaughtered his classmates. "I just mowed them down, and I didn't feel any guilt until I woke up."

A mythology class was one of the few bright spots. He fell in love with Latin and Greek, plowing through Homer, Virgil, and Ovid. Jonathan took his SATs early, and at sixteen he was admitted into the great-books program at St. John's College in Annapolis, Maryland. His parents didn't have tuition money, though, so instead he accepted a full scholarship to Rose Hill, a tiny Greek Orthodox college in South Carolina, delaying his enrollment until his mother gave birth to his youngest brother in September 1996.

Watching his baby brother come into the world was the most beautiful thing he'd ever seen. His brother was smaller and more fragile than his other siblings, and as he held the tiny child, he remembered the sign he had worn as a kid. That aborted baby didn't look so different from his brother.

When he left for college, he took along a pistol. By day at Rose Hill, he read Aristotle, Plato, and Plutarch; by night, he surfed the internet at the campus library, trying to educate himself on the anti-abortion movement.

On a website called Prisoners of Christ, he discovered Shelley Shannon, the thirty-seven-year-old housewife whose spree of abortion bombings ended in 1993 after she shot a doctor in both arms outside his Wichita, Kansas, clinic. Jonathan wrote to Shannon in prison, sending his prayers and telling her that he supported her actions. "I could tell by her letters that she took pleasure in what she did," he says. He loves that she kept pictures of burned clinics in her cell.

"I was really ashamed of myself, reading about this woman who had the courage to do what I felt like I oughta been doing—her all alone, and she's a woman."

He talked with other students about terrorizing abortion clinics, and his talk scared people. After thirty of his classmates held a special meeting to discuss their fears, Jonathan left school and returned home to his parents, taking the job at the animal shelter where he was injured. As part of his rehabilitation, he practiced shooting a .22

rifle out his bedroom window. Even with his mangled arm, he could hit a moving squirrel from sixty yards.

***

When he was in prison, Bob Lokey tattooed a woman's name on the head of his penis. Actually, he meant to spell "Charlene," but it hurt too much, and he is left with the letters CHAR hanging there forever, unless he should choose to have them removed. And that's unlikely, because Charlene was the only woman he cared anything for, the mother of his two children and his former wife. He lost her after he went to prison in 1962.

He was still in prison in 1973 when the Supreme Court rendered its decision in *Roe* v. *Wade*. The legalization of abortion changed Lokey's life. God spoke to him for the first time and told him to do something about it.

Now Lokey is fifty-eight years old, a powerfully built, gray-bearded man with massive forearms flecked with other fading jailhouse tattoos. He doesn't eat red meat. He does yoga most every day, even when he's on the road. He's a black belt in tae kwon do. When he steps out of his Tempo in Neal's driveway, he is wearing blue jeans and sandals with white socks. He looks like a cross between Hemingway and Popeye.

Jonathan overslept, and he is still pretty much asleep when he meets Lokey, who shakes his hand—grabs it and really wrings it out. On the inside of his right forearm is a baby angel blowing a horn, surrounded by fluffy clouds. "I read your poem about the use of force on the website," Lokey tells Jonathan. His voice is a deep southern rumble. "That's a powerful poem."

Lokey has not yet loosened his grip. "You love the babies, don't you?"

"Yes, sir. I do."

"I can tell. Never let anybody tell you that babies aren't souls before they are born. I have memories that predate my own conception."

Neal has told Jonathan that Lokey is the best trained and most disciplined soldier of his generation, the cream of the crop of potential assassins. Lokey is obsessed. Only an obsessed man plants a sixteen-by-twenty billboard of aborted fetuses in his front yard, as Lokey had done on a country road between Opp and Elba, Alabama.

Lokey drove five hours up from his trailer there to talk strategy. He's concerned about all the heat Neal is getting. Especially about the death threats. "If they want to kill somebody," Lokey says, "have 'em kill me. There's nothing I'd like more than being nailed on a cross for the babies."

Lokey has his own home page linked to Neal's website. On it, he writes that killing doctors is justifiable homicide. "I'm the one causing you all these problems," Lokey says as the three settle in the den. When Neal holds up his hand to remind him that tape recorders are running, Lokey says, "I don't give a damn. Any of the three of us could be FBI."

"But you must understand what's going on here," Neal says. "The media is trying to say I incited the sniper to kill."

"And that should make you very proud. It sure makes me proud," Lokey says. "I threw out my TV a long time ago. I hate the media."

"Journalists are ball-less, spineless cowards who have been pussy-whipped and vaginally defeated," Neal says, shaking with laughter. "Can I get an amen?"

"Vaginally defeated!" Lokey repeats. "That's why I'm celibate. Can you imagine me—"

"Whupped by the pussy!" Neal yells.

"Vaginally defeated!" Lokey yells back. "God told me to give them up," he says, quieting down. "I haven't had sex myself since 1984. Women are all manner of vileness."

"Lokey, you crack me up," Neal says. "I had some wild sex just last night, right upstairs. Hell, smoking dope, fucking, and boozing— that's who I am naturally. But now I got me a good Jesus. I haven't touched the weed for eighteen years, and I only have sex with my wife."

Earlier, Neal had let Jonathan in on his wild sexual past. "When I was young, anything that gave me penile friction I'd engage in," he'd told him. "Men, mules, I'd fuck anything."

Jonathan couldn't believe what he heard. The closest his parents ever came to suggesting that sex had occurred between them was saying that they had "gotten pregnant."

"I've ridden a mule," Jonathan said. "But you screwed one?"

"Yep."

Jonathan is still a virgin. And until he clicked on Neal's website, he'd never seen another man's erection, much less two guys kissing. He'd never even heard of fist fucking. Neal calls this part of his website the Desecration Digest. It also features photos of a woman sucking off a Rottweiler. There's a snapshot of a woman shitting into a man's mouth. The pictures make a lot of Christians uneasy, but Neal, who also sells JAIL FAGGOTS bumper stickers on the website, says the decision to show these photos was inspired by a passage from the Bible: "Have nothing to do with the fruitless deeds of darkness but rather expose them." The porn is Neal's bait and switch. Mixed in are images of mangled fetuses. "We want to smuggle the images into people's brains." Yesterday, amid the hate emails, he got an email that made him hoot: "More girl-on-girl pix!"

Lokey wants to get down to business. He leans forward, addressing Neal. "There are people that I'm absolutely certain have read my website and have gone and killed somebody or hurt somebody. That was my intention."

"When you say that, Lokey," Neal says, serious again, "can't you see they're organizing now to prosecute me?"

"Look here, buddy," Lokey says. "In my life, I've discovered that sometimes violence is necessary, and if it is, you just have to roll up your shirtsleeves and dive in."

"And so what you just said," Neal says, "is that you're absolutely certain that your website, which is located on mychristiangallery..."

Lokey ignores his concern. He is studying the room, with its country furniture and paintings of ducks. His eyes pass over every object, as if for the last time. Then he looks out the large windows of the den to the pond and into the nearby woods. The smell of brewing coffee is in the air. Finally, Lokey looks at Jonathan. "A man should be safe in his own house, right?"

Jonathan nods.

"Not in a war," Lokey says. "There's nobody safe. And when you kill in a war, it's not murder. People get killed in war. That's what happens."

***

In the evening, Neal and Jesse go on their walkabout through the neighborhood, as they do most evenings, getting exercise and saying hello to the kids, who all love to pet Jesse. As Neal's green sweatpants disappear around a bend in the road, Lokey and Jonathan stand alone on the porch. Jonathan is very impressed with Lokey's uncompromising air. He had Neal sounding like a man who just wants to preserve his comfort. He had Neal sounding *timid*. Jonathan wasn't questioning Neal's commitment, but if he wanted practicality, if he wanted to be *safe*, he'd go back to picketing clinics. Lokey has never picketed clinics. "I can't go near them. I'd kill somebody with my bare hands."

"But Lokey," Jonathan says, "what if God told you to kill? What if that's what God wants?"

"I would kill," Lokey says.

God spoke to him in prison. "I was called to circumcise myself. I obeyed the call," he tells Jonathan. Lokey tried to compromise with God, asked the prison doctor to do the operation. When he was refused, Lokey, who was forty at the time, took a single-edged razor blade and, sitting on the toilet after lights-out at San Quentin, cut away his own foreskin.

"God took and guided my hand. It was the same as if he had done it with his own hand."

Lokey turns to Jonathan. "You don't tell one other person your plan," he says. "Not even Neal—he might say something in his sleep. But when God calls, Jonathan, you answer."

The next day, Jonathan emails Lokey:

Lokey—

I'm enraged within myself. Hatred has become my driving force. It is a hatred which pours out from a fountain of love for the unborn children. . . .

I am very ashamed of myself. I speak about a fountain of love for the unborn, but where is the evidence of that? Lokey, it's building up inside of me. I can't contain it forever. I am containing it now, and trusting that the Lord knows how much I can take.

Lokey's response surprises and disappoints Jonathan:

Jonathan—

I need to caution you about getting too close to these babies. Your time will come. You have to wait for it, and don't push it, don't rush it. You will know when it is here and you will know what to do. It might be any of a number of things. . . . Not being there yet does not spell failure. . . .

Now, I can't expect the babies not to be on your mind twentyfour hours a day, as they are on mine. And I wouldn't have it any other way for myself. We can't do everything alone right at this moment. The world will catch up and then hell will break loose. I give my most solemn word on this.

***

November 11, Veterans Day, has become, to some in the anti-abortion movement, Remembrance Day, the day to commemorate the aborted birthdays of the unborn. Much of the violence against abortion providers in the past few years has happened in the weeks leading up to this date. Dr. Slepian received a faxed warning to this effect on the day he was shot.

On November 9, Neal takes a trip into town to check his mailbox. Since he started becoming famous, he's been receiving checks in the mail. From just a few dollars to several hundred, to support The Nuremberg Files. Today, there's a pretty nice haul, nine envelopes. Sitting in his car, he opens the third envelope, which contains a letter that reads, "You have just been exposed to anthrax." Probably a hoax, but within an hour, Neal is being scrubbed by technicians wearing space suits and oxygen tanks, just in case the letter actually contained the deadly bacteria.

But before getting decontaminated, he calls Jonathan at home. "Send out a press release!" he instructs. "I've been anthraxed!" Back at home, in interview after interview, the story becomes sort of a routine. "Anthraxed! I've been anthraxed!" Jonathan must hear Neal say that to a dozen reporters.

Michael Bray, who served nearly four years in prison for bombing clinics in the Washington, DC, area, emails to say, "I'm glad it was you and not me." The anthraxing puts Neal's picture on the front page of the Atlanta newspaper. Looking at it, Neal says to his daughter, "Good thing I'm married, because if I had to rely on that photo to get laid, I'd be in trouble."

Jesse, the family dog, is dead. Two nights ago, he came into the house, panting, whimpering, clearly in pain, and then he walked off into the woods and died. Neal is sad and says it was just Jesse's time to go. But Jonathan worked at an animal shelter, and he knows a poisoned dog when he sees one.

***

The night before he goes home for Thanksgiving, Jonathan and Kathy go see *The Wizard of Oz*. Jonathan has been careful not to become too friendly with Kathy in the months at Neal's house, but now she is almost like family. On the way to the movie, they get very lost, and Jonathan begins singing Christian praise songs. For hours, they drive the back roads, singing and praying for each other.

They have much to pray about. That day at school, a girl shouted at Kathy across the lunch table, "I know somebody who wants to blow your house up!" The police came to the house after school. Kathy doesn't know how seriously to take the threat, but somebody once threatened to kill Jesse, and now Jesse is dead.

The next morning, Jonathan climbs onto a bus to return to Kansas City, carrying most of the things he owns in a duffel bag.

Neal hugs his neck, and it crosses Jonathan's mind that they may never see each other again.

Raking his cowboy hat low over his eyes, Jonathan settles into a seat in back for the twenty-hour trip home. He waves goodbye to Neal and says a quick prayer for the safety of the Horsleys. He lifts his heart to Jesus. *Thy will be done.*

An older woman with red-haired, Celtic good looks is seated a few rows ahead. She's mid-thirties and slim. As the miles roll by, Jonathan tries to catch her eye. He stretches his legs, drags the heels of his cowboy boots across the floor. He whistles a tune.

Somewhere across the Tennessee border, with the whole night ahead of them, the woman ambles back and sits beside him. "So, are you really a cowboy?"

She'd been in Florida, taking care of an old man and his special needs son, and, like Jonathan, is now headed back to Kansas City. "I love your voice," she says after they've talked for a while, "and your eyes." He tells her that he designs websites for a radical pro-life group. She hardly believes he's still a teenager. By early dark, they are kissing, and after they switch buses in Nashville, they sleep through the night in each other's arms.

Two days back in Kansas City, they meet up at a bar. After Jonathan has four beers, they climb to the roof of a nearby building where the woman used to live. There, on a blanket, near the elevator shaft, Jonathan loses his virginity. Behind him, he can hear the black machinery of the elevator grinding.

Pull out before you come, she had told him. She wasn't on the pill and didn't want to get pregnant. He ignored the request, and as he came inside her, it occurred to him, as it had often occurred to him recently, that he didn't know how long he would live, and that he had an expectation of early death. If God chose to plant the seed, that would be all right with Jonathan. A warrior needs to leave a legacy, he thought.

The next day, Jonathan drove out to a lady gunsmith at Guns Unlimited in Clay County, Missouri, and bought two rifles, a Ruger .22 and a Winchester 30-30. He paid cash.

Later, as he crouched in the woods, using a hedge-apple tree for support, he aimed the Ruger at his target. The crisp early winter air was on his face, and as he looked through the scope and pulled the trigger, he thought only of the babies.

Esquire, 1999

A FEW GOOD NAZIS

For years, Private Jim Burmeister and his buddies proudly displayed swastikas in their barracks at Fort Bragg, North Carolina. So why did it take the murder of a Black couple for the US Army to notice its white supremacist problem? A special report from inside the bunker.

When Private James Burmeister Jr., twenty, left the barracks at Fort Bragg, North Carolina, in early darkness on the night of December 6, 1995, his hair was cowlicked, nearly uncombable. It gave the young paratrooper from Pennsylvania a goofy, sweet, unfinished quality. Gawky and a little too tall, wearing square-framed glasses on his long face, Burmeister looked like an overgrown kid from a Norman Rockwell painting.

Fort Bragg is home to the 82nd Airborne Division, one of the United States Army's elite fighting units. The 82nd, known as the All-American, has served with distinction in almost every war, skirmish, and peacekeeping mission of this century. So many members of the 82nd Airborne served in Vietnam that Fort Bragg's hometown, Fayetteville, was called Fayettenam. But the town has always been proudest of the fact that it was paratroopers from the 82nd who filled the skies over Europe at the end of World War II, helping to liberate European Jews from the most notorious of Hitler's concentration camps.

After piling into a black Chevrolet Cavalier, Burmeister and two 82nd Airborne buddies, Specialist Randy Meadows and Private Malcolm Wright, both twenty-one, drove past the field where six weeks before, another paratrooper from the 82nd had shot up his brigade, killing one soldier and wounding eighteen. They headed fifteen miles out into Harnett County, where Burmeister rented a room from friends for $245 a month in a mobile home set against tall pines. As an unmarried enlisted man, Burmeister was not authorized to live off post, but as long as he showed up for formations, nobody seemed to mind.

Inside the trailer, a German flag with a large swastika dominated the living-room wall. Burmeister loved Nazi flags. He'd hung them above his bunk in the barracks for more than a year before he moved here. He'd never even considered living off post until that drunken night in August when he picked a fight with a Black infantryman and got his nose broken. The Army's Criminal Investigation Division had been a problem even before that, following him into bars and "harassing" him. "I've had fucking government on my ass for the last couple months," he told a friend back home. "They think I'm a racist or something." So Jimmy had been laying low. Let everybody else live at Bragg; he was happier out here in the sticks.

In his bedroom, he had five different Nazi flags, including a Hitler Youth flag, which hung above an eight-by-ten photograph of his sister Lisa. It was nearing the third anniversary of her death, at age nineteen, from leukemia, and her memory was one of the few things, he wasn't ashamed to admit, that could make Jimmy cry.

With Burmeister's new puppy, Zoe, scampering underfoot, the soldiers drained several cans of Milwaukee's Best and cranked up their favorite white supremacist band, Skrewdriver. Malcolm Wright talked about religion and his fear of white genocide. Malcolm had a spiderweb tattoo on his elbow.

You rightfully earned a spiderweb, Jimmy knew, only if you killed somebody, a nigger or a faggot. And though Malcolm hadn't earned his tattoo, Jimmy admired the spiderweb as if it were a medal of honor.

The three popped more beers and got ready to go out on the town. The black Ruger 9mm pistol that Burmeister's father had given him after his nineteenth birthday lay on the coffee table. As he was leaving the trailer, Burmeister stuck the pistol into his belt and said, "Maybe I'll earn my spiderweb tonight."

Burmeister insisted on driving. Wright climbed into the backseat, and Jim handed the gun to Meadows, who stashed it under the front seat.

Ever since his fight, Jim had been growing his hair so that he'd be harder to peg as a racist skinhead. Tonight, he didn't even wear red laces in his Doc Martens, which would have marked him immediately. He was wearing his black flight jacket, but since he'd removed the Nazi patches, he could be just about anybody in Fayetteville, a city with forty-two thousand active-duty soldiers.

They could deny him the outside symbols, but inside he knew his allegiance. When he sent off for promotional materials from the skinhead 'zine *Blood and Honour*, he'd signed his name "Jim Burmeister, 88." *H*, the eighth letter of the alphabet. Heil Hitler. Sometimes when he was alone, listening to Skrewdriver, he'd do the Nazi salute, and it made him proud to be of use to a movement that was about truth. Malcolm was good to have along. He'd taken the Church of the Creator loyalty oath, and he abhorred the impure races who were not white, the mud races. They both believed in the inevitability of the racial holy war—Rahowa they liked to call it.

But first, they needed some dinner, and a little more beer muscle. They headed to Squire's Pub, a cozy, woody joint a couple of miles from base that serves kidney pie and Guinness stout. Just down the street from Squire's, they passed Luigi's, an Italian restaurant where two years before, a young 18th Airborne sergeant named Ken French had a bad night drinking and killed four people with a pump-action shotgun. After that, folks in Fayetteville started teaching one another how to spot "killer eyes" before some other nut from Fort Bragg made his presence known to the world.

At about ten o'clock, the soldiers headed for the Cue and Ale Lounge, a topless club on Bragg Boulevard. They drank three or four pitchers of beer. When a Black dancer strutted onto the stage, Jimmy and Malcolm turned away. "I don't want to see that nigger," Jimmy said, and then, at 11:30, abruptly announced, "Hey, we're going." Meadows got behind the wheel this time. Burmeister sat in the passenger seat, and Wright in the back, next to the beer cooler.

"Drive where there are niggers and not a whole lot of people around, where it's dark," Burmeister said, according to sealed police reports. For the next half hour, fortified by a twelve-pack purchased at a convenience store, they hunted Blacks—first in a trailer park and then down Murchison Road through other Black neighborhoods.

Burmeister and Meadows had done this before. It was fun to knock somebody in the head and run. Hookers or crack dealers were the best targets—they'd walk right up to the car. Whenever they saw a Black person, Jim cocked his finger as if he were shooting and said, "Die, nigger." But with each sighting, there was too much street light or there were too many people around.

Wright gave directions to another downtown neighborhood. Burmeister reached under the seat and pulled out the pistol and held it in his lap. Suddenly, Jim said, "There's a nigger couple right there."

Jackie Burden, twenty-seven, and Michael James, thirty-six, were out for a midnight walk. Meadows drove past the couple, who were walking down Hall Street, a dirt road in a neighborhood of old mill houses. He eased the car around and drove past them again. Malcolm said, "Let's get out here." Wright left his flight jacket and beeper in the backseat and directed Meadows to park around the corner. If they weren't back in fifteen minutes, he was to return to the trailer. Burmeister tucked the gun into his belt.

The two soldiers left the car and approached the couple. Burden and James were friends. Jackie Burden was planning to become a nursing assistant. Michael James, a welder by trade, was disabled from a construction accident; he'd just gotten out of prison in August on a drug charge and had a plane ticket to New Jersey so he could be with his wife and three children for Christmas.

The soldiers walked past them on the dirt street, stopped, and turned back toward the couple, who were less than seven feet away. Burmeister drew his 9mm. Raising his long, skinny arms, he closed the gap by three feet. James was hit first, with two shots to the head, the second from within eight inches. Wright would later tell police that Burmeister tried to hand him the gun but that he refused it. Burden tried to run and was reaching into her pocket to clasp a small brown-handled knife, coins spilling onto the ground, when a bullet smashed into her back. According to police records, one of the soldiers then walked over, holding the pistol at close range, and fired three shots into her head. "Execution style" is the phrase that would resonate sickeningly in Fayetteville.

Meadows, parked a block away, had barely shut off the car when he heard gunfire. Not seeing his friends, and thinking they had perhaps been shot, he was walking toward the bodies on Hall Street when the first police cruiser showed up.

Burmeister and Wright, meanwhile, were running away. Police dogs tracked them for nearly three quarters of a mile until the trail ended at Gillespie Street, heading out of town. For the next two hours, the soldiers stole through backyards and open fields, walked along the railroad tracks, and hid in stands of small hardwood and scrub oak. Wright vomited behind a shed. Burmeister hid his gun in a tree. Finally, they decided to walk into downtown Fayetteville.

At a pay phone along the road, Burmeister tried calling friends, hoping someone would pick them up. Wright called his pager, which was in his flight jacket back in the car.

Later, around 2:30 a.m., just three blocks from the county jail, they would flag a taxi driven by a guy named Cowboy, who gave them credit because they were soldiers. But first, Burmeister hiked back to retrieve his black Ruger.

"All right," Jim said, tucking the blood-spattered pistol back into his belt. "We're happy now."

***

Jackie Burden and Michael James were killed by active-service soldiers who were part of a culture at Fort Bragg that was more important to them than any imperative of military life, a community of racist skinheads numbering at least twenty-two and as many as sixty that has operated in plain sight on the base, often seeming to challenge the US Army's right or will to curtail its activities.

Jim Burmeister was a new and zealous convert to the skinhead cause, which the Anti-Defamation League now calls the most dangerous white supremacist movement in America. Burmeister was not a skinhead until he was recruited by a fellow soldier in the 82nd Airborne, but his course may have been set years before in a sleepy little town called Thompson, carved out of the Endless Mountains in northeastern Pennsylvania, forty miles up from Scranton. Jimmy moved here with his family when he was six. His father, James Burmeister Sr., a rangy Texan, resigned from the Los Angeles County Fire Department in 1981 to raise his children away from city living and crime. A crack mechanic, he started Burmeister Auto Repair in the old creamery and soon had a good business. The family—Jimmy and his sisters, Michelle and Lisa—lived in the white farmhouse that Jimmy's mother, Kathy, grew up in, on wooded acreage just outside town.

There's not much for a kid to do in this town of three hundred with no stoplights, one grocery store, and two churches. Jimmy Burmeister was content to ride his bike until he was old enough to peel out in his car and annoy Police Chief Tom Rivenburgh, a career West Point man who retired to Thompson and became the town's police force.

Over the years, James Sr. developed a reputation in Thompson as a frustrated man who tended to blame others when things didn't go right for him. He had a morbid sense of humor and enjoyed playing out petty vendettas. Once, when he had an ax to grind with the proprietor of Eats, the town's hot-dog stand, Burmeister changed the portable sign outside his auto shop so it read: RATS ON A BUN, 500 FEET AHEAD. A neighbor recalls him shooting songbirds off his wife's bird feeder with a .22 rifle and hanging them from the clothesline. And although Black faces are rare in Thompson, other neighbors remember Jimmy's father talking about Black people as subhuman; they blamed it on his being from Texas.

Jimmy worked beside his father in the shop and would bring along his close friends, who liked Mr. Burmeister. The boy was shy and artistic, and he liked to write poetry. In 1989, when he was a freshman at Susquehanna Community High School, he published a poem in *Discovery*, the school arts magazine:

SHADOWS
Nothing to be afraid of.
Just curious.

Always following you around.
"Stay here,"
You say—
But they do not listen.
You move, you run,
They follow, they chase.
You stop, you look,
They try to hide.
Motionless . . .
Your every move they follow.

There were guns around the house, though to Jimmy they held no particular fascination. But when his father returned from a gun show with *The Poor Man's James Bond*—a how-to manual of soap-flake-and-gasoline bomb recipes and other explosive devices you can make in your utility room—Jimmy was mesmerized. He and his father and his best friend, Scott Ficarro, the local high school computer whiz, would spend hours talking about how to make bombs.

During his junior year in high school, along with Ficarro and a couple of other friends from school, Jimmy started an anarchist group and called it the Angels of Darkness. The group spent hours lying around Jimmy's room, smoking Camels, studying the book, and talking about a world without moral consequence.

A running feud with a schoolmate culminated in Jimmy's first documented act of violence, on October 30, 1992, when he tested one of the book's more rudimentary recipes and firebombed the boy's dune buggy with two Molotov cocktails, almost setting a nearby house on fire.

In his senior year, the local Army recruiter pulled up to Police Chief Rivenburgh's house with Jimmy in the passenger seat. Like many people in Thompson, the chief liked Burmeister and had tried to help him out along the way. When Jimmy had wanted to take up drumming in high school, Rivenburgh, who had played in the West Point band, lent the boy his own drum. Later, when Jimmy drove his Mustang recklessly, the chief gave him only warnings. But Rivenburgh also knew that Jimmy was the main suspect in the firebombing, and that's about as big as crime gets in Thompson, Pennsylvania.

When Rivenburgh was coming up, judges often gave delinquents the choice between jail or enlistment. Maybe the Army would give Jimmy a sense of direction.

Jimmy told friends that the Army was just a step toward his ultimate goal—to be a police officer in a state that had the death penalty. "If I put them in prison," he said, "I don't want them coming back after me."

When he graduated in June 1993, Jimmy decorated his mortarboard with a large peace sign he had made of masking tape. As he accepted his diploma, the six-five Burmeister looked winsome, and the peace sign gleamed in the sunlight. The Army awaited.

After basic training at Fort Benning, Georgia, Burmeister arrived at Fort Bragg as a paratrooper and mortarman. He traveled back to Thompson frequently his first year, usually by bus, homesick for the Angels of Darkness and for his high school girlfriend. At least once, he shared a twelve-hour car ride home with a Black soldier from nearby Binghamton, New York.

Adjusting to Army life was not easy. Repeated mortar concussions injured one of Jimmy's ears, and less than a year into his Airborne career, he could no longer jump out of planes. He'd been proud of his assignment to the mortar platoon, but after the injury, firing mortars literally hurt him. Unable to perform, he was ostracized by the platoon. They called him an "oxygen thief." He wanted to change assignments and even considered transferring to the mess hall, but his ear couldn't take the banging of pots and the loud hood fans. Eventually, Burmeister would be assigned to the armory, where he was responsible for maintaining and breaking down all weapons available to his unit.

Humiliated because he was a paratrooper who couldn't jump and a mortarman who couldn't shoot, Burmeister turned increasingly to alcohol and was rarely seen off-duty without a beer in his hand. It was around this time that he met a charismatic young paratrooper from Chicago named Brian "Lobo" Lobianco, who had a tattoo of Hermann Göring on his chest.

Lobo considered himself a student of Hitler and tried to influence impressionable soldiers by aping the Führer's body language. "Even the way Hitler held his arms was a form of power," he would later say. "Hitler would put his left hand on the outside of his right elbow and his right hand on the outside of his left elbow, which allowed him very easily to straighten his right arm and point and yell. When your hands are underneath your arms, it's a sign of weakness. I had studied this."

In Burmeister, Lobo saw a potential recruit into the neo-Nazi skinhead movement that he was involved with at Fort Bragg. "You could tell he was just screaming out for someone, for friendship," he says. "I could just pull out his brain and mold it into what I wanted."

Lobo talked in earnest with Burmeister about "where I was in my belief, that if things don't change, there's never again going to be one pure race; it's going to be a mixture of everybody, and you lose your ancestry."

Lobo brought Burmeister into the world of *The Turner Diaries*, which would later inspire Timothy McVeigh, although Hitler's writings were more important here. "Anti-Jew was a big part of what we talked about," Lobo says. "I told him to read *Mein Kampf*. People in general want to blame their problems on something; they all want a scapegoat. Blame the Jew, blame the Black. I knew how to play him."

Out drinking one night in October 1994, Burmeister told Lobo he wanted to shave his head and publicly identify himself with the goals of the racist skinhead movement. "I told him that's something you do when you're sober," says Lobo.

The next day, Burmeister shaved his head. A week later, he began wearing Doc Martens strung with red laces, and then he got the flight jacket, thin red suspenders, and Nazi insignia that would make up his new uniform of allegiance.

Lobo also showed him the ways of skinhead fun, introducing him to a network of other racists and to white-power music. And when they wanted to mosh, elbows flying, they went to Purgatory, an underground club three hundred yards off base, or to the Flaming Mug, where one night, at a wet-boxer-short contest, Lobo, clad in jackboots, flight jacket, and wet boxers, goose-stepped onto the stage, executed a Nazi salute, and then twirled his coat above his head in a garish promenade and threw it into the frenzied crowd, where Jim scrambled to collect it.

In February 1995, Burmeister was reprimanded for poor work performance. During this evaluation, his commanding officer found that Jim wasn't wearing his dog tags but rather a German Iron Cross. It wasn't his only display of Naziana. His NCO knew he was flying flags. Soldiers on Burmeister's barracks floor remember how a sergeant teased him: "Hey, Burmeister, know whose birthday it was yesterday? Adolf Hitler's!"

Lobo eventually passed Burmeister on to Tom VanHoose, who, along with two other 82nd Airborne soldiers, both possessing spiderweb tattoos, was organizing a clandestine white supremacist group at Fort Bragg called the American Wiking Regiment. (*Wiking* is German for "Viking.") Among the members of the regiment were Malcolm Wright and Randy Meadows. Burmeister shaved his head again. He was home.

Lobo left the Wiking Regiment last summer and claims to have experienced a Christian conversion. "What scared me," he says, "was their cold heartlessness, and so much talk of genocide."

***

This is not your daddy's Army. The sign posted on the wall of the 82nd Airborne barracks reads: VISION 2000 DOES NOT GIVE SOLDIERS CARTE BLANCHE TO LIVE AS THEY SEE FIT. Vision 2000 is a policy adopted by the Army in 1994 to, among other things, make military life freer and less regimented than in the past. Next to the sign is a memo dated December 7, 1995, the day after the murders of Jackie Burden and Michael James:

> Response to soldier questions raised during class on racial sensitivity—
> Q: Are religious icons allowed to be displayed in soldiers' rooms?
> A: Yes, that doesn't mean the commander will allow devil worship, bestiality icons, etc. You do not have total freedom

to display any "religious" symbols which purport hatred or violence.

Q: Can I have flags in my room that show pride in my heritage?

A: Yes, if the flag does not enflame the people living in that room with you or is not patently offensive.

A last memo, dated December 8, 1995, and posted nearby, announces the Army's policy on extremist organizations:

Army policy does not prohibit passive activities such as mere membership, receiving literature in the mail, or presence at an event, though strongly discouraged as incompatible with military service.

Specialist Michael P. Fallon, a member of the American Wiking Regiment and one of Jim Burmeister's closest Army friends, panicked when he returned to his barracks room one day last summer and found that his Nazi flags had been stripped from his walls. He marched down and complained to his sergeant, who barked, "Fallon, you keep your key above your door, don't you?"

"Yes, sir."

"Did it ever occur to you that one of your friends might be playing a prank on you?"

"No, sir."

Later that night, to his relief, Fallon found his beloved silk flags safe under his pillow, and he put them back on his wall, so that his barracks room again looked like a Nazi outpost. "I had four Nazi flags hanging on the wall," he says today, "and five World War II German recruiting posters."

Had you walked into Fallon's room in this barracks on any given night during the past year, you'd have seen a scrum of drunken skinheads plotting the ultimate separation of the races. One night, you'd have heard Fallon, polluted on Goldschläger, bellowing at the top of his lungs out in the hall, "Sieg heil! Sieg heil! Niggers, go home! White power!"

Tonight, January 14, Fallon is joined by two other members of the American Wiking Regiment, Specialist Steven Manseau and his wife, Chrissy, the newlyweds who rented out the room in their mobile home to Jim Burmeister. They've brought along their seven-month-old son, Ian, who is named after the lead singer of Skrewdriver, the late Ian Stuart. These people watched Burmeister through the most significant changes of his life. During at least one inspection, Fallon even hid Burmeister's 9mm Ruger in this room.

"My fingerprints were on the gun," Fallon says now.

"Don't worry," Manseau says. "Jim cleaned it a thousand times."

"Any one of us could have been with them that night," Fallon says. "I would have been with them if they called and asked me if I wanted to go."

"I can understand why the gun came out," Manseau says. "Jim can't fight. I watched him get his ass whipped in his barracks one night. By a Black guy."

After the murders, Fallon took down his flags and unstitched the swastika armband that he had openly worn on his flight jacket. "I'm undercover. I don't dress like this," he says, pulling at his rugby shirt, which hides a racist tattoo on his forearm. "I usually wear short-sleeved shirts, my tats showing, my suspenders. I had a big swastika armband. It took me two hours to take that fucker off."

Fallon's concrete barracks walls are now bare, the recruiting posters rolled up in his closet. His head itches from growing out his hair, and he's looking forward to wearing his skinhead uniform again but says that now that he's incognito, he's getting laid more often.

He passes around bottles of German beer. "We're Airborne," Steve Manseau says, "the most physically fit alcoholics on earth."

A muted television plays *The Last of the Mohicans*. Ian chortles happily on the bed with his mother. Steve sits in a chair near the door of the narrow, dorm-size room. Laconic, self-possessed, and not at all boastful by nature, Steve Manseau is quite important in the lineage of the American Wiking Regiment. It was Manseau who recruited Lobo into the skins and who shaved Lobo's head for the first time two years ago. "I've been a good soldier," he says of his seven years as a cook. "The Army said we could have our beliefs." Manseau took the American flag off his flight jacket when older skinheads told him it was the "Jew flag, because Jews run the government."

On the television, the local evening news is now showing 82nd Airborne paratroopers in full gear boarding a plane for a six-month peacekeeping mission in the Middle East.

"Shit, that's Tom!" Fallon shouts. "That was Tom, dude! Off to the Sinai."

Fallon and Manseau identify the soldier as Tom VanHoose, commandant of the American Wiking Regiment. "Tom's a skinhead and a Klansman," Fallon says gleefully, "and he's going to Israel!"

A month earlier, on December 13, when questioned by police at the Army's Criminal Investigation Division, VanHoose admitted organizing the Wikings and provided numbers in the range of "about twenty to sixty members."

Fallon was drunk when he was interrogated and readily identified regiment members in snapshots confiscated after the December murders. In one photograph, Burmeister sucks the barrel of a pistol held by a paratrooper. In another, Wiking soldiers are standing before a swastika, making the Nazi salute.

The most dangerous and committed of their confederates, the soldiers all agree, were not on Fort Bragg's original list of suspected extremists. One of Burmeister's mentors in the months prior to the murders is a former member of the notorious Confederate Hammerskins who was getting advanced training in demolitions at an air-force base in Florida. Known as Big Steve, he had been promoted to E-4 specialist on January 10 and was scheduled to be posted to Camp Shelby, Mississippi, later this year.

"Big Steve's got a serious commitment to racial war," says Manseau.

"He's got more than that," adds Fallon. "Big Steve's got a plan."

"The reason he joined the Army," whispers Chrissy, "is to gain skills to further the movement."

In honor of their devoted friendship, Big Steve and his wife have vowed to name their next son after Jim Burmeister. In the days after the killings, both VanHoose and Big Steve sent word to the Wiking regulars. Steve counseled all to "stand by your white brother" and raise money for his defense. VanHoose, mindful that they all could come under scrutiny, admonished them to "grow your hair, don't be conspicuous."

How many racist skinheads are there in the 82nd?

Counting on his fingers, Fallon rattles off names. "Derick, Dan, Sean, Big Jim, Big Steve, Matt, Tim, Tom, Trent, the two brothers, Duncan, the dude from another country, Ed, Spaid . . ." He continues for a moment. "That's twenty-one right there," he says. "There are maybe thirty-five of us who are in still or who have recently gotten out."

Manseau sees racial holy war as inevitable, but he regards Jimmy's actions as premature. "It's counterproductive, going bashing," he says. "Makes us look bad. It hurts the cause of separation." Fallon points to the baby, now sleeping peacefully on the bed. "He's what it's all about. That's what the whole movement is about." He quotes the Fourteen Words of David Lane, the imprisoned leader of the Order, the now-defunct armed wing of the Aryan Nations: "We must secure the existence of our people and a future for white children."

These are the words that Burmeister once painted on his barracks walls, alongside a swastika. He'd use White Rain shampoo as a medium, an old girlfriend says. Under normal light, the symbols were invisible, but they glowed defiantly under Jimmy's black light.

To these soldiers and their white supremacist confederates, the exploits of the Order are heroic and serve as a prototype for action. Fallon, like Burmeister, regards white supremacist Robert Matthews, who was killed after robbing armored cars for the Order, as a martyr who stole from the government to further the white cause.

"They are the Robin Hoods of the white race," Fallon says. "They robbed, they kept a little to support themselves. They gave the rest to other like organizations. I have a song about it at home."

As if to save himself from complete skinhead withdrawal, Fallon pulls out a Skrewdriver tape from his white-power stash. "This was one of Jim's favorites," Chrissy says. "He played it constantly."

As the song cranks into a thrashing chorus, all three sing along, eyes closed, trancelike, as they mouth the echoing refrain: "Hail!

Heil! Hail victory." Fallon and Manseau thrust their arms upward in repeated Nazi salutes.

On the muted television, the local ABC station begins its celebration of Dr. Martin Luther King Jr.'s birthday with a midnight showing of *King*, starring Paul Winfield.

In this room, there is no Martin Luther King's birthday, only "National Nigger Day." And yet, when Gary Jones, a Black soldier with high-level security clearance, enters to return a video, Fallon engages him about the plight of the embattled skinhead. "It's a witch-hunt, pure and simple," Jones says. "If they're going to kick out the racists here, they need to start with the brass."

"You think they're looking for Black racists?" Fallon asks Jones. "We have a Crip right on this floor."

"We've got Crips all over Bragg," Jones answers. "They just want *this* to go away, so they're just busting everybody who looks like a skinhead. There is no real investigation."

Steve cradles his infant son in his arms and begins feeding him with a bottle. Compared with the more voluble Fallon, he has been fairly quiet all night. As a soldier who preceded Burmeister into the movement and nurtured him in it, he now wants to make sure his views are clear. "My wife and I are for separation of the races, not for genocide," he says. "Most of the guys we hung out with were for the genocidal view. I think Jim pretty much wanted genocide."

"Yeah, he did," Chrissy says softly. She then tells of the night last fall she found Jim and Randy Meadows thumbing through the Yellow Pages, looking for a "Jewish synagogue to destroy."

"I didn't think anybody would be that stupid," she says, "so I didn't pay them any mind."

The next morning, returning from town, she noticed that a car that had been abandoned on the roadside for a long time was no longer there. Back at the trailer, she mentioned this to Jim and Randy. "They smiled at each other," she recalls, "and then told me how they had busted the windows with pool balls in a sock and doused the car with gas and set it on fire. They watched it burn and explode."

Later, she drove by the spot. There were burn marks, and the grass was charred where the car had been. It was then that Chrissy

Manseau, driving home in her Geo Metro with the Heil Hitler bumper sticker, began to realize that these ideas had consequences.

That evening, she watched the news to see if Fayetteville's synagogue had been firebombed.

***

At 9:05 a.m. on December 7, 1995, the morning after the James and Burden murders, Fayetteville police raided the Manseaus' mobile home. Jim Burmeister was sleeping in his bed, and Malcolm Wright was on the couch. A round was chambered in Burmeister's pistol, and a sawed-off shotgun was within reach of Wright. The soldiers didn't resist arrest and were escorted, wearing boxer shorts, to separate squad cars.

Among the evidence gathered in the search of Burmeister's room, the police listed a dish of "vegetable matter." The dish actually contained a quarter pound of smokeless gunpowder mixed with a half pound of fertilizer. Nearby were wires and specialty glue. Private Burmeister had been cooking a bomb.

This news should not have come as a surprise to either the Criminal Investigation Division at Fort Bragg or to the FBI. Both agencies had been informed months before that in James Norman Burmeister Jr. they had a budding terrorist on their hands.

In August 1994, Fort Bragg received a call from the district attorney of Susquehanna County, Pennsylvania. Because a couple of locals were in the habit of recording phone calls off their police scanners, the DA's office had in its possession a taped telephone call made from within the barracks of Fort Bragg by Jim Burmeister in which he conspires to blow up Thompson police chief Tom Rivenburgh. The chief had, in Burmeister's view, excessively ticketed one of his old Angel of Darkness buddies. In the same conversation, Burmeister boasts that he can smuggle grenade launchers and armor-piercing bullets out of Fayetteville. Despite the fact that authorities at Fort Bragg were apprised of this conversation, Burmeister was later assigned to work in his unit's armory.

A year later, the CID at Fort Bragg was informed by the FBI of another, even more disturbing Burmeister conversation. This one was taped by Chief Rivenburgh himself. On August 12, 1995, Burmeister requested technical assistance in the construction of a powerful C-4 bomb, which he was planning to transport across state lines. Jim's father was told of this tape and immediately called his son. "I want my gun back," he said plaintively. "The FBI is watching you. Whatever you're doing, stop." But in the fall of last year, the CID and FBI proved only a mild inconvenience to Jim. He became aware that someone would occasionally tail him on a night out, but he seemed to derive pleasure from the cat-and-mouse game. "What can they do?" he said to a friend. "I haven't gotten caught doing anything."

Given all that was known or suspected about Jimmy Burmeister, the question begs: Just what does it take to get expelled from the Army? Had he been openly homosexual, Burmeister would have been chaptered out immediately. But the true beneficiaries of the military's "Don't ask, don't tell" philosophy seem to be political extremists. As for the FBI, "It seems they were waiting for Jimmy to do something, because they thought they had another Timothy McVeigh," said Chief Rivenburgh. "They wanted to grandstand." In a country informed by the experience of Oklahoma City, the fact that someone as potentially dangerous as Burmeister was not taken more seriously is unfathomable.

But for the murders of Jackie Burden and Michael James, swastikas would still adorn barracks walls at Fort Bragg, the American Wiking Regiment would still be recruiting vigorously, and the entire skinhead culture in the military would still be tolerated or ignored. The Pentagon has now acknowledged problems on at least four army bases and is investigating.

All the soldiers photographed by *Esquire* are being "chaptered out" of the Army, chiefly, it seems, for being photographed and not necessarily for past skinhead activities. American Wiking Regiment commandant Tom VanHoose didn't make the peacekeeping mission to the Sinai but had been scheduled to go until the murders. And on

February 9, Big Steve was recalled to Fort Bragg to be questioned in the Army investigation.

Burmeister, Wright, and Meadows await trial in Fayetteville. And Brian "Lobo" Lobianco, Burmeister's father in the movement, says he hopes Jimmy gets the death penalty.

Esquire, 1996

THE HUNTER BECOMES THE HUNTED

You don't know his name, and you've never seen his face. But as America leaves Iraq for good after eight years of war, we also leave behind a man believed by our military and intelligence agencies to be the best terrorist hunter alive. He's still there, hunting. And so are the terrorists.

VIRGINIA, SUMMER 2010

Omar Mohammed hunts terrorists in Baghdad. Hunts them and kills them. A few months ago, he killed two big guys in Al Qaeda—Abu Ayyub al-Masri and Abu Omar al-Baghdadi, the two most-wanted terrorists in all of Iraq. But when you hunt Al Qaeda, they also hunt you. The more you kill them, the more they want to kill you. They've shot Omar, blown him up, and killed dozens of his men.

Omar is a senior officer in the Iraqi Counterterrorism Unit. He was doing police work when the Americans invaded in 2003, and he volunteered his services to the occupiers as the insurgent war overwhelmed the American presence, enveloping them in a kind of warfare for which they were not prepared. To America's military and to many intelligence operatives in Washington and in Iraq, Omar is the best terrorist hunter alive. His photo has never been published. His face doesn't exist in any database linked to his real name. It's a broad, handsome face, and he's thick as a bull across the neck and shoulders.

At this precise moment he's not in Iraq, though; he's in a red canoe on a river in Virginia, heading fast toward a waterfall.

In the back of the canoe is Tim Clemente, a former FBI agent who until recently served on Washington's Joint Terrorism Task Force and is himself regarded as an excellent terrorist hunter. He trained Omar to hunt terrorists. Like a lot of FBI agents, you don't notice Clemente at first. Not too tall, not too short. Hair close-cropped but not military. Calm, kind hazel eyes. As can happen with those who bond in a common purpose under threat of death, Omar and Clemente are best friends, and they are here on the Rappahannock, as far from Baghdad as you can get, for a vacation with their families. In a month, the United States will pull all but fifty thousand troops out of Iraq, effectively ending all combat operations there, and the White House has announced that all American troops will be gone by the end of 2011, bringing an end to the eight-year US military engagement altogether.

That's why Clemente has invited Omar here. (*Omar's name has been changed to protect his identity.*)

Because of Omar's great success at killing terrorists on behalf of the United States, his chances of dying a natural death in his country are very slim, and so Clemente wants to show him all that America has to offer, thinking maybe he can persuade Omar to bring his family here and make a new life. He wants to take him to Washington, maybe show him California. He doesn't want him to be bombed, shot, or beheaded when the American troops leave for good.

Clemente steers the canoe over the waterfall, both of them whooping. Omar has been trying to take in this beautiful scenery. Having just arrived from Baghdad last night, he finds it's almost too much. The white water is tricky here, not deep but very fast. As they shoot the rapids, Clemente yells, "Go left!" He j-hooks hard, but the canoe spins sideways, taking water. Large rocks ahead. They both spill out into the chest-deep water, and the submerged canoe, caught in the fast current, swings around hard and catches Omar off guard, smashing him against a large rock. The canoe buckles around the rock, pinning Omar's leg, trapping him.

"My leg," Omar yells. "It's broken!" He's trying to laugh, but panic flashes across his face, too.

"Oh, stop crying like a baby!" Clemente yells.

"I'm not crying!"

The harder he works to get free, the more surely he is trapped. "I need to get to the hospital!" Omar says, and screams in pain, which alarms Clemente, who is trying to use his paddle as a lever to move the damn canoe off him but seems to be making things worse, and the churning water is just too strong.

Clemente falls down in the water, laughing. "I may have to cut off that leg," he says.

"It hurts worse than anything!" Omar shouts. He knows pain. A couple years ago, militia gunmen shot two bullets into his leg. Then they blew him up in his car. He doesn't remember that pain. He was in a coma for three weeks. Woke up with a beard. Now he's wide awake, and not completely sure he'll make it off this river.

"You're trying to kill me!" Omar hollers. "I see your plan now!"

"Come on, infidel, there are worse places to be!" Clemente yells. It's a joke from their days in Baghdad. *Infidel.* The truth is, to the jihadis, Omar is an infidel, marked for death because of his work with the Americans. Al Qaeda has been killing Iraqi cops with terrible frequency, and those are ordinary cops. Omar is no ordinary cop, and the terrorists he just killed were among Al Qaeda's top leadership in Iraq, responsible for murdering hundreds of Iraqi citizens and many American soldiers. If he goes back, Clemente is certain Omar will be killed in retaliation, in short order. Just today, Omar received word that Ali Lutfi al-Rawi, a sadistic killer whom Omar had put away for life, escaped from prison. And even if Omar lives, what kind of life is that?

"Why are you trying to kill me?" Omar howls.

"Better you die here than in Iraq!"

BAGHDAD, 2004

One morning in January 2004, a man drove a white pickup loaded with a thousand pounds of explosives toward the main entrance of the US military headquarters in Baghdad. Clemente heard the blast from Camp Liberty, where the FBI is housed, grabbed his pistol and long gun, hauled himself into the back of an SUV with the FBI's hostage-rescue team, and raced toward the smoke and fire. He'd been in Iraq for three days.

American soldiers had already cordoned off the blast area when the SUV pulled up. Clemente marked the location of a severed hand far from the blast, then walked to the edge of the smoldering crater. He'd been early on the scene at the Pentagon on September 11 and was among the first generation of FBI to operate internationally to combat terrorism; he had also seen this before in Kenya, Tanzania, and Yemen. It was to be his job in Baghdad to prevent things like the Assassins' Gate bombing, as the blast would come to be known. But Clemente didn't know a thing about Iraq. He'd quickly need to find somebody who did.

Two days earlier, Clemente had made his way to the former jail that housed the Major Crimes Unit of the Iraqi police. He saw AK-47s and grenade launchers strewn all over the floor, and more leaning against the barred windows. The Iraqi cops were deferential to Clemente but they were wary, too. No one spoke.

Finally a young cop stepped forward and offered his hand. Clemente shook it and looked into Omar's face. "What's with all the weapons?" he asked.

"We got in a shoot-out here last week," Omar answered in unbroken English. "Insurgents blasted us from the minaret across the street."

"You kill them?"

Omar nodded.

"How many guys are you?" Clemente asked.

"Just us." Omar pointed to a small clutch of cops. They seemed to have no interest in Clemente and turned back to their work, whatever work a cop can do without computers, maps, or even pencils.

"What's wrong with them?" Clemente asked.

"No, they're great," Omar said. "They just don't speak English. Watch this." He yelled at the cops, "Hey, you piece of shits!" He turned to Clemente. "Do I say it right?" Omar yelled at them again. "I'm going to kill all of you!" Nobody even looked up. Omar grinned.

"Where'd you learn English?" Clemente asked.

"A beautiful woman," Omar said. "I followed her into a night class. She dropped out, but I stayed." Omar ushered Clemente to a jail cell, his makeshift office.

Eight months earlier, Paul Bremer, the American administrator in Iraq, had fired the entire army and police force. Unemployed and angry, some of those armed men would join the insurgency, planting some of the deadliest improvised bombs ever seen in warfare.

But not Omar. When the national police force was dissolved, Omar drove a cab, keeping an AK-47 under the seat to protect himself, waiting for the chance to be a cop again. His father, a highly decorated army general during the war against Iran, had been murdered by Saddam Hussein when he voiced opposition to Iraq's invasion of Kuwait in 1990. "We only find one of his boots, half burned. We put it in the casket. To this day, my mother thinks he was buried."

Omar had gone to the prison to press charges against Saddam's armed forces chief of staff, who he believed ordered the hit, only to find that thousands who'd also lost fathers and brothers were there ahead of him. Even when Saddam was in the hole, Omar was still terrified of him. Saddam believed he was coming back, and until he was arrested, Omar had the same feeling, that Saddam would come back and kill all of those who had betrayed him.

Clemente had been in Iraq long enough to learn that Iraqis couldn't be trusted. At least that's the warning he'd received from some of his FBI colleagues: All Iraqi cops are dirty and in bed with Saddam and the terrorists. But Clemente, himself a former St. Louis cop, had no choice but to trust someone.

"I don't want to spend weeks reading files," he told Omar. "I need a partner here who can help me identify terrorists."

"I can do that," Omar said.

Clemente looked around at the AK-47s and rocket launchers stacked in Omar's office. "You killed those guys and recovered these yourself?" he asked.

Omar smiled and nodded.

The next day, the two started working together. Omar would drive, as he knew the neighborhoods, the culture, and could immediately distinguish Shiite from Sunni. Clemente grew a beard to blend in a little and took to wearing a kaffiyeh. Together they built an informant network from nothing, and before long they had people in bakeries, driving taxis, sweeping floors inside mosques. Omar's men started bringing in low-level terrorists, locals who were being paid by the insurgency to set bombs and provide intelligence on the Americans to Al Qaeda.

By American standards, Omar didn't have much formal police training, but he was eager and seemed fearless. Under Saddam, police loyalty to the regime was valued much more than detective work. At the police academy, Omar's class was ordered to skin and eat a live dog. After that, his instructors believed, no order would be too repulsive to carry out.

Hunting terrorists, Clemente told Omar, is just good police work. But doing police work in a war zone complicates things somewhat. Leads disappear or get shot, so it pays to act fast. Some days, Omar and Clemente would interview a source in the morning, identify a suspect, tap the phone a few minutes later, have a unit doing surveillance in the afternoon, make an arrest, and be interrogating by evening.

Slowly, they began to trust each other. One day, when Omar had been on the job for just a couple of weeks, his car got hit by fifty-five AK-47 rounds on his way to meet Clemente at the American base. He wasn't hurt, but it told him that militants had discovered that he was working with the Americans. The next time Omar drove to the base, he saw Clemente ambling down Route Irish, the deadliest stretch of road in Iraq, wearing shorts and a baseball cap, with a gun tucked into the back of his waistband. He was waiting for Omar, to ride with him for the most dangerous stretch. From then on, most days Clemente would walk out to ride in with him. During a dust storm, Omar called to warn Clemente that insurgents might use the weather as cover to fire mortars into the FBI operations center at Camp Liberty.

And they began to catch bombers. Two months on the job, one of Omar's sources, a baker, called in to report a suspicious man carrying a duffel. The baker's street was one that US convoys used every day. The man was now digging a hole, the baker said. Just minutes away,

Omar raced over with one of his cops, parked, and approached on foot, trying to look casual, and then wheeled around and jammed his pistol into the guy's stomach while his partner gingerly grabbed the bag containing the bomb.

Clemente arrived to interrogate the suspect, a handcuffed middle-aged man named Zaid, and underneath a napkin on the table, he found a small device, the size of a brick, with a hand crank and wires with alligator clips at the ends. Clemente shut down the interrogation, took Omar for a walk.

"Is that how you do police work?"

"Of course. We torture them."

"Don't you try to figure out what they are doing first, and who they work for?" Clemente asked.

Omar said, "No, why should I? This guy is a terrorist—he was going to blow up people."

"We can flip him," Clemente said. "Let me talk to him."

Back in the room, he uncuffed the man. "Zaid, did Al Qaeda pay you to bury the bomb?"

"Yes."

"How much?"

"$150."

"Do you have a job?"

"No."

Clemente pulled out a photo of his children. "I have eight children," he said, "and if my kids were starving, I would do anything to put food on the table." Clemente put a hand on Zaid's shoulder.

"What if I could pay you more money to not make bombs?" Clemente had convinced the FBI to give him plenty of cash to pay informants to make his plan work. Zaid took a breath. Omar gazed at him intently.

"I'll pay you to tell us whenever you see bad men planning or doing bad things."

Finally, Zaid said, "How much can you pay?"

Clemente looked at Omar. *Bingo.*

And it was this moment—the moment that he learned to be clever rather than brutal—that was the most important moment in

Omar's life. With this new skill, he felt that maybe his job wasn't so futile after all. He felt as if, just maybe, he could help save his country.

Along the way, Omar and Clemente became inseparable and began to build a deep friendship. Clemente heard that Omar liked fishing and brought him to Camp Slayer, an American base on the grounds of one of Saddam's former palaces, where the dictator had dug lavishly stocked lakes. No rod and reel for Omar; he just wrapped the line, which he called the "lion," around the thick of his hand. And once he hooked a fish, he didn't let go. One day he caught a sixty-pound carp by hand, waded into the water, and gaffed it. Clemente snapped pictures. And they would talk movies for hours. Omar loves anything with Robert De Niro, but his favorite movie is *Die Hard*, because a cop is the hero, and it has a happy ending. He doesn't care for *Serpico*, which is one of Clemente's favorites. Too dark.

One day they took the baker fishing at Camp Slayer, and he told them that jihadis in his neighborhood were recruiting blue and green-eyed Iraqis to walk into police stations and army bases wearing suicide vests. Two weeks later, Zaid called to tell them that someone named Ahmed was in town. "He's a guy whose father was part of the former regime."

Turns out that was an understatement. The father was Muhammad Younis al-Ahmed, known to investigators as M.Y.A., a member of Saddam's inner circle and a leader of the Ba'ath Party military wing. No insurgent action in Iraq, from suicide bombings to kidnappings, happened without M.Y.A.'s green light. He controlled billions of dollars stolen from the Iraqi treasury to fund the insurgency. So wily that he never showed up on Washington's original deck of cards. Eight weeks before, when they'd captured Saddam in his hole, he was holding letters to M.Y.A. They included how to run the insurgency, how to reach out to Al Qaeda, what kinds of attacks to execute, where to concentrate. These were Saddam's orders to his commander as to how to conduct the war. Through their new network, Omar and Clemente had stumbled upon the guy at the top.

In short order, Clemente got a call from a Delta Force leader. He wanted to see Clemente immediately.

The Delta commander wanted to know about Omar. He said they were impressed by the intelligence he'd been able to gather. "We've been chasing M.Y.A. for months but have nothing." He wanted to know how much Clemente trusted Omar.

"With my life," Clemente answered.

"Bring him in. We want to meet him."

"When?"

"Now."

This is how Omar found himself walking into Delta's top-secret compound, which he would come to call Disneyland—the first Iraqi cop ever to set foot inside.

VIRGINIA, 2010

Having survived their canoe adventure with just scrapes and bruises, Omar and Clemente go driving through the Virginia backcountry. Clemente's behind the wheel for a change, and as he rounds a bend, he sees a for-sale sign and slows down—*What about that one? It needs a little work, but nobody will be trying to blow you up.* Not long ago, a truck bomb blew up across the street from Omar's apartment in Baghdad, killing ninety-five people and injuring six hundred, and parts of the engine landed in his apartment. "That sort of thing doesn't happen around here," Clemente says as he pulls up to his property. They get out and walk under the old beech trees. Tim's not rich. He bought the land in 1998 for $89,000, making the down payment with overtime he'd earned working the embassy bombings in Africa. Since his retirement in 2007, he has found work in the movies, doing some screenwriting and consulting on a few films and TV shows, "so that they get the law-enforcement stuff right." But just look at this spread. The house is on twenty-eight acres that was a Union encampment in advance of the bloody Battle of Fredericksburg. Homemade swings now hang from the high branches. Omar's three-year-old daughter runs toward them through the trees and hangs on Omar's legs as they walk. Clemente built his own house here, and he wants to build one for Omar, too. *The bad guys will not find you here,* he tells him. *A homemade version of witness protection. We can do this. You, your family, you'll be safe. We'll find you work.* Clemente's own grandfather, a stonemason, came over from Italy with nothing.

In the meantime, Clemente has plenty of room for them to stay. There are some visa problems, a bit mysterious given Omar's service to America, but Clemente's hired a lawyer and has a stack of letters to support Omar's petition, including from top American generals. Omar wants the visas for his wife and daughter, wants them to stay here where life is good. He's less certain about himself, as he has unfinished work in Baghdad, where the situation is still so dire.

Omar picks up a call as he makes his way to the porch. Clemente watches his friend's face turn grim. More news on the escape of al-Rawi, who has been an obsession of Omar's since he kidnapped and killed Margaret Hassan, an Irish aid worker, in autumn 2004. The video al-Rawi made of her death shows him shoving a green apple onto the muzzle of his pistol as a silencer before shooting her at point-blank range. Omar had watched the video over and over again and had come to care about Hassan, who had spent thirty years in Iraq, working among the poorest. Omar hunted al-Rawi for three years and put him in prison for life. He turns to Clemente: "If I'd been in Baghdad, he wouldn't have escaped."

"Who are you, Superman?" Clemente says. "There's nothing you could have done, Omar."

But then the bustle of Clemente's household envelops Omar and his wife, Amira, and their daughter. Clemente and his wife, Karen, have eight kids, ranging from six years old to twenty-three, and the kids are lounging around the kitchen on stools pulled up to wooden counters and spilling over into easy chairs and couches in the adjoining family room. They have all been homeschooled and there's no TV, but there are always a half dozen laptops going.

In Iraq, Clemente always carried a "family" cell phone, and Omar recalls that unless he was on a mission, when that phone rang, Tim always picked up.

Clemente's middle daughter, Grace, is eighteen and has a diamond nose stud and wants to be an FBI profiler like Tim's older brother, Jim, who retired in 2009 after twenty-two years with the

Bureau. As she dries the dishes, she asks Amira how she and Omar met.

"He saved my life," Amira says quietly. "It was very romantic."

Omar leans against the counter. "I got shot twice in the leg."

Amira, an electrical engineer, had done some work for the Americans in the Green Zone when she started getting threats. She was living with her parents, and her family took the threats seriously because her sister, who was also working with the Americans, had already been shot in the chest three times by militants at a roadblock. Army doctors worked fifteen hours and saved her life.

"Friends in the FBI asked me to check up on Amira," Omar says. "So I went to see her. . . ."

He gave Amira his cell number—and told her to call anytime, day or night.

"I'm on night shift when she calls," Omar says. "She's terrified, whispering that men with guns are in her house looking for her."

Amira had locked herself in the bathroom. The gunmen were ransacking the house and yelling, Which one works for the Americans?

Omar grabbed a vest and an AK-47 and raced to the house in his SUV, lights flashing. There were two cars parked at her front gate, and an armed lookout. Omar crashed straight into the first car.

"My SUV landed right on top of it, killing the getaway driver inside. And then I shot the lookout."

Clemente's youngest son asks, "You killed him?"

Omar looks to Tim, who nods, *It's okay.*

"Yes, I killed him," Omar says softly. "The gang was shooting at me from inside the house. I kept firing, killing two of them, and I saw a third go down. I ran inside the gate, trying to get to the house. That's when I felt the first bullets hit me."

As Omar was falling, he returned fire, killing the last gunman. By that point his backup had arrived.

"So you know what he does?" Amira says. "He tells his guys to carry him inside. So they do, and he knocks on the bathroom door."

"I wanted her to hear my voice," Omar says. "So she'll know she's safe."

"I opened the door," Amira says, "and saw him, leg bleeding and shattered, being held up by his men."

"She squeezed my breath out," Omar laughs, "and we fell to the ground."

"I waited at the hospital all night outside his room."

"In the morning she kissed me. And three months later we got married! That's Baghdad romance."

By now it's late, and Omar's feeling a little sore from the river, leaving aside the jet lag from having just flown in from Iraq.

"You should just stay here," Clemente says. "We've got seven bedrooms."

"No, thank you, we're good at the hotel," Omar says. "There's a swimming pool."

Omar carries his sleeping daughter out into the darkness.

Later that night, after his wife and daughter are asleep, Omar walks across the freeway to the Burger King for a snack. He is the only customer, and he sits on the curb with his burger. In Baghdad, he ate at least one meal a day at a Burger King at Camp Liberty, sitting on picnic tables under camo netting, surrounded by concrete blast walls and sandbags; sometimes he and Clemente brought informants, some who were low-level terrorists they had flipped, and they'd eat Whoppers as they plotted how to stop the bombings.

But now Omar worries that nothing's going to stop the bombings, not when the Iraqi army's chief of staff today announced that the Iraqi military won't be ready until 2020 to stop foreign insurgents. Maybe Tim's right, maybe it's crazy to go back.

Omar looks at the nice new Burger King. In another life, he'd like to be the burger king of a tranquil Iraq, own franchises all over the country—he'd make millions. But that Iraq doesn't exist, and may never again. And what would he do in America? Are there terrorists to hunt? It's beautiful here, very peaceful, the abundance is dazzling, and Tim and his family are so good to them. But there's the unfinished work of his own country that just won't leave Omar alone. His teeming mind will scarcely let him sleep.

Omar walks back across the freeway to his hotel room, and he will stay up and lurk for hours more on a jihadi website. When he finally falls asleep, it's the deepest sleep he's had in months.

The next afternoon, Omar's talking to Clemente when his phone rings again. He excuses himself and comes back a few minutes later. "I need to be in Washington tomorrow. Our friends there would like to see me."

"Take me with you, Omar," Clemente implores. "You need someone to negotiate for you." As hard as he's been trying to persuade Omar to make Virginia his home, there are others in the US government who are convinced that counterterrorism in Iraq simply won't function if Omar decides to accept his friend's offer of a comfortable retirement in the country. For several years, Omar has been working closely with the CIA and Special Forces and the "Delta boys" in Baghdad—on most significant operations outside the Green Zone—and it has come to the attention of some very senior agency officials that he is vigorously pursuing a visa for US residency. This has them concerned that he isn't going back to the fight. And so the urgent meeting.

In spite of Clemente's pleading, the next morning, Omar goes on his own. And that night, Omar returns after dark and announces he wants to get drunk. Clemente takes him to a hotel bar in Fredericksburg. Omar wants to try a margarita, maybe two. Clemente's never seen Omar drink liquor before.

Finally, Omar turns to Clemente and says, "I'm going back, Tim."

"Fuck you," Clemente says. "No, you're not."

They promised Omar that American special ops would stay in Baghdad for as long as he needed them. He wouldn't just be abandoned.

"Bullshit! It's a lie! I know the agency and I respect them. But you're just an asset to them, now, Omar. And you'll just as easily be a casualty. Their obligations are to the institution, and never to the individual. That's why I want you out of there." Clemente is livid. "Did they offer you a visa for your family?"

Omar shakes his head. "I didn't go there to negotiate," he says.

"They should have. Getting you a visa just takes a phone call. This is a dirty CIA trick, Omar." He's pleading now, eyes brimming with tears. "Don't you see? They need you back in Baghdad to help prove the withdrawal plan can work—even if it kills you."

The evening dissolves into a drunken emotional blur.

The next morning Clemente picks Omar up at the hotel. He's just stirring. "How you feeling?" Clemente asks.

"Ahh. Dizzy."

"Headache?"

"Big headache."

"I have the best cure for a hangover." They grab some egg sandwiches from the Wawa and drive over to the Bass Pro Shops for fishing gear. Omar comes to life, selects his tackle. *I'll take the ninety-pound test.*

Clemente has chartered a deep-sea fishing boat. "You've fished enough carp in Saddam's moats, buddy," he says. "Let's find you a tidewater Virginia house, Omar. Or something down the road from us. Hell, you can have a piece of my land! It's yours. I'll give it to you. We'll build the prettiest house for your girls. But please, just don't go back."

Even out on the Chesapeake, Omar wraps the line around his hand, and when he feels a bite, he lets the hook set with a tug. His pain threshold is extraordinary. With an upward stroke of his hand, a rockfish arcs through the air and crashes on the deck.

"They promised if I stay three years, I can get a job at Langley as an analyst," he tells Clemente.

"Bullshit, Omar. They won't even get you a visa!" Clemente yells. "You go back and you and your family will be killed. And they'll do nothing to protect you. I can get you a job tomorrow, teaching at Quantico. Who knows more about Al Qaeda? You should be advising the president!" Clemente is searching, desperate. And then, a ridiculous plan occurs to him. "Let's go to Hollywood!" he says. "Let me take you there. I'll introduce you to movie people. I'll introduce you to Robert De Niro! You can meet them all. Just don't go back to Iraq. Please. Let's get you a job in the movies."

BAGHDAD, 2004

On the way into Disneyland, Omar had to pass three checkpoints. He walked into the Delta command room, where flat screens showed real-time footage from all across Iraq.

On the wall was a large photo of M.Y.A. Underneath, a notice that the reward for his capture was $1 million. Omar, stunned, took a closer look. "One million for him?"

"That's the official number." Unofficially, he was told, America would pay $5 million in cash. Omar looked at Clemente. Twenty soldiers sat down on folding chairs and the meeting began.

Clemente explained that M.Y.A. had a real estate problem. He had properties all over Baghdad that he needed to sell before the Iraqi government seized them; the funny part was that he needed a lawyer to negotiate the sales for him and backdate contracts. He had sent his son, Ahmed, to take care of things for him. Tracking Ahmed offered an excellent opportunity to kill or capture M.Y.A.

The Delta team agreed to help on the operation, and they offered beacon trackers, drones, and a couple of assault teams.

A week later, when Ahmed pulled up to the lawyer's house in his white BMW, geo-positioning satellites locked in on the car. The whole house was wired for sound, and an assault force waited, hidden nearby. A Delta operator put a tracker on the BMW. Clemente and Omar waited back at Disneyland, listening.

"Do you have the money?" the lawyer asked.

"It's here," Ahmed said.

"Your father needs to sign these documents."

"I'll take them to him."

"I have to see him sign them. How do I know this is being done with your father's approval?"

"Do you know who my father is?"

Ahmed sounded agitated, upset. He told the lawyer he'd get back to him and walked out of the house. Afraid that he'd vanish, Omar and Clemente gave the signal to snatch him. As Ahmed walked toward his car, an assault team of Delta operators on the ground and in the sky descended on him. He was brought to Camp Cropper, the military detention center by Baghdad Airport.

At Ahmed's interrogation, Clemente, another FBI agent named Sutton, and two Delta boys were in the room, with Omar watching from the back. Ahmed was a big guy, twenty-six years old, spoke good English, and was very arrogant. Designer jeans and lots of cologne. Omar became offended at his behavior. After an hour, he asked permission to speak to the prisoner. He walked up to the handcuffed young man and said in Arabic, "My friends were killed in your father's operations. Now you're going to pay for the blood you spilled. I'm going to make you pay."

Ahmed smirked. "Fuck you. You can't touch me, the Americans have me." Omar rocked back slightly on his heels, and before Clemente could react, he windmilled his right hand and slapped Ahmed so hard that he lifted him off the floor. Just as quickly Omar hit him hard with his open left hand. Clemente grabbed Omar in a bear hug and pushed him back. But Omar strained forward into Ahmed's face and said in Arabic, "No! You are *my* prisoner."

With that, Ahmed wasn't so composed anymore. "You can't let him take me," he begged Clemente. "He'll torture me, he'll kill me."

"Well, I can help," Clemente said. "There's another way this can go. Just tell us how you contact your father."

Ahmed slipped off an Italian loafer. Stashed under the insole were three SIM cards. He asked for his three phones back, put the SIM cards into each of the phones, and showed Clemente what he thought was an untraceable method for contacting M.Y.A. It involved initiating contact with one phone, talking on a second phone, and listening on a third. Ahmed dialed the first phone. He let it ring once and hung up. This signaled his father that it was him calling. He dialed the second phone and said hello. A few seconds later, his third phone rang. His father's voice was on the other end of the line. "Where are you?" he asked Ahmed.

"I'm in Baghdad. I'm getting ready to do that thing."

Hearing something in Ahmed's voice, he said, "Tell me what's wrong. Are you with the Americans? Do the Americans have you?"

"They do, father, and they want you to give yourself up."

"Die like a man" was all his father said, and hung up the phone. Both lines went dead, and Ahmed broke into sobs.

Delta had traced the calls to a village just across the border in Syria.

"Let's go!" Omar shouted. He was ready. M.Y.A. was within reach. "That won't be possible," said the Delta commander. Delta didn't have authorization to cross into Syria, by order of the president of the United States.

In private, Omar implored Clemente. "Let's go anyway," he said. "If your government won't do it officially, we can go ourselves."

"I'm an FBI agent, I can't go," Clemente reminded him. "I can't invade a foreign country." Omar looked him in the eye. "Then quit. That's what I'm doing."

"You're quitting the police force?" Clemente was incredulous. Omar nodded.

"What are you going to live on?"

"A $5 million reward."

"I can't, Omar. I have a job to do here. And there are rules. You know that."

Omar was so angry that he didn't talk to Clemente for two days. But he'd learned from Clemente, and he set about finding out all he could about where M.Y.A. was and how he spent his time. By the time he saw Clemente again, he'd found a villager who knew the farm where M.Y.A. was hidden and had learned a back way onto the property. "We can drive an old livestock truck with goats and sheep across the border. We'll dress like shepherds. We can hide all of the weapons in the back. We'll take the smuggler's route. When we get there, we can take him dead or alive."

Clemente made a decision. "I'll go with you. Even if it means I have to quit the FBI to do it." Clemente went to his barracks and yelled for Sutton to come down. Sutton came out in his underwear. "I'm quitting the FBI. I'm going with Omar to Syria tonight. I have to. This man could be the most important target of the war."

"You're fucking crazy," Sutton told him. "What about your family?"

Clemente looked at him and said nothing.

"Do what you have to do," Sutton told him.

And that was as far as Omar's plan went. Moments later, Delta was informed that the two were planning to freelance a cross-border mission.

"If you were to do this," a senior Delta operator told them, "it would look like we approved your mission. Our explicit orders are that we cannot cross into Syria. It will make things worse. That'll be on your head." It was clear that if Omar and Clemente were to cross the border, they put Delta operations at risk throughout Iraq.

To Omar, this was incomprehensible. It's a one-night job, a piece of cake, he told Tim, weeping. For several days he didn't answer Clemente's calls. He finally came back around, but he made it clear that M.Y.A. was unfinished business.

After that, Omar changed. A grimace settled in. Tim had trained him in counterterrorism, but Tim's deployment would eventually end. Over a period of months, even as Omar continued his work as a Baghdad cop, Delta welcomed him into its fold, and as he became a full-fledged Delta asset, his work marked him. Omar started traveling with bodyguards. Dogs searched his car before he went anywhere. He switched cars several times a week and moved apartments every few months. One of his closest cop buddies killed himself, and Omar, in shock, crashed into three cars on his way home. When another anti-terrorism cop had two of his children kidnapped by insurgents, as a unit they voted not to negotiate or pay ransom. Otherwise, every cop and his family would be vulnerable. After the kids were murdered, Omar stopped going home, sleeping mostly at the office.

An insurgent whom Omar sent to jail for life sent him a message: "I have four sons and three brothers. My family will hunt you down for the rest of their lives." Omar had seen the beheading videos; he knew what vengeance looked like. But when Clemente began to express his worry, Omar would laugh. "There's an Iraqi saying," he would tell him. "If you are already wet, there's no reason you're afraid of rain."

On the wall of his office Omar kept two large boards. On one, a whiteboard, was an official list of his targets, the most-wanted terrorists in Iraq. On the other, a red board, was the list of those who had tried to kill Omar or his men. Every day that list was growing longer.

LOS ANGELES, AUGUST 2010

Straight from LAX, Clemente does his best to roll out the lures of dreamland. A hot young director screens an early cut of his action film for him and Omar. There are steak dinners on Sunset, and after-hours casinos, and heady talk of the Rock playing Omar in the movie version of a story that has yet to end—*no matter, we'll make up a good ending!*—but they may have to set it somewhere else, because, really, does anybody care about Iraq anymore? In Santa Monica one perfect evening, as the sun slips into the ocean, Omar sips Coronas on the green of a grass badminton court, and shows incredible prowess at the game, which he calls "featherminton." It seems the war couldn't be further away. But there's a look in Omar's eyes that tells Clemente he's already gone. There are not enough miles in the world to separate him from the marauders who are loose in his country. And whether the entropy was set in motion by the American invasion, or now by the American withdrawal, or by something essential to the Iraqi character, or all or none of these things—matters not at all to Omar. "Imagine if it were your home," he tells Tim. "Nothing would be able to keep you away." And then the sunset and the featherminton are interrupted by a call from Iraq: Two convicted Al Qaeda terrorists, just freed from prison, have publicly vowed to kill Omar.

There is so much unfinished business, and Hollywood has nothing to offer that could possibly change his mind. The face that Omar sees at night—the woman who broke his heart—is Margaret Hassan. He keeps photos and videos of her on his laptop and looks at them every day. It's an Irish face, fifty-nine years old, looking into a camera that is held by those who will kill her. This is the movie Hollywood will never make. Her kidnappers taunt her, forcing her to beg. Eyes lined with fatigue and fear, she pleads for her life. She'd been on her way to work in her Toyota when two cars of gunmen blocked her. She had a driver and a bodyguard, but that didn't matter. Not when eight gunmen, including one dressed as a police captain, raced toward her car, weapons drawn. They savagely beat her bodyguard and driver, leaving them for dead. Hassan was thrown into the back of a white Land Rover. The vehicle had two doors, her bodyguard told Omar. Which became his first clue—most Land Rovers have four doors.

Omar watches a video of Hassan pleading for her life—she faints, a bucket of water is poured on her. She is wet, helpless, lying on the floor, struggling to get up. It didn't matter that for twelve years she'd been the head of CARE, and devoted to the people of Iraq, or that she'd married an Iraqi and converted to Islam. She was still an infidel. Knowing that he was racing the clock, Omar hunted for the two-door Land Rover. There were maybe fifty white Land Rovers in Baghdad. He and his men knocked on doors, worked his informants. They followed white Land Rovers every night. He kept charts on the wall, thousands of surveillance photos. He slept at the office.

The kidnappers asked for ten million in cash, and then weeks after she was kidnapped, they sent the video of her execution. Al Jazeera refused to broadcast the video, but Omar studied it, looking for clues.

In the video, the leader of the gang, later identified as al-Rawi, keeps his face covered. He pushes a green apple onto the muzzle of the gun, an improvised silencer. He then puts the gun to the back of Margaret's head and pulls the trigger. The apple doesn't silence the gun completely, but it's the clue that changes the focus of Omar's investigation. Who needs a silencer in the country? Her executioners were here, in Baghdad.

Six months later, Omar's investigators followed a white Land Rover as it drove up to a small house in a quiet neighborhood, and the surveillance photos showed a man at the door. The man's face matched that of the kidnapper in the police uniform. In the raid on the house, Omar killed one of the suspected kidnappers in a shoot-out, and two others were arrested.

Al-Rawi, the man behind the kidnapping, wasn't there. It would take Omar three more years to hunt al-Rawi down. Maybe he thought everyone had forgotten. But Omar hadn't.

At the Santa Monica Pier, the next morning, Omar plays arcade games and redeems yellow tickets for a key chain. He gives his extra tickets to a young girl. Later, as they amble down the beach, he tells Clemente, "You're walking with a dead man." For all his bravado, Clemente feels a desperate sadness, mixed with other emotions, too. It was he who got Omar started in the counterterrorism business. And it is he who has now abandoned Omar to a country in chaos. He feels he has betrayed Omar and left him surrounded by the enemy to be killed. Iraq was once the front in America's "war on terror," but no longer. It was once Clemente's war, but no longer.

Clemente spends the night on Omar's hotel couch; he just wants to be in the same room. He pleads again for Omar to seek asylum. "For God's sake, man, you have a wife and a kid."

Omar shakes his head no and tells Clemente a story about the night he watched Uday Hussein and his thugs kidnap a woman, and he didn't stop them. The woman was standing in front of one of Baghdad's best hotels with her husband. Uday was known to take women off the street and rape them. Her husband tried to resist, but Uday's men beat him with the butts of their guns. Uday's red Ferrari idled nearby. The woman screamed and clawed as her attackers shoved her into a waiting SUV. Omar, just out of the police academy, saw this from down the street and grabbed for his gun.

But two older cops held him back. "Don't get involved," they warned. "You'll get yourself killed. Think of your family."

The shame he felt that night has never left Omar. And he has never walked away again.

BAGHDAD, FALL 2010/WINTER 2011

On Halloween, as Clemente is at a party in Los Angeles dressed as Maverick from *Top Gun*, Omar is outside Our Lady of Salvation Church in Baghdad. Inside, five suicide bombers have taken a hundred Christians hostage. They are demanding the release of all Al Qaeda prisoners in Iraq and have already killed a priest and several children who cried. Omar hears machine-gun fire and grenades exploding inside and gives the order to go in. The suicide bombers detonate, and in the end, scores of worshippers and six of Omar's men are dead, along with the insurgents, four of whom were foreign jihadis.

Omar calls Clemente from the hospital.

There's a lot of static on the line.

You heard about the attack on the church?

Yes. Clemente had just heard on his radio—the deadliest attack on a Christian target since the war began.

That was us, Omar says. My team.

You were at the church?

Yes. Silence.

Where are you now?

I'm at the hospital.

Are you all right?

I'm all right.

You're sure?

Six of my men are dead. I'm here with the wounded. The suicide bombers blew themselves up. Fifty or sixty of the Christian people inside the church died.

You made the call?

Yes.

You made the right call, Omar. The bombers were going to blow themselves up no matter what. You saved some lives.

A long pause. *Omar, who did this?*

The Dentist. You know who the Dentist is?

Clemente knows. The Dentist is the Baghdad leader of Al Qaeda in Iraq. Omar captured the last Al Qaeda leader in Baghdad months ago, and the Dentist, so called because he fixed teeth before the war, is his replacement.

Omar, you gotta get out of there.

Not until I hunt down the men who did this.

Omar, there are too many of them, and only one you. At least your family—they can come to my house.

Your country won't give us visas.

The next day Omar and his police unit walk in a procession from the bombed church through the neighborhood as a show of force and respect. At the cemetery, he gathers his men and vows to hunt down those responsible for the attack.

Three weeks later, Clemente is at home in Virginia. It's Thanksgiving, and his phone rings. It's Omar, elation in his voice.

It's done. We caught the Dentist.

How'd you catch him?

Police work.

They both laugh. It's what Tim always said, hunting terrorists is just good police work.

There was a white car at the church bombing, Omar says. We track the registration. We did stakeouts all over Baghdad. We waited. They had five dens, they moved between them. We got the Dentist and eleven others. They had tons of explosives and cars rigged with bombs, ready to go. We found intel on foreign insurgents planning big bomb attacks—they were waiting up by the Syria border, in the Badlands. We gave them a big surprise.

You went to the Badlands?

I flew in your helicopters.

With our friends from Disneyland?

It was like the old days. We fight side by side. We were hunting every night. For two weeks. Camping in the desert. Big fights, but we catch thirty-nine insurgents, all foreigners. We catch them and load them onto the helicopters back to Baghdad to be interrogated.

Were they the ones who bombed the church?

They helped, and they were going to do many more bombings. Same one paid them all.

Who paid them?

You know. There is only one name Omar will not say out loud, not over the phone. *I have another mission. I'm going back after him.* Clemente knows he is speaking of M.Y.A. *Have they approved the mission?* he asks. *Soon,* Omar says. M.Y.A. is still operating his terror network out of Syria, but with Al Qaeda contacts around the world, he is more powerful than ever. He's back at the top of the most-wanted list. No terrorist operation in Iraq, including the church bombing, occurs without his approval and funding.

Clemente fears that hunting M.Y.A. will bring brutal retaliation, and that Omar and his men alone will never be enough to stop the madmen. The Americans are leaving within months. Omar will soon be alone.

Watch the news, Omar had told him. *You will see.*

Sure enough, a few days later Clemente opens up his laptop and sees a picture of Iraq's interior minister parading thirty-nine terrorist suspects wearing orange prison uniforms in front of the news cameras. Al Qaeda's third-highest-ranking leader in Iraq, Hazim al-Zawi, is brought in wearing a black hood. In a rare appearance, Omar's counterterrorism boss is there. The minister says that while the capture of the insurgents is a serious blow to Al Qaeda, many of the men have been arrested in the past by US forces and released as a result of political deals and have gone back to the insurgency. By design, neither Omar nor the Americans are credited with the arrests. It's important that Omar stay invisible.

The new year begins, and still no visas for Omar and his family. Moktada al-Sadr returns to Iraq from his three years of self-imposed exile in Iran to exercise a greater degree of control over affairs in the country. Things are now so dangerous that Omar's wife for the first time begs him to get them to America, for their daughter's sake. A famous counterterrorist cop in Mosul, a lieutenant colonel, is killed when three suicide bombers dressed as police come into his station and blow themselves up. The colonel, who was Omar's friend, had been sleeping at the station to protect his family, as Omar often does. Omar goes to the American embassy in the Green Zone to strike a bargain: If they give his wife and daughter visas, he'll stay in Baghdad to fight. He is told to come back later. The embassy official is not hopeful.

To Tim Clemente, this is no mere bureaucratic intransigence. As a special agent in the FBI, he had an easier time obtaining visas and other special favors for the rankest criminals, once gaining safe passage to America for a drug-cartel money launderer and his stripper girlfriend. Omar is nothing of the sort. He may be unknown to Americans, but his anonymity makes him no less an American hero. That he cannot get the proper documents to protect his wife and daughter is a scandal and a disgrace to Clemente, who is not giving up on his campaign to persuade Omar to come to America.

And so it is that on January 3, Omar is behind the wheel on a highway far outside Baghdad with two prisoners and four Delta boys in his Humvee when his phone rings and he hears a familiar voice. He pulls over, too excited to drive. "Hi, Omar, this is Bob De Niro. I just want to make sure you're okay over there, that you're staying safe."

"Robert De Niro!" Omar blurts out. "I love your movies!"

"Thank you," De Niro says. "Tim's told me all about you."

They talk for a couple of minutes, none of which Omar will be able to recall later. The actor invites Omar to come see him in New York.

"Inshallah," Omar says. *God willing.*

"Inshallah," says Robert De Niro.

Esquire, 2011
Longform — Best War Stories, 2011

RIOT BABY

In the wake of the Rodney King verdicts, American society ruptured in South Central, L.A., resulting in the worst riots in our nation's modern history. This is the life story of ten-year-old Jelani Stewart, who came into this world as his city burned.

The Black circus is dark and smoky and magic. And it is loud and it is *Black*. The ringleader, Casual Cal, is Black, and he's got a Black midget sidekick, and the trapeze artist is Black and the guy on stilts is Black and the guy who vaults thirty feet high and flips and lands on a tiny chair perched in the air is Black and the magician is Black and the showgirl he makes vanish and who reappears in the tiger cage is Black. The audience is Black, too, and at the moment, to a person, all two thousand are going completely nuts, especially Jelani Stewart, who is not quite ten years old.

Look at this boy, Jelani. He's about to have a heart attack, y'all! He screams, *No! No! No!* as the girl contortionist from Africa bends over backward, curving her spine back, back, back until her perfect brown face is between her thighs and she is smiling up into the audience and rolling her eyes. Jelani grabs his cousin Kiana's hand. *Oh, my gosh!*

Casual Cal pumps the crowd. "I say, Big Top, you say . . ."

Circus! Jelani shouts, leaning his head back, staring into the heavens of the circus tent. It's like it's not real! A family is up there on the high wire riding bicycles without nets. The deejay is spinning, and it is *loud!* "I'm a sucker for cornrows and manicured toes. . . . Mommy . . . what's poppin' tonight?"

Jelani's been waiting all year for the UniverSoul Circus to come back to Los Angeles. For one thing, he gets to eat cotton candy and nobody says a thing about cavities. For another thing, all of the people who matter the most are here. There's LaTonya, his mom, who loves him beyond words; Nana and Paw-Paw, who let him play on their computer at home; his seventy-five-year-old great-grand-mother, Elouise, who raised seven kids in Watts and South Central; his auntie LaTrice and his uncle Tommy, who works at the airport, and his other cousins Tarik, Karlie, Karol, and Tommy Jr. The big-top tent is up across from a cemetery in the parking lot of the Hollywood Park racetrack. Paw-Paw sprung for ringside seats at $18.50 a pop.

Paw-Paw has a round, bearded face, short dreadlocks springing off his head, wire-rim glasses, and an earring. His name is Cornelius Reffegee, and he's LaTonya's stepdad. He is forty-nine years old and has been married to Pat, LaTonya's mom, for fifteen years.

"*Soul Train* time!" Casual Cal announces. "I need volunteers over thirty!" Before Jelani can sing, "We're gonna get funky, funky, funky!" Nana—who is old, y'all, she's fifty-one!—is center ring, shaking her booty in a *Soul Train* line. The whole family is up, stomping their feet, chanting, "*Go, Pat, go! Go, Pat, go!*"

Jelani's never seen Nana onstage before, but this is the circus, and all things are possible. He looks over and sees his mom howling with laughter, tears rolling down her cheeks. Three elephants gallop into the ring, and one stops short. Jelani pokes Kiana in the ribs. Look, he's taking a poop. The elephant wraps its trunk around the waist of a pretty girl in glittering tights and picks her up. Look, he's got her legs and stomach inside his mouth.

What if he bites her?

He don't got no teeth!

A light-skinned acrobat scampers onto the high wire. "Brother looks like a half glass of milk," purrs Casual Cal, who is really on now. "I want all the large-sized women to stand up and let us see you," he hollers. "We're proud of you sexy ladies. And young men, pull your pants up! Nobody wants to see your underpants!"

Outside it's bright California sunlight, but inside the big top there's a chalky smell in the air from the smoke machines, and the colored lights are spinning, and everything just glows. Jelani was born just up the street from here, and he and his mom live a few miles east, in the heart of South Central Los Angeles, just past the intersection of Florence and Normandie. And that's what this story is all about, Jelani being born. Because the boy's about to turn ten, and y'all, what a ten years it's been! Because people sometimes tell him that something weird was happening when he was in his mom's stomach, waiting to come out, and when he was little, his Nana used to call him Riot Baby. Because he was born in fire. But he doesn't really know much about that. What does he know? "*I never ever want the circus to ever ever end!*" he says. Casual Cal is worked up, too. "A man has to want to change!" he shouts in benediction. He is drenched in sweat and gleams in the purple air. "Never conceive in your mind to do anything evil to another human being."

***

April 29, 1992, evening, and LaTonya Potts, aged twenty-five, is in labor in Centinela Hospital in Inglewood, squinting up at the TV between contractions. An angry crowd is shouting and beating people on the TV and somebody says that you can smell smoke in the hospital and LaTonya wants her mother, who is there trying to help, to just *back off*. The nurse has been saying *Any time now* for five hours. And now, smoke and fire.

The pain is worse than anything LaTonya's ever felt. *Can somebody just turn the damn TV off?* She tells herself she'll make good choices from this point on. She just wants the baby to be born, soon, and naturally. No getting cut open. She knows it's a boy from the ultrasound but has kept this a secret, even from her mother.

Her family has begun to drive in from all over South Central. She hasn't seen the baby's father, Daryl, in six months. She hadn't trusted that man and hadn't meant to get pregnant, and she's only going to stay with people she trusts from now on, period.

Not far away, a man LaTonya has not yet met, Bo Noble, thirty-one and still on parole from a drug conviction, is racing his gray Cadillac toward Florence and Normandie. He's been watching the verdicts on television, and then the images, live from a news chopper, of a mob looting Tom's Liquor at the corner there. Bo picks up his gun, chambers a bullet, clicks the safety on, and tells his homegirls: "I'm gonna get me some."

As he approaches the intersection, a Latino couple with an infant is attacked in their car. Helicopters fly overhead, broadcasting live. Anyone who is not Black, and even some light-skinned Blacks who are unlucky enough to enter the intersection, are pulled from their cars by the mob and beaten to a pulp on live television.

LaTonya recognizes the intersection on the TV. Florence and Normandie is only a couple blocks from where she grew up. The contractions pound. *This baby is big.* A white man is being dragged out of a truck and beaten. Reginald Denny, hauling twenty-seven tons of sand in his rig to an Inglewood cement-mixing plant, had rolled into the intersection of Florence and Normandie at 6:46 p.m. He was listening to an all-music country station and didn't hear news of the Rodney King verdict, but something is going on up ahead of him. Rocks and bottles fly past. As Denny slows, rocks and chunks of concrete smash his windshield, his doors are yanked open, and he is pulled from the cab. He is knocked to the ground and beaten in the head with a hammer; when he tries to move, another man crushes his skull with something that looks like a fire extinguisher. *Mommy, please turn off that damn TV! Oh my baby, oh my baby.*

Bo parks his car off Normandie and pushes through the crowd. The corner is Eight Trey Gangster territory. It feels like a party. Bottles of Olde English 800, looted from the liquor store, are being passed around. A gantlet has formed, and guys with baseball bats are smashing all the car windows. Bo knows some of these guys from his days living in the neighborhood. There's Football Williams! He and Bo are both Crips, though from different sets, and they smoked a little weed together when Bo was living a few blocks from here with an old girlfriend. Football was always a big guy, and there used to be talk that the pros might be interested. Now Football grabs something that looks to Bo like a cinder block and smashes a white guy in the head. There is no sign of the police.

An hour ago, the police field commander for the 77th Street Division ordered his thirty officers in the area to retreat. "I want everybody out of here!" he shouted into his radio. "Florence and Normandie. Everybody get out! Now!" When two officers in a lone squad car return to rescue a Korean woman who has been beaten unconscious in her car, the officers are pelted with rocks and bricks and almost can't escape. The crowd chants, "It's Uzi time!"

At 6:30 p.m., as the worst riots of the century are developing in his city, Daryl Gates, the Los Angeles police chief, leaves headquarters to attend a fundraiser in Brentwood. The city has known since early afternoon that the verdicts would be delivered, but Gates did not put his department on tactical alert, and a dozen of his captains are out of town at a training seminar. Gates and Los Angeles mayor Tom Bradley haven't spoken in more than a year. After the field commander for the 77th Street Division orders his officers to withdraw from Florence and Normandie, they retreat to a command center thirty blocks from where Reginald Denny lies. During the next few hours, the police lose the city. Pawnshops that stock weapons are looted, putting thousands more guns on the street.

LaTonya's family is being told that no one should leave the hospital. Mayor Bradley imposes a citywide dusk-to-dawn curfew. Cornelius, Pat, and the rest of the family will sleep in the waiting room.

Once the sun sets, looting and burning and killing begin in earnest. Bo kicks in store windows, grabbing what he can. Sunday Mays, who is thirty and has been in the gang life since she was twelve, rides shotgun in the Cadillac. Sunday grew up slashing and shooting, but she also loves Barbra Streisand, and she's singing "I Want Everything" from *A Star Is Born* as they ride. She and Bo feel the lawlessness like a drug, and it's euphoric. Children ride stolen bicycles; women lug bags of shoes and toilet paper. Whole families. *Retribution, baby*, Bo says. *Payback time*. Liquor stores, corner groceries, and fast-food restaurants are torched. A new fire is reported every four minutes. Firefighters are shot at and can't put the fires out.

Bo holds his fist out the window of his Cadillac. Ash falls like snow. Fire on every corner. A laundromat is lit, now a fish market, crowds moving from building to building with torches. The Kmart and the Sav-on are looted and the Newberry's burned down. Korean shop owners, armed with shotguns, are on rooftops. Bo jacks a woman at a gas station, steals her wallet. Some Mexicans put a chain around a cash machine and pull it down the street, sparks trailing behind.

It pisses Bo off that Latinos have joined in the looting. "Rodney King wasn't no Mexican," Bo says as he puts a pistol to a guy's head and steals his wallet.

Bo and Sunday bring in their first haul. When Sunday's landlord asks her where she got all the TVs and boxes of shoes and electronic equipment that she's carrying up her stairs, she answers: "I'm a Black business owner. I'm just trying to protect my stuff." Bo fills his bathtub with meat, stacks his bedroom with TVs and VCRs and liquor. Open season. Once in a lifetime, Bo says. He's dreamed of something like this since he was a boy back in Ohio.

LaTonya's baby doesn't come all night, as if he knows.

***

In the morning, the second day of the riots, the doctor breaks LaTonya's water, but it doesn't help. Nobody told her it would hurt this much. The doctor drips Pitocin into her vein, and the contractions come with more force now, but the baby is not moving. Then he takes what looks like a pair of spoons, and he reaches inside with them and tries to pull the baby out, but nothing works.

Bo can't believe there are no police in the streets, and it's late afternoon by the time the National Guard shows up (having had what the governor calls an "ammunition problem"—their bullets had failed to arrive). The looters—Black, white, Latino—are swarming the stores with a crazy sense of exhilaration. Gang members and mothers with children. At 4:00 p.m., the first national guardsmen take up position at Martin Luther King and Vermont and other hot spots, armed with M16s, but it's easy for Bo to avoid them. The looting spreads toward Westwood, up Hollywood Boulevard. An eighteen-year-old Korean is killed trying to protect a pizza parlor.

"Let's go to Beverly Hills," Bo tells Sunday. "Shit, yeah, we fixing to bust into Tiffany's, get us the good stuff."

But Beverly Hills is one of the only neighborhoods protected by police in riot gear. Bo wants to pull out his pistol, but Sunday says it isn't going to help against that heat, and they turn around.

The riot spreads throughout Los Angeles County and up into the Valley. The TV shows a department store with no police around, and looters show up five minutes later. The city is burning. There are no cops. People come up in taxicabs, keep the meter running, grab VCRs. Police cars are turned over and set afire in the street. Flights can't leave LAX because of the smoke.

As evening falls again on the city, LaTonya, after thirty-two hours of labor, asks for a C-section. *Get this baby outta me, please.* At 5:49 p.m., while the city burns outside and the sirens wail and gunshot victims, the dead and the dying, are being treated in the emergency room downstairs, LaTonya is cut open and the boy is taken out. He weighs eight pounds, ten ounces. He is footprinted and cleaned and brought back to his mother's arms.

As LaTonya takes the baby to her breast, in a speech announcing that thirty-five hundred federal troops have been dispatched to Los Angeles, President Bush vows to use "whatever force is necessary to restore order." She names the baby Jelani, from a book of African names. It means mighty and strong. She talks to him all that night. "Now I understand why you didn't want to come out," she says. "When you get older, you're going to hear people talk about this day."

Making his way through the roadblocks and the fires, Jelani's father, Daryl Stewart, arrives the next day. Cornelius meets Daryl at the door. "Don't you go in there unless you plan to stay with her." Daryl shoulders his way past him. He says it is the happiest day of his life and he wants to make things work. He's gotten himself a job, and can't they try again? LaTonya wants her son to have a father, but for now she wants to stay with her family. On Monday, the curfew is lifted, and the city returns to work and school. Returning home from the hospital, most everything she sees out her window has been burned down. Plywood is being nailed up. Folks are sweeping. Fifty-four people are dead, making this the most violent urban uprising in modern American history. Twenty-three hundred wounded. Twelve thousand arrested. One thousand fires. Eight hundred businesses burned down.

LaTonya and Jelani stay with Cornelius and Pat for six months, and then they move into a one-bedroom apartment. LaTonya decides to give

Daryl Stewart another chance. Daryl got himself a job, pest control for Orkin. Every morning he goes off to work, kisses her goodbye, a man in a uniform. But when she calls his job one day, she learns that Daryl was fired, weeks ago, actually. "But he dresses and goes to work every day," she says to his boss. Then her phone rings and it's a drug dealer, telling her that Daryl has traded her car for crack cocaine, and would she like to buy it back? She files a police report, and apart from a brief visit in Las Vegas years later, Jelani has never again seen his father, nor has LaTonya ever received child support. "If I saw my dad on the street," Jelani says, "I wouldn't know what he looks like."

***

Jelani wakes up slowly. He goes into the bathroom. He's got to get through his mom's room to get there. His mom's boyfriend, Bo, is snoring in her bed; he'll be snoring for hours. Jelani doesn't think it's right that Bo sleeps all day and watches TV. Not that Jelani doesn't like watching TV, he sure does, but a man gets up and goes to work or school or something. There is a list taped to the wall next to the bathroom sink: "Jelani's daily bathroom chores. Good morning! 1) Wash face 2) Brush teeth 3) Put deodorant on 4) Pick up clothes off floor 5) Hang wash towel up 6) Make sure water is turned off and lights are out. Thank you son. I love you." Jelani's mom believes if you write things down, especially dreams, they come true. She learned that from the Bible, and her list is thumbtacked to the kitchen wall: "1) To own my own daycare business 2) For my business to be successful 3) To own a black shiny new Pontiac Grand Am, with a license plate that reads:

CALIFORNIA
PRYR WKS!

4) To own my own home 5) To be the best mom and provider I can be."

Jelani's mom is in the kitchen making oatmeal. She is dressed in nice pants and loafers with tassels. Jelani is walking around the house in his long underwear. A couple TVs are on in different rooms, as always, and he is not getting dressed. "Put on your clothes. Now!"

The walls of Jelani's house are decorated with squares and circles cut from colored construction paper. They are labeled CIRCLE, SQUARE, TRIANGLE. On the stove, a handwritten sign says STOVE, and underneath in red letters is the word HOT! Jelani's mom is getting ready to run her daycare business out of the house, and he has helped her make the signs. She told him, *I'm an entrepreneur.* He liked that word, and it felt like a project they were doing together. When she had to learn pediatric CPR, they practiced on each other, and now her certificate is framed on the wall.

As Jelani and his mother head outside, he's shoving his homework into his backpack. Divine, a pit bull that lives in the backyard next door, throws himself against the chain-link fence that separates the yards. Jelani's mom wants to be saying, Don't be teasing that dog, but what's the use, she's said it a thousand times. She's worried that the pit bull will scare the families that she hopes will come to have her baby-sit their kids.

Oh, shit, she needs Bo to pay the electric, and she'd better remind him because he'll never remember otherwise. Jelani waits by the gate as LaTonya sticks her head back in the door. Of all the places they've lived, this little South Central rental with the palm trees outside is his absolute favorite.

After Jelani's father disappeared, LaTonya found another apartment, for less rent, and for the next year and a half, she raised Jelani alone. She loved feeding him and washing his clothes. She didn't have much furniture, just a bed for the both of them, but she kept the place spotless. It felt good to be on her own, but sometimes she got lonely. She got a job with the school district at a daycare in Venice. Sometimes she took Jelani with her, and other days she walked him to a babysitter who lived around the corner.

Bo was dealing crack out of an apartment on Highland when he saw LaTonya walk by holding her son's hand. She was slim and pretty, wearing a pantsuit. She seemed from another world, a better world. Bo was living the gangster life, and mostly he met girls who wanted drugs for sex—strawberries, he called them. But this girl was different. She didn't seem to want or need anything. "There goes an angel," he whistled. "That's my future."

And so the next morning, Bo raced outside when he saw her at the mailbox. He was still in his pajamas. He introduced himself and told her she smelled nice. He asked if he could call her. She just laughed. "Don't you got a girlfriend?" He was out there again the next morning, and every morning for the next week. Sometimes he'd walk beside her a ways. He made her laugh. Finally she gave him her number. Sure, he was probably wild, she knew that from the start, but he was handsome, and, well, he was paying attention to her.

The scar is not the first thing you notice about Bo, but once you get past the bulk of him—he's six feet and 225 pounds—then you might notice it. It's a dark, jagged line across his forehead. He got it back in Lorain, Ohio, when he was hit by a car at age three. His head was busted open, his arms and legs broken. He was in a coma, hooked up to life support, and his mother sat at his bedside even when everybody gave up hope. Sometimes he still hears her voice— *Why you playing in the streets? You gonna be okay, I'm with you. Junior, I'm gonna whup you when we get home.*

Jelani stayed with his grandparents when Bo and LaTonya had their first date. Bo blended her a drink with gin and ice cream and pink lemonade; he put whipped cream on top—pink panties, he called it.

LaTonya never knew what crack looked like until she met Bo. She'd never known a gang member. Before Jelani was born, she'd been a nanny for seven years, starting with an affluent white family in suburban Chino, an hour outside Los Angeles. She'd gotten the job through church. Bo called her square. Her daddy had smoked weed in front of them as children, funny-smelling cigarettes that he would roll in the car as he drove them to school. She didn't like it then and she didn't like it now, but nobody had ever paid her this much attention before, and it felt good to have somebody think she was pretty. Soon he was staying overnight.

"Bo was extroverted, and I was Bo's girl, and nobody could touch Bo's girl, and I was made up to be some kind of queen," she says.

Daryl had been introverted and sneaky, stealing off for his drugs. Bo was more out with it, and she liked that. He was upfront: This is who I am.

For the first time in his life, Bo felt that, in LaTonya, he really had something special. And for the first time, he felt like he had a lot to lose. But a man's got to make money. He worked the alley behind their apartment, selling crack. "He had twenty cars in that alley all lined up," she says. "White folks, every color." She was always telling him, "You got to put up that money, invest it." He thought it was going to last forever. He always told her, "I know what I'm doing."

LaTonya never smoked crack. Bo told her if she ever did it, he'd beat her up. He wanted her pure and clean. Crackheads brought furniture and stereos and jewelry as payment, and these things furnished the apartment. LaTonya had rules: She didn't allow Bo to deal in the house while Jelani was home. Crack addicts didn't scare LaTonya; some were middle-aged men who just a few months earlier had families themselves and had held down jobs. Her own father had been a family man until he'd tried crack.

Jelani spent most weekends with his grandparents, and often during the week he'd be with LaTonya's grandmother, a retired nurse. "I knew it wasn't good for him to be with me, the way things were going," LaTonya says. Paw-Paw bought a refurbished computer from Nana's younger brother, Joseph, who opened a successful computer-training business after the riots with the goal of helping Black youth enter the technology age. With Jelani on his lap, Paw-Paw ordered CDs and books online. Paw-Paw introduced him to jazz recordings, the more obscure the better, and for laughs, they'd tune in Dr. Demento. Jelani was the son Cornelius never had and the grandson he'd always hoped for. Most Sundays, Jelani went to church with Nana, who sang in the choir, and LaTonya sometimes came along.

When Jelani wasn't around, she'd be out in the alley with Bo, but when her son was home, she stayed inside. Bo's idea of how to play with a child was to crush things between his hands and shout, "This is Bo!" At three, Jelani started preschool at a local daycare. A teacher there said that Jelani was hyperactive and that he should be checked by an expert. So LaTonya took Jelani to UCLA, where he was diagnosed with attention-deficit disorder. The doctor prescribed Ritalin, but when LaTonya researched the drug, she didn't like what she learned, especially that some kids seem to turn into zombies. She refused to give it to her son. And he seemed to settle down fine.

LaTonya wanted to believe Bo would outgrow selling crack, especially when his gang friends started going to jail. Dre, who brought Bo into the life, got twenty-five in Pelican Bay after he was picked up twice for robbery and selling crack. But Bo figured he was smarter than the police. "Don't be trippin', baby," he told her. "Everything's going to be okay." At night, he'd count out hundreds of dollars, sometimes thousands. She told him, "You should buy a house with that." "We got this place, baby, what I need a house for?"

Sometimes the police came around and jacked Bo up against the wall, and sometimes they took him downtown for questioning. LaTonya was with Bo in the alley the first time she saw the police handcuff him. They wanted to talk to him about a murder. "Don't worry," he said. "I ain't trippin' on this." Bo promised he'd be home that night, and he was. The police rattled Bo's cage every now and then, but it wasn't until 1997 that he was arrested again, and this time it was LaTonya who filed the complaint.

***

Almost a hundred thousand Blacks have left Los Angeles in the past twenty years. A good many have gone to the cemetery, a good many have gone to jail, a good many more have made it to the suburbs, some have made the migration back home to the South. But South Central is LaTonya's home. This is where she's staying.

To get to the house where Jelani lives, you exit the Santa Monica Freeway at Vermont Avenue and drive south, passing first the red brick buildings of the University of Southern California and then the new Science Center, built since the riots, and the L.A. Coliseum, before crossing Martin Luther King Boulevard, where national guardsmen were stationed with M16s. A block farther south is where the first person was killed. As you drive, consider that many of the businesses on Vermont for miles south of here were reduced to ashes—a mix of storefront groceries, mom-and-pop shops, and the occasional Korean-owned liquor store. Notice that Payless Shoes and Taco Bell, as promised, have rebuilt, as have a couple banks.

Jelani's street intersects with Vermont just before the railroad tracks at Slauson Avenue. A pink storefront church is on the corner, and there is a laundry just up the alley, and also a barber college. During the riots, while many businesses were gutted, not a single house was burned. The low-slung wooden bungalows, built in the 1920s, remain the pride of South Central. Should one come on the market, it will fetch upwards of $150,000.

There are palm trees on both sides of Jelani's street. They are very tall and skinny palm trees. The sky is pale blue overhead, the air very still. Most front lawns are well kept. Most windows have burglar bars. There are no high-rises here, nothing more than a couple stories. Even in the neighborhood known as the Jungle, off Crenshaw Boulevard, four miles west of Jelani's street, they've got lawns. Jelani and his mother live in a small brown house in the back-yard of a larger bungalow owned by Miss Allbirdie Jones. They have been here for two and a half years now—the longest they've been in one place since Jelani was born. LaTonya feels lucky to have found the house, and she pays $400 a month for rent. Jelani likes living behind Miss Jones's house, set back away from the street. He feels safe back here, and if trouble comes through the door, he knows to hide in the closet.

Jelani is looking out the screen door. A few kids have gathered in the driveway next door. "What are they doing, Mom?" he asks.

"Is that your business?"

He shakes his head.

"That's right," she says. "It's not your business."

LaTonya doesn't let him play with neighborhood kids, except his cousins when they come to visit his great-grandma, who lives across the street. If LaTonya could keep Jelani inside forever, she would. She only recently began to let him walk the five blocks home from school alone. She used to wait at the school door, until he said, "I want to walk all the way home by myself." That five blocks is Jelani's favorite part of the day. He'll walk home with Brittani and Jahnae, who tease him and tell corny jokes and sometimes hold both his hands. They're all in the fourth grade. Jelani has a bounce to his walk and big, brown, long-lashed eyes. "Jelani, all you has to do is change that little smartie attitude into a positive attitude," Brittani tells him. "Like today we were doing history and you made us laugh—that was not a good opportunity." She's got braids and long legs in bright pants and a great attitude, and Jelani's in love with her. She's not going to marry him because he's not serious enough.

Fart is Jelani's favorite word. As in, "Bo likes to fart" or "All Bo does is sleep, eat, and fart." Jelani has a slight Louisiana accent from his grandma's side of the family, and he elongates the vowel: *faaabrt*. When he giggles, his shoulders shake. Jelani likes words, and has since he was a little boy, when his mom first read him *Curious George*. Some nights, for homework, he must learn a dozen new vocabulary words and use them in a sentence. "I *slew* my enemies," he says, balancing on the curb. "I will not *indulge* in bad behavior."

Now here's LaTonya waiting on the corner of their block. She has heard that a ten-year-old kid in the neighborhood is already gang-banging, and she says that drugs are being sold from two houses on the block. The 77th Street Division is the deadliest in California, with eighty-two homicides last year, about fifty-five of those gang killings. But there is no safe place anywhere, LaTonya says. "I *like* my neighborhood. I don't want my son to think he has to move out. To where? Everywhere there are bad apples."

When Jelani saw the Columbine shootings, he wanted to know if it was real or just TV. Then he wanted to know how the students got guns. LaTonya told him about gun shops and background checks. If he ever saw a gun, he promised, he'd come right home and tell her. She wanted to know how it made him feel to see those kids shooting. "Maybe they needed their moms and dads," he said. He thought, Yeah, it's dangerous here, but look at *that*. He felt sorry for those white kids.

***

Bo is sleeping as LaTonya and Jelani leave for church. Sometimes LaTonya thinks that Bo is just using their place as a safe house, a retreat from his thug life, and all he seems to do is sleep. He says he's not living the life anymore, but last night he was washing blood off his hands and face in the shower. And last week, she found a deep bruise on his sternum where somebody had tried to stab him in the heart. She'd long ago stopped asking him to join her in church, or in anything; but it's Bo she is thinking about as she listens to the soloist. *Storms they keep a-raging in my life*, goes the song. The congregation is on its feet; the snare drum and the organ are keeping tempo. LaTonya is up, rocking back and forth, and she hears herself shouting out loud with the others, *Amen!*

The family church is in Watts, a fifteen-minute drive. Jelani's great-grandmother kept coming here even after she moved to South Central; she is up in the choir today, in African garb and headdress, looking regal. The usher at the door wears white gloves. Outside is Nickerson Gardens, one of the most notorious housing projects in America. It was near here in 1965 that the Watts riots, which killed thirty-four, began. To this day, cops are not easily trusted. Last week officers came to serve a warrant and were confronted by a hundred angry residents, some throwing rocks and bottles; extra units were called in to protect the officers from what was described by police as a "near riot."

Every Sunday, the women in LaTonya's family drive here for church. LaTonya's mother also sings in the choir, and once a month, Jelani sings up front with the children's choir. Today, along with thirty other kids, Jelani is in junior church.

"Good morning, junior church!"

Jelani wears corduroy pants and a checked shirt. He slouches and twists, all shrugs, like a boxer ducking punches. He is in the front, sitting with his cousin Kiana. The stained-glass window is etched with white orchids. Men in suits move among the children, keeping order. Brother Saunders, a volunteer Sunday-school teacher with a bushy mustache and suspenders, is up front, asking questions.

"How many of you pray?"

Jelani raises a hand.

"How many of you pray every day?"

Jelani doesn't raise his hand. He pulls at his cousin's shirt.

"How many of you do things that are wrong?"

Jelani looks around, then puts up his hand.

"God says, 'If you do things wrong and you come to me, I'll forgive you.'"

Brother Saunders walks over like he might hit Jelani, rears back his open hand.

"If I hit Jelani, what is he supposed to do?"

"Forgive you!" the children shout.

"That means Jelani is not supposed to hit me back, right?"

"*Why not?*" a kid asks, totally perplexed.

Yeah, why not? thinks Jelani. In karate class, the teacher says, *Jelani, your body is your house, your arms are your gates, don't let anybody in your house. Protect your house!* Nothing about forgiveness there. And there was that time last year when the bully was all over him. What was he supposed to do, forgive the kid, who was twice his size? Uh-uh. He got somebody twice the bully's size. Bo went and had a serious talk with him, and *poof*, no more bully. Isn't that the way the world works? And that's when it's good to have Bo around, too. That's when it seemed to Jelani that they were almost a real family. He wasn't much good for doing stuff or playing ball—*Tomorrow*, he would always promise Jelani—but having Bo in the house made Jelani feel secure sometimes. Except a couple times, when he was so mad that it seemed like he was going to do violence against LaTonya, and maybe Jelani, too.

"Now, I'm not saying that Jelani should not defend himself!" thunders Brother Saunders. "Jelani, you say, 'Brother, I will defend myself, and then at an appropriate time, I will forgive you. And I will do both of these things vigorously.'"

The real trouble with Bo started in 1997, when Jelani was five. Up until then, Bo had been the man of the house, Jelani's real father figure, except of course for Paw-Paw Cornelius, who was such a good man and who hovered over LaTonya and Jelani as much as he could without interfering. Cornelius said that of all his grandkids, it was Jelani he worried over most, because of that man Bo.

Bo had always been volatile. When his mother died a few years before, he went back to Ohio alone for the funeral. He broke down at the funeral home and pulled out his gun and waved it around until everybody cleared out, including the preacher. That's what Bo said happened; LaTonya was never sure. But now he became moody and violent at home. He started lighting his crack pipe in front of LaTonya, and he would dip his cigarettes in a mixture of embalming fluid and PCP that he called sherm. It got to where she felt safer around the crackheads than Bo, and one of Bo's regular customers even told her, "You need to leave him—he's going to bring you down." Things got so bad that LaTonya went to court and had a judge issue a restraining order to keep Bo away.

"Defendant has been physically violent toward me throughout our three-year relationship," the complaint stated. "He has punched me in the nose, blackened my eyes, slapped and hit me on numerous occasions, and has thrown a chair at me. He also repeatedly makes threats to harm me, my son, and family members."

The legal voice then gives way to Bo's voice: "I'll kill you and your family."

When LaTonya's mother read the restraining order for the first time, she was devastated. "Why didn't you tell me?" she said. When LaTonya was growing up, Pat had been beaten up by her first husband and later by a boyfriend. LaTonya recalls looking "into my mom's room, and her boyfriend is sitting on top of her, just punching her, and the next day, he's this nice man in the house who did things for us and bought things for us."

On the nights when her father was violent, LaTonya would gather her sisters in the other end of the house and read them stories as loud as she could. He had a job at the hospital, and nobody was a more careful dresser or responsible provider. Before her daddy turned to drugs, he was Mr. Clean. A piece of lint outraged him. One night when he was threatening, Pat and the kids fled, and LaTonya still remembers standing in the rain and the dark, waiting for the bus.

After LaTonya got the restraining order, Bo's luck began to run out. He was arrested five days later for possession of cocaine with the intent to sell. He called her collect from the county jail. "I got stuck and I'll let you know what happens," he said. He was sentenced to

270 days in jail. Within weeks of getting out, he was arrested again, this time in Venice with a 69th East Coast Crip named Lil Too Cool, for possession of crack. A few months later, he was busted again for drug possession, and in September 1998 he was sent to prison.

Jelani was six. He didn't know anything about crack cocaine or jail. All he knew was that Bo was gone and there was no money left to pay the rent.

***

At around age ten is when it will start for Jelani. *What gang you from?* is the most dangerous question he can be asked in this neighborhood. The question is coming, and there is no right answer. *I don't bang* is the answer mothers tell their sons to say. "Jelani, you say, '*I don't bang,*'" LaTonya says. And hope for the best. *I don't bang* got two kids killed just before Christmas. For all his swagger in the world of gangs, Bo cannot protect Jelani; in fact, Bo is a liability. Gang violence is spiking again, and Jelani's street is Hoover territory, and the Hoover Crips are a large and serious gang known for their ruthlessness. Bo's a Crip, too, but his set and the Hoovers are sometimes enemies. One neighborhood gangbanger puts it this way: "When little niggers from Hoovers see Bo, if they smoke him, they get more stripes because they got a OG. So Bo in more danger than a little homie."

The mothers in this neighborhood attribute all this business to the Devil. *Devilment* is a big word here. The police officers beating Rodney King was the Devil's work, and the riots were the Devil, too. Damian "Football" Williams hitting Reginald Denny in the head with the cinder block was the Devil. When Williams was arrested thirteen days later, he sobbed and said, "I never seen my daddy. I bet if I had a father, I wouldn't be in this predicament that I'm in right now." He told his mother that he was guilty, and she said, "Dame, you know you were wrong, but that was the Devil."

Gangs are the Devil. Selling crack is the Devil, and smoking it is the Devil, too. It was devilment when Bo hit LaTonya, and it was devilment that one time when he hit Jelani square in the face, and it is devilment to just sit there and not do anything about it.

LaTonya decided to do something about it.

***

Jelani's house is in the flight path to LAX, and from his yard he has always loved watching planes come in low over the palm trees. Until September 11 he wanted to be a pilot and would get Paw-Paw and Nana to take him to the airport to watch takeoffs and landings. But after the skies go quiet, Jelani doesn't want to be a pilot anymore. He wants to be a judge with a gavel, like the Black lady judge on TV who sends people to prison. The planes crashing got Jelani thinking about his own life, and this is what he realized: 1) that he, Jelani Stewart, is the man of the house, and 2) the world is made up of good guys and bad guys and very little in between. Jelani wants to judge people and pronounce them bad if they're bad. After September 11, when LaTonya meets him on the corner after school, Jelani will ask her, "Is he here?" And if Bo is at home, LaTonya will nod her head yes, and Jelani's face will just fall.

Jelani's started talking back to Bo. "When you gonna stop making my mama cry?" he says to him. "When you gonna leave us alone?"

"Jelani talks so intelligent," a fourth-grade mom tells LaTonya at school.

"You think so?" LaTonya laughs.

"He's always polite and well-mannered," the mom says. "How'd you do it? Mine talks back to me. He's ten years old and he's already sagging his pants, cussing, and looking like a thug."

"Mine grew up with a thug," LaTonya says. "So he's already seen the life and decided he didn't like it."

***

Bo got out of prison two and a half years ago. He had been calling collect and writing, *I'm gonna change. I just want my family back.* He said he'd go to counseling with LaTonya. He had gotten strong in jail, and

Jelani was impressed when he saw him. "Here's the thing about jail," he told Jelani. "If you sleep and drink a gang of water, you won't age much. I'm in the best shape of my life."

Bo settled back into LaTonya's little three-room house, and the romance rekindled for a while, and she even had fleeting thoughts that maybe they'd get married. When he was in jail, LaTonya had had fantasies of taking Bo away from his homeboys and the three of them just living a simple life, but where? She even searched the internet to find an apartment in Lorain, Ohio, where they all could live. But she knew better. And Bo began to stay away at night, and soon he was back in the thug life. The restraining order from years before had done some good, though; if Bo was still a thug, at least he was a mellower thug.

LaTonya will never quite understand what happened next. It may have had something to do with the night two years ago when she was mugged.

It was a Friday night, and LaTonya was wearing her uniform when she got off the bus and began her walk home. She'd been training for a $7.25-an-hour housekeeping job at the Marriott in Manhattan Beach and had cleaned twenty rooms that day. It was her birthday. Her house was just ahead when she heard footsteps behind her; a kid walked past, a sweatshirt hood over his face. His hands were in his pockets, and when he got in front of her, he turned and pulled out a gun. He pointed it at her face, stepped toward her. It all happened so fast. Then he reached out and grabbed her purse. A car pulled up and the kid was gone.

Jelani and Bo were home waiting to celebrate her birthday when LaTonya pounded on the door. "Bo opened it and my mama was crying and she hugged him," Jelani says. "Bo said, 'What happened, what happened?' She could barely breathe. I thought she got shot. I was crying, too. I was crying so hard."

Bo ran out to the street to see if he could catch the robber or find the purse. LaTonya called the police. "If the police are coming," Bo said, "I can't be here. I can't have nothing to do with the police."

Bo left, the police came, and Jelani's stomach got sick that night. "I thought that man was about to come to our house."

And LaTonya lay awake, holding Jelani, feeling abandoned, thinking, How many times has Bo done that to people—scared them, pulled a gun, maybe killed? And from that night on, LaTonya has said a prayer. She might backslide, and the Devil will try to make her fail, but please, God, deliver me and my son, Jelani, of this man Bo. He's not meant to be here. I cannot do this alone. I am a sinner, Lord, and I have only myself to blame, but I ask your mercy. Thy will be done.

***

Finally, this is what happens:

One recent weekend, LaTonya drives into the desert in a rental car with her mother, on their way to Palm Springs to attend a women's prayer conference. A few thousand African American women are there, filling an auditorium, hands in the air, some warbling prayers in tongues LaTonya can't decipher. She is hoping that God will give her a sign.

When Jelani feels fear, he always feels it in his stomach. The day before his mom leaves for the desert, he goes with her to the laundromat on Vermont. He is riding his scooter in the parking lot when he sees the man with the gun. LaTonya is inside, folding laundry. The man is in the alley next to the laundry with his back to Jelani. The man pulls the gun out of his pants and aims; he does this again and again. Jelani gets a good look at the gun and at the man's hand and the way his hand fits around the gun. Jelani doesn't want the man to catch him looking, so he takes his scooter inside the laundry and stands next to his mom. He doesn't want to tell her about the gun, doesn't want to scare her. All night he has a stomachache.

LaTonya left Bo the key to the house. "Don't be bringing none of your friends here while I'm gone," LaTonya said.

"Don't you worry, nigger."

"I'm not worried. I'm telling you."

"Okay."

"I got spies."

Jelani is staying at Paw-Paw's while LaTonya is gone. It's fun at Paw-Paw's, like a vacation; Jelani gets to play on the computer, and

Paw-Paw always cooks. Paw-Paw is just about the opposite of Bo. He and Nana take Jelani on trips, and Paw-Paw always has a project for Jelani. Today's project: build a shed.

Bo walks into the American Barber College on Vermont to get a shave before heading to see his parole officer. He pays his two bucks and sits in an old-fashioned barber chair. The apprentice barber is nineteen years old and just out of jail; his pants are belted low on his hips, and four inches of striped boxers show, FREAK is hand-jagged on his left forearm in wide Old English lettering. "You in a gang?" he asks as Bo sits down. Bo nods. "First Street. East Coast." The barber is a Crip, too, like Bo, but from another set, the Watergate gang on Crenshaw and Imperial. Bo is wearing a crisp blue shirt with a moto-cross design and wide blue pants and blue Converse All Stars. When the barber sees Bo wearing Crip colors, with his hair pulled back in a tight ponytail, he sees an OG, an original gangster, a term that signi-fies a leader, a survivor. The barber tells himself: *This nigger's been doing this shit twenty years longer than me. You've got to respect him. Even though he's not from my hood, he's still a G.*

Out at the desert hotel, LaTonya prays, and others pray for her, a chorus of voices: "Let him go. . . . You're strong. . . . There's no good for you there. . . ." She catches herself feeling sorry for him but then remembers how she sent him to pay the electric bill last week and he kept half the money.

Paw-Paw and Jelani set to work clearing the back for the new shed. But soon after he starts raking and piling leaves, Jelani begins to wheeze—a deep, gasping, desperate wheeze, like a drowning boy. First, Cornelius just thinks it's dust, and he sits Jelani in his car with cool air running. "I need my inhaler," Jelani says. "It's at my house." Jelani's house is locked up, and when Cornelius knocks on the door, Bo isn't there.

Bo is at the parole office, sitting through a mandatory job-training seminar. The jobs lady up front has a list of places that might employ ex-convicts. "When you go for a job, don't announce right away that you're a convict," she tells them. "Somewhere down the line you're going to have to tell them. By then maybe they'll be on your side."

In Palm Springs, songs of praise are bouncing off the rafters, and the lady evangelist is up front exhorting her sisters to "Rejoice and surrender!" LaTonya is in the middle of the crowd, but she feels alone. So many choices she wishes she'd made different. "I want you all to get up now, sisters," the evangelist says. "I want you to jog around this hall. Feel God's energy, His love for you." LaTonya starts to move.

Taking the bus back from the parole office, Bo stops at the Home Depot. For a moment, he feels inspired. Maybe he'll get a job. When he first came to Los Angeles, before he started slagging crack, he worked as a security guard, first for Bank of America and then for an art gallery. He worked construction for a while, helped build a Howard Johnson's. I'm not afraid to work, he tells himself; but as he walks into the massive Home Depot, with its endless neat aisles of lumber and nails, he feels something like fear. He goes toward the counter, where the manager is standing by a stack of applications, and blurts out, *Do you hire convicts?*

The manager shakes his head no, resigned, and even as Bo watches the manager, heart racing, he is not sure whether he just said those words or imagined it.

That night when Cornelius checks on Jelani, something's definitely not right. The boy's breathing is still labored, and he's sleeping with his eyes open, which he's never done before. By dawn, he seems a little improved, but later, as Paw-Paw barbecues outside, Jelani starts wheezing loud enough for a neighbor to suggest that Cornelius take him to the hospital.

LaTonya is up on her feet, like the other women in the auditorium, and yes, she's jogging, wringing her arms, trying to shake off the old, the depression, the sense of failure. *Surrender and rejoice!* She can feel the energy in the air. Moving down the aisles, threading past the stage. Suddenly, out of the whole crowd, the lady evangelist reaches out her hand and touches LaTonya's shoulder, anointing her. She looks into LaTonya's eyes. "You are going to make a change in your life. Let the walls come down. Trust God." Out of thousands, it is LaTonya who is anointed. It has happened, the sign she has been waiting for. And she weeps, each new breath filling her with hope.

When LaTonya gets back to her hotel room, an urgent message: *It's about your son.*

On the phone, LaTonya can hear Jelani's lungs fighting for breath. Asthma is serious in the neighborhood. Jelani's friend Jahnae would die from an attack. "We've done this before," she tells her son. "Everything's going to be okay. Just breathe."

"Can you come home?"

"Let me speak to Paw-Paw," she says, and she instructs Cornelius to a nearby hospital where they've got Jelani's records. "Call me as soon as you get back," she says.

Bo is heading to the corner of Washington and Rimpau, the corner where he became a gangster. He slagged crack here for five years out of the laundry, which everybody called the wash house. It's a clear day, and he can see the Hollywood sign to the north. He used to stash his rock cocaine in a broken washing machine, and the man working the cash register was on his payroll. All the money went straight into the cash drawer, so when the police came, which they did every other day or so, frisking Bo up against the window, he never had drugs or cash in his pockets. Bo was a natural businessman. Back in Ohio, he had worked as a hospital orderly, and sometimes when old folks in that hospital were getting ready to die, they asked for Bo to sit with them. He had a gift with people that way, the same gift that made him a good drug dealer.

Cornelius and Jelani tear through the streets to the emergency room at Midway Hospital. Jelani is hooked up to machines, blows into a tube to test his lung capacity.

People respect Bo in this neighborhood. This is his turf. Wherever he's lived, he's always come back here. It's his corner. He's got nothing to sell tonight, and nobody's got any money, but this is where life happens. Bo climbs into a van.

Hey, it's me, Bo!

Damn, Bo.

Bo smokes a little Thai stick with the guy in the van, Tupac's on the radio, they pour something into a cup, drink it. These days he doesn't hang out here so much. There are other destinations at night, cryptic journeys and transactions, minor hustles. This is the street, this is the life, he tells himself, and I'm a Crip till I die. LaTonya knows it; her mother knows it. I'll be representing till the casket drops. He takes another hit. I'm a thug, a killer. I'm a gangster. I'll blast you. I'll shoot you. I'll rob you. I'll kill you. They all know it comes along with the gangster life. They don't want that in their family! He stomps like an angry bull, and then comes a low wail, like a wound.

LaTonya has a choice to make, whether to leave now and return to Jelani. But she prays and prays on it and decides she must stay in the desert. When God is getting ready to bless you, the evangelist says, the Devil always attacks the person closest to you, trying to take you off your path. *Don't give in.*

She can feel the rising voice, all that is ahead, and it scares her. She does not want the confrontation, she does not want to say *Go!* Jelani sucks the inhaler, a deep breath, a gasp, forcing his lungs open. Paw-Paw holds his hand. Bo lights his crack pipe, sucking the smoke into his lungs. *I'm a thug. I'm an* OG. And Jesus got angry at those that would desecrate his house! LaTonya knows what's ahead, and it is terrible. When she returns from the desert, she makes a small sign with a colored marker and tapes it to the front door: CAUTION! GOD IS AT WORK IN THIS HOUSE.

And he says, *You're worthless.* He calls her a bitch; that's the least of it. It's all *f*-this and *f*-that. But Jesus got angry. She calls him a bitch back, just to let him know that she's not going to back down from the Devil. Then he says, *I'm going to smoke you.* The wind is howling, her own voice yelling back. He says, *I'm going to bust all the windows!* She knows he is in despair, angry at himself. He wants her to fight back. She feels the rising heat convulsing her body; letting go is like childbirth itself. I can't forgive you anymore, *I'm not your mama.* I have a son.

***

"You sad, Mama, when I was born?"

"No, I was happy. I was tired and in pain, but I was happy."

"I thought you didn't feel anything."

"I did feel, but not when they was taking you out, 'cause I was asleep."

"I never know a baby can be in your stomach. I never know that."

"Yes. Remember on TV when we watched *ER*, and they were cutting the lady's stomach to get the baby out?"

"They cut you open with scissors?"

"Knife. They had to cut through six layers to get you out."

"They cut you open all the way around?"

"Yes, like a smile."

Jelani doesn't know what else happened when he was born; she hasn't told him yet, and nobody seems to talk much about the riots anymore anyway. All he knows is, "I came out of her all wet." But he does have some questions. "I heard at school that babies come out of your butthole. Is that true?"

The other morning, Jelani made snacks for the four new babies in LaTonya's care, and then he read them a book. He's about to start baseball. Paw-Paw will take him to practice. He's taking Brother Saunders's etiquette class, which teaches young men how not to behave like thugs. LaTonya now believes that you can't protect your child from devilment in all its forms, but when you invite the Devil in, you can invite him to leave.

And she packed Bo's bag and he's back on his corner. He's been gone a month now. She hadn't wanted to tell this story. She'd hidden Bo at first, embarrassed by those years when Jelani was little and she was too comfortable with crack and thugs. But LaTonya decided that telling was testifying, and testifying is a Christian act, and that maybe this is all a part of God answering her prayers. So here it is, the story of the life of her little boy, good and bad. Jelani Stewart is ten years old. On April 30, there will be a big party at a park near LaTonya's house, with a Black clown and a piñata. Everybody he loves will be there. He made the guest list himself.

Esquire, 2002
Best American Nonrequired Reading, 2003

INTO THE HEART OF WHITENESS

A month on the run in South Africa, during the election of Nelson Mandela, with the mad bombers of the ultra-right wing Afrikaner resistance.

It's the oldest rule of hunting—if you wait at his watering hole, the lion will come to you. The rumor is that Eugene Terre Blanche, leader of the Afrikaner Resistance Movement, the largest white militant organization in South Africa, is on the run. At dawn, a police anti-terrorist unit arrested thirty-two of his right-wing soldiers, charging them with 21 counts of murder and 139 counts of attempted murder, along with possession of explosives and illegal weapons. It is Wednesday of election week in South Africa, and a miracle seems to be happening. Factions that had promised bloody war here, even Chief Buthelezi and his Zulu warlords, have called a truce—at least temporarily—to elect a Black president. All except white diehards like Terre Blanche, who is boycotting the elections and promising to disrupt the new democracy, using "any means necessary."

Not so long after the sun sets, Terre Blanche walks into the pub at the Ventersdorp Hotel, a beer-drenched lair of brownshirts and armed right-wing misfits in South Africa's rural platteland, about one hundred miles outside Johannesburg. Frans, the bartender, and the regulars stop playing darts and greet the Leader, hands clasping forearms, as is the custom in these parts. A burly *oke* in his fifties, white beard neatly trimmed, camouflage cap pulled low, Terre Blanche does not look like the most dangerous man in South Africa. No gun visible, just a screwdriver sticking out a side pocket of his work pants. He ducks into the gents, returns, spots me before he sits at the bar.

"Hello, cowboy," he says, ordering a whiskey for us both.

His blue, usually ardent eyes ("They burn with a pure flame of my people's desire for a white homeland") are now bloodshot; and his voice, a rumbling, gravel-pit-deep baritone, has quieted to a whisper. We talk about the raids on his organization, which, in his native Afrikaans, is called the Afrikaner Weerstandsbeweging, or AWB. He says among the arrested are Nico Prinsloo, his right-hand man and secretary general, and the leader of the Iron Guards, his elite paramilitary unit. His fist slams the bar. "The bastards!"

Yes, he expects to be arrested, but no use running. "I've just come from my farm, where I told my Black workers that I may be gone for a long time. I told them to feed the sheep and the cattle."

"And your horses?" (Terre Blanche—French for white earth— was once a playwright, and I know my part in this drama: I am the writer who seeks his confession, and like him, I will play my part shamelessly.)

"*Ja*, I said goodbye to my horses." He downs his drink, buries his face in his huge hands. ("He's got such *fokken* big hands," one of his enemies marveled. "I mean, you should see those hands. Big as *fokken* lavatory seats.") His fingernails are caked with dirt. "I am a lonely man," he says, "a simple man, a Boer farmer."

Four major bombs have gone off in the days before the elections, including a car bomb in downtown Johannesburg, which killed nine; another at a taxi rank, killing eleven; and a blast at Jan Smuts airport, which caused ten million dollars in damage. Now that his men have been arrested, will his organization, which claims to be the IRA of South Africa, take responsibility for the bombs? There have been deaths, I say, and people want to know if you were part of those deaths.

"No," he growls, shaking his huge, bearded head. "I won't take credit for those bombings." He hunches deeper into the bar. "Our men have never killed anybody, except a few Blacks."

"Then who planted the bombs?"

"You tell me," he bellows, clearly exasperated. "Who is Father Christmas?" He orders cigarettes from the bartender, settling for Chesterfields. A second whiskey is ordered.

Frans's young daughter runs across the bar, wanting to be kissed by the Leader. For a beguiling moment, Terre Blanche is indeed Santa Claus, lifting her high into the air, and then she is gone, scampering across the room. He turns to me, his voice somber. "What will her future be like under a Black government? We taught them what was gold, we taught them what was diamonds, we taught them what was trains—and now they will kick us in the face. They will burn our flag and throw our books into the streets."

I tell him he looks tired.

"I hardly sleep at night," he says, lighting another cigarette. "When I close my eyes, I dream of betrayals."

For Terre Blanche, who has cast himself as military savior of Afrikaner nationalism, these are indeed trying times. I understand the desire for a few stiff drinks. Not only were his top generals locked up—perhaps for life—but, even worse, today the enemy breached Ventersdorp, his hometown. Right around the corner from his bunkered headquarters, where he's spent the last years declaring that a Black government will never rule his people, local Black voters—protected by the army and the police—cast their votes in South Africa's first democratic elections.

Most of South Africa's five million whites, including the vast majority of the 2.7 million law-abiding Afrikaners, believed former president P. W. Botha when he said that they must "adapt or die." In a whites-only referendum two years ago, more than 65 percent voted for a measure that started the country toward this week's all-race elections. And now, the AWB, which claims sixty thousand dues-paying members—with a hard core of armed, racist soldiers—finds itself on the other end of the gun and the legal system.

Clearly, the apartheid system, designed to remove South Africa's thirty million Blacks to bleak tribal "homelands," had not worked. Millions of Blacks, flouting apartheid's pass laws, had poured into the sprawling megatownship of Soweto, outside Johannesburg, and into squatter camps around Cape Town rather than live in the homelands. And the South African economy desperately needed the workers. When Botha's successor, F. W. de Klerk, also an Afrikaner, brought African National Congress leader Nelson Mandela out of prison in 1990 and began negotiations for a democratic election, he irrevocably split the Afrikaner tribe.

Right-wing ideologues like Terre Blanche, unwilling to give up apartheid's central belief in separateness, hit upon the idea of a *volkstaat*, a separate Afrikaner homeland within South Africa. The *volkstaat*, in Terre Blanche's fondest hopes, would include roughly the territories of the old Boer republic—parts of Orange Free State, the Western Transvaal, and northern Natal, with Richard's Bay as its port. It is the land of their forefathers, the white tribe of Africa, who arrived from Germany, France, and Holland in the 1600s. Land they fought and died for in battles against the Zulu and Xhosa tribes, and finally the British. This is a sizable chunk of South Africa, roughly 20 percent of the country. "Our own little Israel," championed former defense minister General Constand Viljoen: He had a military plan for how the *volkstaat* could be accomplished. It was a boon for Terre Blanche, a former policeman who wanted the world finally to see that he was no neo-Nazi, but a patriot, one of those Afrikaners who wasn't so citified that he'd lost his roots.

And at root, Terre Blanche reckons, the true Afrikaner is a Boer, a man of the earth, a farmer; the rest, such as de Klerk, are traitors who betrayed the *volk* to the CIA, the Jews, and Jane Fonda. Others might choose the ballot to decide their fate in a country where Blacks outnumber whites six to one, but Terre Blanche didn't like those odds. He roared that the election would never take place. The borders of his people's *volkstaat* would be drawn in blood.

But here he sits on a barstool, impotent king of his own right-wing castle, without even the dignity of arrest or martyrdom. A month ago, in less desperate times, the Leader was the cause célèbre of the international right-wing set. One day, he answered the phone in his office, spoke for a minute in Afrikaans, then, cupping his hand over the receiver, asked me, "Who's David Duke? Is he a right-winger?" While Duke, the American white supremacist, sought an audience with Terre Blanche, out of the fax machine spun an invitation from Russian nationalist Vladimir Zhirinovsky: Come, establish your new white homeland in Russia!

But tonight, when the police commissioner—currently dodging investigations of his own complicity in anti-ANC hit squads—appears on the television screen to announce, "We've arrested the brains behind the bombings," the insult is not lost on old Terre Blanche. He bellows back, "The bombings will continue! The Boer will fight! We are heading toward revolution, not toward peace and prosperity."

***

Once the cortex fuse is lit, you have about thirty seconds before the car bomb explodes. And if you've packed the trunk of the stolen Audi with two hundred pounds of explosives (stolen from the gold mines, where you've learned your lethal trade) all tamped into short lead pipes, you'd better run like hell. That's enough explosives to level a few square blocks of downtown Johannesburg. As you run, you pass two white policemen, just a blur. You jump into a getaway car around the corner and are three blocks away when you first hear the blast. You did not expect the sound to be so beautiful, to echo around you in the Sunday-morning air.

You listen to the radio for news of soft targets—humans. The two cops are okay, just injured, but a white woman is dead, which snags in your gut until you hear that she was ANC. You are at war, and, well, war is politics; didn't even the white traitor President de Klerk, who handed over the country to the Black communists without firing a single shot—wasn't he the one who said politics isn't for sissies? Drive slow, but not too slow, ambulances and cops still flying in the other direction. It won't matter if they catch you: Didn't Barend Strydom, a true right-wing patriot, kill eleven kaffirs, and they gave him amnesty—and before he killed them, didn't Barend go up to the Voortrekker Monument, that testament to Afrikaner survival, and pray, "Dear Lord, if you don't want me to do this, please give me a sign"? And then Barend made his vow to God, just as you did this morning, in the name of the volkstaat, *the white state, that this day might be an anniversary.*

***

That Sunday morning, three days before the elections, just after dawn, I am standing on a balcony in Johannesburg with three press photographers. They are debating whether to wear bulletproof vests. Even the Zulus have quit threatening civil war and climbed aboard the election train, and the quiet is making us nervous. Last week in Tokoza, a Black township outside Johannesburg, the bang-bang had been intense. Photographer Ken Oosterbroek wasn't wearing a vest, and now he is dead. Kevin Carter, who'd just won a Pulitzer, as if that matters now, says a vest wouldn't have helped—the bullet entered under Ken's arm, pierced his heart. Ken had been his best friend. A war zone last week, kids with silver AK-47s on both sides. Another photographer, Greg Marinovich, took a round to the chest; if he'd been wearing a vest, the bullets would have dinged off the ceramic plate, and he wouldn't be in the hospital now. Kevin models a dark-blue vest—very slick, very security police, we fear. Still, we all put them on and head out.

Into the Black townships on the East Rand, just outside Johannesburg, where whitey comes in at his own risk, we search for dead bodies in the golden light of morning, the best light for photographers. Charred barricades, streets still smoldering. Neighborhoods of burned-out houses. In the past year, hundreds have been shot, hacked, burned, and necklaced to death on these streets in tribal and political fighting—mostly between local ANC comrades and Zulus loyal to Buthelezi's Inkatha Freedom Party. Last week, twenty-seven were killed in one day: proof, right-winger's carp, that Black South Africans don't want peace.

Hey, *Com.*

Hey, cameraman, the kid says, waving us past.

Today, whitey with a camera is okay. Today, whitey with a camera is cool. We drive on through a scorched no-go zone of charred structures that separates the ANC residents' homes and the barrack-like Zulu hostels, some of which hold several thousand men—an area known as Beirut. Kevin Carter rides shotgun, an illegal police scanner pressed to his ear, listening to the cops talk in Afrikaans. We watch rooftops for snipers at their usual posts. But all is quiet this morning. Army troops in casspirs—armored vehicles designed to withstand land mines—rumble past cows eating garbage alongside the dirt roads.

Instead of the familiar *tat-tat-tat* of AK-47s, we hear bugle calls and see ranks of Zulus, shields and traditional weapons held aloft, *toi-toiing* up the hill from the hostels, toward us, a high warbling in the air. We drop to our knees, shooting pictures. Spearpoints touch our chests as the Zulu *impi* claims the ground, moving forward, warlike but jubilant. They are off to an election rally, escorted by the army casspirs. All hail Chief Minister Gatsha Buthelezi's call! Finally, in the eleventh hour, he has asked all Zulus to put aside their guns—at least for now—and vote Inkatha! In the front ranks, a male Zulu warrior wears a tattered black bra. We laugh for the first time in days.

Kevin picks up a report on the scanner. A bomb in downtown Johannesburg, a block from ANC headquarters, a hundred yards from my hotel. Welcome to the new South Africa. We've all seen bombs— 110 have gone off in the past month—but nothing has prepared us for this.

Two hundred pounds of explosives packed into a cream-colored Audi. Nine killed, ninety wounded. Flying shrapnel, severed limbs, a blinded child. The wounded carted into ambulances as we arrive. The Audi still on fire, upside down. Glass everywhere, rusty water pouring through the streets, reddened with blood. Twisted steel, shattered windows, raging fire. Two prostitutes in terry-cloth robes, dumb with shock, stand in front of a corner massage parlor. I walk on, as if I know where I am going. Bomb-sniffing dogs strain at leashes. A woman crumbles in a corner. An angry Black crowd pushes at the police barricades.

***

Mannie Maritz, legendary Afrikaner nationalist and former junior heavyweight wrestling champion of the empire, has for this week converted his farm, an hour east of Pretoria, into a right-wing refugee salon, a rest stop for Afrikaner Resistance Movement members on the run.

It might be dangerous to show up unannounced at the Maritz farm on this election eve, two days after the Johannesburg bombing, so I call. If there's one thing an Afrikaner respects, it's a chap with a sense of politeness. Maritz, who once defeated an American who was 102 pounds heavier and a foot taller, invites me over for "soup with the blokes."

Among the blokes is Terre Blanche's secretary general, Nico Prinsloo. Within hours, he will be arrested for allegedly masterminding this bombing campaign. But for now, he offers me a cigarette while a commando of thirty AWB soldiers lounge nearby in khaki uniforms with pistols stuck into their belts. Prinsloo, thirty-two, wears blue jeans and a dress shirt; his eyes are calm today, focused. He is soft-spoken, married, and is himself a farmer. Like most white males of his generation, he spent mandatory army service in the South African Defense Force on the northern border during the heyday of an official government paranoia called Total Onslaught, which blamed all unrest in South Africa on communists stealing across the border.

A pack of barnyard dogs are sniffing and rolling underfoot; Malay gamecocks strut the lawn. Before we serve ourselves from giant kettles of soup and platters of white bread, the sixty-nine-year-old Maritz—whose father was a general in the Anglo-Boer War and whose great-great-grandfather was one of the original trekkers who led his white tribe into the African interior—asks us to bow our heads in prayer. Invoking the Vow of Blood River, which "protected our forefathers" in their epic stand against the Zulus more than a century ago, Maritz asks God's protection in the days of unknowing ahead. The vow ends: "Deliver our enemies unto us."

We take our bowls to the edge of the lawn, and in the company of bantam chickens, swans, several peacocks, and a pair of ostriches, all penned nearby, Prinsloo asks me about the size of the first bomb.

I say two hundred pounds, and Prinsloo shakes his head as if surprised. "*Jissis, dis'n fokken groot bom.*"

But there isn't a look of satisfaction in his eyes when I tell him about the blasts, which killed mostly Blacks; instead, he seems a little squeamish when I describe the severed hands and bloody fingers I saw on the pavement, and how among the dead was a fifteen-year-old white schoolboy and a thirty-year-old white woman.

Maritz suggests that the bombs are a kind of warning—"while the rest of the world is euphoric over the elections, they show the real tension. Small fuses are lit everywhere, do you know what I'm saying?"

"Who do you think set those bombs?" Prinsloo asks. "Do you think it was the Zulus?"

A white man, I tell him, was seen running from the car before it exploded in Johannesburg, and another white was caught yesterday with explosives rigged in his car. The police say it's a right-wing conspiracy to disrupt the elections and have offered a half-million-dollar reward, hoping the money will entice a few unemployed right-wing canaries to sing.

Prinsloo's brow furrows. "Anybody who goes to jail now will be forgotten. They'll throw away the keys."

I never do see the trailer of mortars or the cache of machine guns Maritz is rumored to have stashed on the thousand-acre spread. Police sources tell me that such caches are buried on farmland all across South Africa. But Maritz keeps insisting that this farm is not a paramilitary base but a refugee camp for terrified whites who don't feel safe in the city.

Fear mongering has become a national sport in South Africa, and for the AWB, talk of the *swart gevaar*—the Black threat—is a useful rallying cry; it doesn't help that in the recent past, isolated white farmers have been killed by Black militants who chant, "One settler, one bullet" and "Kill the Boer." At a closed meeting of the AWB faithful I attended a few nights back in Durban, on the Indian Ocean, the local general had revealed a top-secret defensive plan in anticipation of "two million Blacks rising out of squatter camps with AK-47s." Code-named Operation Thunder, the plan included cryptic phone calls, defensive *laagers*, safe houses, exodus routes, and, yes, indeed, a ship in the harbor.

As I leave Maritz's farm, he is still overseeing preparations for the apocalypse, convinced that thousands of white refugees from Johannesburg will flee. Two Black workers—one wearing a Bing

Crosby hat at a rakish tilt—are lifting another massive soup pot off the back of a truck. He calls out to me, "We're safe out here in the platteland. We know our Blacks—they're like family."

***

To reach AWB headquarters in Ventersdorp, you cross the great fertile platteland of the Western Transvaal, through dazzling fields of maize and sunflowers. It was on this stretch of road one night last December that six AWB members, wearing stolen police uniforms, set up a fake roadblock and forced ten Blacks from their cars at gunpoint, seating them on the tar road and shooting them at point-blank range.

A CNN crew waits at the corner. After weeks of shunning the media, Terre Blanche has invited journalists to join a two-hundred-car convoy of heavily armed AWB supporters who are heading to a rally fifty miles away, where he will talk about the arrest of the bombers. CNN is hoping for blood. "Do you know what AWB stands for?" the CNN cameraman asks, punching me in the arm. "Afrikaners Without Brains." At AWB headquarters, a bunker of sandbags is stacked eight feet high around the entrance, and steel mesh slants down to deflect grenades and petrol bombs. A large sign, in green letters, is taped to the outside wall: BEWARE MEDIA! AWB grunts hate the press, and as we approach them, I am reminded of the Zulu king Dingane screaming, "Kill the Wizards!" before he slaughtered the party of whites he'd invited to his kraal in 1890.

At noon, the church bells toll, and the convoy heads north out of Ventersdorp: bearded men in khaki uniforms, on the backs of trucks, some wearing ski masks, shotguns held high. The CNN crew races ahead to get a long shot. I get a flat tire, which I fix with the help of a Japanese television crew, and we are cut off from the main convoy, which had been given military escort. We crest a hill and find our cars surrounded by a rogue group of AWB Wenkommando, the Victory Command. I am taking pictures when they leap from their pickups and begin smashing at windows with rifle butts, trying to strip us of cameras. They are especially intent on halting the Japanese in the next car from filming, but the TV crew accelerates onto the shoulder and speeds away. The snarling Wenkommando turn their attention to me. The barrel of a pump-action shotgun presses against my window, centimeters from my face. *One picture, one bullet.* Another masked soldier jumps onto my hood, crouches with his R-1 assault rifle. *You take a picture, I'll kill you.* I slide my camera under the seat and put my hands up. *I can blow your head off.* I drive on, dogged by them the whole way. At the rally, before Terre Blanche is introduced, a Black reporter from the New York *Daily News* is beaten and chucked out. The AWB crowd cheers, and journalists, who now outnumber Terre Blanche supporters, threaten to walk out but don't. CNN leads the evening news with Terre Blanche sounding his familiar refrain that the bombings will continue. "We will use any means and ways to keep our people free and independent in the fatherland, which my ancestors paid in installments of blood and tears and the bodies of our children."

***

The thirty-two suspected bombers, including Prinsloo, sat in jail for three weeks before coming up for their bail hearing at the Magistrates Court in Johannesburg. At the hearing, the defendants are not chained or manacled. They come in jackets, denim, knit suits. Their heads shake, a few smile. They all stroke mustaches and beards. The gallery is packed with wives and family.

The courtroom is not so different from the one where Nelson Mandela, then a young lawyer and head of the ANC's military wing, stood in 1963 at his famous treason trial and made his case for a campaign of violent resistance against the apartheid state before being sent away to prison for twenty-seven years.

Twenty of the accused are members of the AWB's elite Iron Guard, a unit made up mostly of former South African special-forces experts, many of whom have explosives training; four are members of the AWB's Wenkommando; eight are regular AWB members. A police colonel testifies that the accused were also planning to detonate a five-ton bomb at Jan Smuts airport on the day of Mandela's inauguration. (The bomb that devastated the World Trade Center in New York in 1993 was a tenth that size.) The confiscated evidence includes assault rifles, machine guns, revolvers, 150 pounds of explosives, stolen cars, false registration plates, nine parachutes, and a black wig. The police admit now that in their dawn raid, twenty-one escaped and are still on the run.

This will be the largest right-wing trial in South African history, and its procedures are governed by a new bill of rights. Under the apartheid legal system, ninety thousand Blacks were detained without trial, often for months or years, and confessions were routinely coerced through torture so intense it left prisoners dead or maimed. Restricted now to interrogating prisoners in the company of lawyers, the colonel admits frustration; the defendants have not been forthcoming.

The suspected AWB bombers lean over the dock, kissing wives and girlfriends. The defense attorney bows to the judge, then addresses the state's chief witness.

But how, colonel, do you know it was these men?

Well, sir, the bombings have stopped.

The thirty-two accused bombers sitting on benches before the judge do not look so much different from sepia photographs of Boer commandos who fought British rule nearly a century ago. Add a few pipes, strange hats, and carbine belts over the shoulders, and these are the armed farmers whose collective will the might of the British empire couldn't thwart. This gallery of rogues descends from Boer farmers who invented the commando: small, quick-reaction units of snipers and horsemen whose hit-and-run attacks on British supply lines prolonged a war in Africa that had whites killing whites. And even back then, the Boers were explosives experts, blowing up bridges, sabotaging waterworks. The British suffered staggering losses to these farmers, finally resorting to the infamous scorched-earth policy of burning farmland and incarcerating Boer women, children, and old men in concentration camps. Twenty-six thousand perished in the camps. Even as the Boer War ended in defeat for the Afrikaners, roaming commandos refused to concede. Those Boers came to be known as the *bittereinders*.

***

There are more than forty militant right-wing organizations active in South Africa, and though the AWB is the most notorious, even locking up its leadership would not stop future bombings—or so most experts believe. In the days before Mandela's inauguration, while Terre Blanche's men were in jail, twelve hundred pounds of explosives were stolen from a gold mine. (About fifty-five thousand tons of commercial explosives are manufactured in South Africa each year. Most of it is destined for the gold mines, which have become the training ground for bombers.)

The Boer Republican Army, another right-wing splinter group, numbering perhaps two hundred, is well known to the police as a bombing organization. Andrew Ford, leader of the BRA, arranges to meet me one midnight at his rural hideout, and when Ford and his dogs greet me at the end of a dirt road, he lets me know that I've been tracked by radio and infrared goggles since turning off the asphalt a couple miles back. He refuses to take credit for the recent blasts, but admits that he has issued a general directive for his men to go after "soft targets." He doesn't believe the bombs were set by Terre Blanche's people, whom he finds "too defensive for my taste." His own group, he says, believes that "one must attack one's enemy."

The Boer Republican Army, sources in military intelligence tell me, works like the IRA, in cells of three or five. Cells do not know each other, and soldiers are known only by numbers. If a soldier gets caught, he can take out only his cell. And in one of the more cynical right-wing ploys, the BRA has trained units of mentally handicapped bombers.

Ford will not be satisfied until "every house, every block, every town" becomes "a front line in the war." The enemy is not just Blacks, but also whites, especially those, such as de Klerk, who have betrayed the *volk*. Ford pledges that white businesses and homes will be future targets. "We're going to hit the big companies because it will throw our people out of work and then they will fight. If you take away the whites' luxuries, they'll have to fight. We must accept that we're in a war."

***

The bearded AWB soldier, hands up, stared into the television camera, pleading for someone to call a *fokken* ambulance. He was wounded, unarmed. Behind him, stretched on the backseat of their blue Mercedes, a companion was bleeding to death. The four doors of the Mercedes were wide open, windows smashed by bullets. Another soldier sprawled in the dirt, facedown, already dead. A howling Black soldier crossed in front of the photographers, pointed his R-5 rifle at the white man's thick torso, fired two shots, and proceeded to the other man, executing him also.

The bearded man's name was Alwyn Wolfaardt, and in the final weeks before the elections, his execution—broadcast on television around the world—symbolized the agony of the right-wing Afrikaner. The image remains central in the gallery of Afrikaner fears, as I found in the diary of a young Afrikaner woman who told me she'd saved a news photo of the execution, along with these words:

"We're going to be shot like this. We're going to plead for our lives. It's going to be like a holocaust. It's going to be 'Chop off the Boer's head and throw us aside.'"

To understand what led to the execution, which also effectively killed any hope of a unified right wing, I pay a visit to one of the most decorated generals in South African history, Constand Viljoen, a man Eugene Terre Blanche has branded "a political Judas goat sent to lead us to slaughter." They had once been allies in a broad movement called the Freedom Front, which had threatened a pre-election right-wing coup. The plan had been for AWB regulars and Viljoen, who claimed twenty thousand loyalists in the South African Army, to take a white homeland by force.

But after a botched military excursion to "liberate" the Black homeland of Bophuthatswana ended in defeat, with Afrikaners being executed, Viljoen instead withdrew from the alliance, cursing "Terre Blanche and his undisciplined men." Instead, he negotiated a deal with the ANC, effectively splitting the right wing. The ANC's agreement with the Freedom Front called for "substantial proven support" in the elections to continue negotiations around the "idea of self-determination, including the concept of a *volkstaat*." Speaking with a velvet voice and an iron fist, Viljoen threatened to mobilize his forces even on the eve of signing the accord. Other right-wingers thought him naive and a sellout. Terre Blanche privately inveighed that Viljoen had been planted by de Klerk to destroy the right wing all along.

When I visited Viljoen, he'd just won a seat in Parliament and two hundred thousand votes for his beloved *volkstaat*. Backed by those votes, he was hoping to propose boundaries for a homeland, but the problem was that some of the areas he was hoping for had voted overwhelmingly ANC. He still clearly hadn't figured out what to do with Blacks. For example, how would Black residents be compensated for moving out of the *volkstaat*, and what would be the rights of Blacks who chose to stay, and if any did choose to stay, wouldn't that defeat the very purpose of a white state? He admitted that these were questions he hadn't yet worked through. And though in theory whites might like the idea of a *volkstaat*, why would they give up houses and jobs and beachfront property to move to the dusty Transvaal? "We are only asking for some piece of land that is ours," he answered, "even if we don't live there." And he continued to insist that the *volkstaat* could have been taken by force before the elections, although he admits his soldiers could not have held it for more than two weeks.

Viljoen's right-hand strategist, Pieter Mulder, admitted to me that "the *volkstaat* idea stinks too much of apartheid for Mandela's nose, but we're thinking five, ten, fifty years down the road, and Mandela won't be here, but the forces for self-determination will be. Just look at Bosnia—the great melting pot doesn't work."

***

The scene inside the Soweto stadium, a victory celebration, is a right-winger's worst nightmare: seventy thousand *toi-toiing* ANC comrades, feet pounding, arms swinging, as *songomas* light sacred tribal smoke pots to rid the stadium of evil spirits and bless the Old Man, *Madiba*, the incoming president, who steps now, in a bright-yellow shirt, onto a makeshift stage in the middle of the soccer field, his fists pumping the air. The undulating, surging, hands-to-the-heavens crowd sings out his name in praise, one great chorus of—hold-that-note-as-long-as-you-can—*Man-del-la*. And then from this side of the stadium, then from over there, a volley of gunshots into the air. The Spear of the Nation honor guards, in camouflage uniforms, are leopard-crawling across the infield—duck, dive, duck, dive, rolling. The gunshots continue, harmless as fireworks, and the crowd greets each sharp pop with a resounding cheer. But Mandela, surrounded by bodyguards, is not amused. He announces in a stern voice that "criminal elements have infiltrated our organization, and I will not have it." The crowd hushes and sits down on the concrete steps of the stadium. "If we find out who they are, we will expel them from the ANC."

And now the young comrades have come to Mandela's most notorious lieutenant, Robert McBride, their lips trembling in confused anger. The Old Man had insulted them.

McBride, who is of mixed race—in South Africa's new politically correct lingo a "so-called colored"—is a hero to these kids. He was sent to death row in 1987 for a bomb he planted under orders from the armed wing of the ANC. The bomb exploded at a nightclub in Durban, killing three whites and injuring sixty others. He was released in 1990 as part of an amnesty swap that also freed Barend Strydom, the white neo-Nazi who killed eleven Blacks in a shooting spree in Pretoria in 1988.

Now McBride, a candidate for the Johannesburg provincial parliament, wearing a pinstripe suit, stands outside the Soweto stadium, cupping his hands as if holding a frail bird. "Mr. Mandela is like a little chicken," McBride explains. "Between now and the elections, we must protect him. After the elections, you can worry him."

"But why did he condemn us like that in public?"

"When you are a leader, it is difficult; you will understand," McBride, who is only thirty, says, leaning over and patting his soft Afro. "Look at the gray in my hair."

He tells them that the ANC has received intelligence reports that right-wing marksmen, or Blacks hired by the right wing, are out to assassinate Mandela, and the young comrades, who have been on the front lines with rocks, rifles, and fiery necklaces for the past decade, nod soberly. "We must," he says, "show that we are disciplined."

Mandela has asked his countrymen to throw all their guns into the sea. Instead, they've just been buried. Everyone remembers where his gun is.

"We've all become quite damaged by what's come before," McBride tells me later. "One became accustomed to people dying on streets every day. People carrying guns. Ordinary people became soldiers. Youths became comrades. Violence and intolerance became the order of the day. If you raise children with guns, it's hard to put guns down."

***

On the day the jailed right-wingers had allegedly planned the greatest explosion in South African history—the five-ton airport bomb—Nelson Mandela took the oath of office. From the reviewing stand at the historic inauguration, the Voortrekker Monument was visible on a distant hill across Pretoria, a towering edifice bearing silent witness. After the ceremony, I went to the monument—the Afrikaner holy of holies, which depicts inside on massive friezes the great trek and the subsequent battles that led those early Afrikaners, the white tribe of Africa, to see themselves as God's chosen people. When I pulled up to the monument, I found it closed, all the doors locked. The grounds were being guarded by a platoon of Black soldiers. They had been sleeping in the rough scrub grass at the base of the monument all week. Tomorrow, they said, it would be open for business again.

Terre Blanche was back on his farm, and I'd like to think he was currying his horses, worrying about how to pay the bills, and waiting, always waiting, for the day the police would come to pick him up. Nico Prinsloo remained in prison, and sometime in August—deep winter in South Africa—his trial will start. The police say they have a strong case, but Prinsloo, from the dock at the courthouse on my last day in South Africa, told me he was confident. The judge has declared that if they are found guilty, he will show no mercy. But if Prinsloo and his fellow right-wing soldiers are found not guilty, it will be a consequence of the bill of rights that has been enshrined in the new South African constitution, the same constitution that they so violently opposed, at least in word, if not in deed.

And on the first working day of the new South African Parliament, President Mandela conducted business in Afrikaans—the language of his former oppressor, which he had mastered while in prison. And even General Viljoen, now the official leader of the conservative opposition in Parliament, was moved to tears.

Esquire, 1994

THE RIGHT TO BEAR SORROW

Like many Americans, Bobby Crabtree felt that only a gun could protect his family. Then, one night, he shot his daughter. A journey through the nation's gun culture.

I. Monroe, Louisiana

Bobby Crabtree, fifty-four, of West Monroe, Louisiana, had been picking guitar earlier that night at a family sing-along at his sister Betty's out in the country. Two guitars, a roomful of voices, and his sister playing spoons and the tambourine. And Bobby, well, when he sang, folks quieted down, even in those rowdy Louisiana roadhouses where he used to play in a band, his voice soft and raspy, like that of his hero, Conway Twitty. They ended the night singing "I'll Fly Away" and harmonizing on "What a Friend We Have in Jesus." Bobby had had one or two beers, a couple cups of coffee. They'd eaten at the Piccadilly Cafeteria that evening. It had been a good time, and tomorrow was his wife's birthday.

Just before they left the sing-along, Bobby's fourteen-year-old daughter, Kaye, phoned to say she was staying overnight at her best friend Stacey's house. She was just checking in, knowing how her parents worried over her. Bobby was glad she called, and it set his mind at ease as he started the half-hour drive home.

All the lights were out when Bobby pulled into his driveway just past midnight. He brought in his wife, Tilda, and his mother-in-law, who uses a walker and has a serious blood-sugar condition. They were in the living room when they heard the noises coming from the closet in his daughter's room. Bobby's mother-in-law, Leola, remembers it as a scratching noise, and she remembers being afraid.

Not long before, somebody had "put a brick through the picture window of the house in front," Leola later recalled. "It was a Black boy from the special needs school next door." And then there had been the recent abduction of the young woman at the Super Kmart by a white felon who'd raped her, cut her throat, and left her for dead. When Leola heard the racket in the closet, she was sure it was a burglar.

Bobby said to himself, "Somebody has broken in, and they are in the closet, and they are going to wait until we go to bed to come out and do what they want." He quietly got down his .357 Magnum from his bedroom closet.

He'd traded a Colt .45 for the .357 years ago. He'd bought the Colt from a salesman at the ice company where he works. "I'll let you have this Colt for all the money in your pocket," the salesman had said. Bobby had twenty dollars. He'd never touched that gun in all those years, then swapped it finally for the .357, which he'd fired only a couple times, at tin cans.

"After I had the gun in my hand, I weighed everything in my mind. My daddy always told me, 'Before you get a loaded gun out, you should be able to lay a hand on every member of your family.'"

Tilda was on the sofa in the living room, sitting near her mother. He knew his daughter was spending the night at her friend's house. His family was accounted for; even the cat was in sight.

"My wife said to her mother, '*Shhh*' when she saw I had the gun." He turned on the light in the bedroom, paused to listen for sounds, then walked to the closet door. "I'll admit," he says, "I was scared." He waited for a moment in front of the closet. He was holding the pistol at his side when he yanked open the door. "It happened so fast, the same instant I jerked the door, they jumped at me. All I saw was a blur. The gun came up. It was just reflex; I don't think I even meant to pull the trigger."

What Bobby didn't know was that his daughter, Kaye, wanting to play a trick on her parents, was hiding with Stacey in the narrow bedroom closet, mimicking the noise of burglars. After calling

Bobby at the sing-along, the girls had hit upon the idea of cooking a birthday breakfast for Kaye's mother the next morning. They convinced Stacey's mother to drive them back to Kaye's. Kaye was a natural prankster and had always loved to jump out from behind doors and scare her father. This night, as the closet door jerked open, she sprang up from her crouched position and yelled, "Boo!"

The hollow-point slug from the .357 entered Kaye's neck.

"Lord have mercy," Bobby wailed, dropping to his knees. "I've shot my baby."

At the hospital, Bobby told me, he saw the Angel of Death sitting at a picnic table. "The reason I knew it was him was because he was crying as hard as me. He asked, 'Why are you here?' I told him. He commanded me to sit down, and he took my hands and held them tight, and he prayed. He cried with me because he knew what was coming. It was the most beautiful prayer I'd ever heard, and I've heard the great preachers—Billy Graham, Charles Stanley, you name it. I went up to get my wife, and when I came back, he was gone."

Kaye lived for twelve hours after the shooting, and her last words were "I love you, Daddy."

***

I first met Bobby Crabtree around Christmas, six weeks after he shot his daughter. His house was my first stop on a journey into America's gun culture, away from the big cities, where voters are showing overwhelming support for gun control. As I left my home in California, a poll in conservative Orange County showed that 66 percent of residents favored stricter gun laws. This is not the case in the middle of the country, where the right to bear arms is held sacred. Much of our national identity depends on the free trade of personal weapons; Crabtree's .357 Magnum is one of an estimated 220 million guns owned privately in the United States. Central to any discussion of gun freedom or the Second Amendment is an understanding of the very impulse to own a gun, as well as a single question: What are Americans so afraid of?

When we met, Crabtree and his wife were living with her parents in a yellow house on the edge of cotton fields in a rural parish far from Monroe. The house had no phone. It was early morning on an overcast day when I arrived. Smoke was rising from the kitchen chimney. Bobby, a slight man with blue eyes, a mustache, and graying hair, was wearing a gray sweat suit and moccasins. He sat on the couch beside Tilda.

The swarm of media with offers of cash had long since gone. Bobby had refused all interviews. I said I'd go, too, and I meant it. But his wife said quietly, "No, stay on."

"It might do some good to talk about it," his father-in-law said, sitting in a rocking chair near the heater under a mantel crowded with family photos, his eyes leaking tears as Bobby began to talk.

"Everyone called her Kaye," Bobby said quietly, "but to me she was always Dobber, the nickname I gave her when she was a child." He brought out Kaye's photo album and turned to the last page, an eight-by-ten print of his blond daughter at fourteen, a class picture of the girl he loved "more than my wife, more than life."

The Crabtrees hadn't spent a night at their own house in West Monroe since Kaye's death on November 6. Bobby asked if I'd drive with him to that house; he needed to pick up mail. His wife showed me a box filled with letters from strangers who'd read of Kaye's death. "I plan to answer them all," Tilda said.

Bobby changed into a plaid shirt and blue jeans. His family was concerned that he might try to take his own life: Just two nights ago, a local Baptist preacher spent hours trying to keep him from suicide. In the car, Bobby told me the only reason he's living now is that he's got to see his daughter in heaven. "Do you think it's true," he asked, "that you don't go to heaven if you kill yourself?"

The question hangs in the air as we pass the ice factory in south Monroe. Each morning at 4:00 a.m., he and his wife begin their workday here. As Bobby explains the ice business, his grief passes momentarily. "Every twenty-four hours, 110 tons of ice are bagged from this little plant. Sixty bags a minute come off the conveyor. That's the truck we drive." Every day, the Crabtrees deliver eighteen hundred of those bags themselves on a route that takes them up into Arkansas. They make five cents a bag.

One day last week, it began to rain at sunrise as Bobby drove the ice truck, his wife asleep on the seat beside him. "I cried for twenty-six miles in that rain," he says quietly.

We cross the Ouachita River and drive toward the outskirts of West Monroe, past bait shops, a taxidermist, and a sawmill. Turning into his own cinder-block house set back from the road, Bobby shakes his head. "We moved over here from the south side to get away from violence, to be safe, because people were shooting each other over there." There were twenty-three murders in Ouachita Parish last year and twenty-six the year before. Most occurred in the south Monroe neighborhood Bobby had left.

Inside the Crabtrees' tidy two-bedroom house, Bobby shows me where he kept the .357 Magnum. His daughter was taught not to touch the pistol. A box of ammunition had come with the used .357. According to the sheriff's office, the hollow-point bullets were "designed for maximum damage."

"You can walk in there," he says, pointing to a bedroom off the hall. "That's my Dobber's room. . . . I can't go in there." On the door, a sign reads, KAYE'S ROOM. Inside, on paneled walls, are Pearl Jam and Nirvana posters. An assortment of tapes, some of them country. The desk where Bobby put the surprise hundred-dollar bill that allowed Kaye to join the pom-pom squad at West Monroe High. Against one wall, near a narrow, neatly made bed, her own television, stereo, and phone. She loved talking on the phone and dancing. Engraved on her tombstone will be a phone and musical notes.

I stand at the closet door, not wanting to open it, trying to imagine Bobby's fear that night. "I'm not going to lie," Bobby had said. "It scared me when she jumped out. If they'd just stayed still, I wouldn't have fired. Anybody tells you they can trust their reflexes, they're wrong."

When I finally open the closet door, I'm surprised at how shallow the space is. A concrete back wall, an empty clothing rack. Both girls crouched in here, atop shoes and boots. Somewhere in this space, a bullet passed and killed a man's daughter.

Outside the house, on an apron of concrete, sits a second car, a white 1986 Cavalier. "I don't intend to ever get rid of this car," Bobby says as we climb in. "It's my Dobber's. I've got to run it so the battery won't go down and the tires won't go flat." A Conway Twitty tape, *Hello Darlin'*, is in the player. Bobby drives us out onto a country road lined with pin oaks, and he is quiet for a good while as the landscape goes by. Then he pushes the tape in, advances it to "It's Only Make-Believe." "This was her song," he says. "I used to sing it to her as a lullaby." His gray-blue eyes fill with tears, and Bobby Crabtree, who has not played guitar or sung in public since his daughter's death, begins to harmonize quietly with Conway until finally I hear only Bobby's raspy, beautiful, and broken voice. *No one will ever know / How much I love you so. / My hopes, my dreams come true. / My life I'd give for you.*

He drives on, past cemeteries, clapboard houses, into more piney woods. The song fades, but his mouth keeps moving, to music only he can hear.

***

"Had that been a burglar in the closet, he might have jumped out and said, '*Boom*' instead of '*Boo*,'" says Ouachita Parish sheriff Laymon Godwin. "And Bobby Crabtree would be dead. I'm amazed that he was as alert as he was. Most people, quite frankly, would have wet their britches."

I am in the sheriff's paneled office, and the silver-haired veteran of thirty-seven years in law enforcement is telling me that Crabtree, believing there was a burglar in his closet, really had only two options: "Wimp out and run out the door, hollering, 'Oh, my God, come help, there's somebody in my house,' or he could defend his property, as, hopefully, most men would do."

Deputies from this office tested Bobby for alcohol and found only an insignificant amount in his bloodstream. No charges were filed. "People in this part of the country," the sheriff says, "see it as 100 percent justification for shooting. I'd damn sure rather be explaining why I shot you than you being there explaining why I'm six feet under."

Sheriff Godwin doesn't believe gun-control legislation is enforceable in Ouachita Parish. Anywhere from three to ten guns per male here is not uncommon, he figures. When the Brady Law went into effect in February 1994, he assigned an officer full-time to do background checks on gun purchasers. "We did twenty-five hundred background checks; twenty-five were turned down. Have we stopped any serious criminals from purchasing guns? No.

"Honestly," he says, "the issue is not so much guns down here as it is government interference." Just yesterday, after a judge downstate in Lafayette ruled that the background check was unconstitutional, Sheriff Godwin, who is up for reelection this year, announced that the Brady Law will no longer be enforced in Ouachita Parish.

***

Stacey Redding was in the closet with Kaye during the shooting. The giggling girls had called Stacey's mother just as Bobby was pulling into the driveway outside. "We're going to scare Mr. Bobby," Stacey had whispered to her mother. Fifteen minutes later, the next phone call came. "Mr. Bobby shot Kaye."

"I was so close," Stacey said later, "I could feel the bullet go by my head." For weeks afterward, she smelled gunpowder, and the sound of the gunshot rang in her ears.

But don't expect this fourteen-year-old to be a poster child for the gun-control movement. Yes, she has lost her best friend. And yes, she could easily have been the victim. But she has also grown up in a gun culture and is a junior member of the National Rifle Association. "I know for a fact I'll own a pistol," she says. "Not to play with, but for my own protection, because of the world today."

I found Stacey at her house trailer down the road from the Crabtrees' home in West Monroe. Her father, Steve, invited me in and offered coffee. He was wearing his NRA cap.

His own guns, including two assault rifles bought before the federal ban on such weapons went into effect, are in a locked cabinet in the main room of his trailer, where we sit. He has the only key. His arsenal includes a MAK-90—a semiautomatic version of the AK-47—and an SKS with an illegal flash suppressor and thirty-mag clip. The SKS, he says, "is the one the guy shot the White House with." Steve bought it "in case things get bad." He has three thousand rounds of ammunition for his assault rifles. His pistols are a 9mm, a .25-caliber Saturday-night special, and a .22-caliber.

Ever since the abduction at the Kmart, he takes at least one and often two pistols when he escorts his wife or daughter to the local mall. He tucks the small .25-caliber six-shot into his boot and leaves the 9mm on his floorboard. It's either that or "succumb to these punks who want to thump you on the head and you're supposed to like it." It's Blacks he says he's most leery of, but "there are white folks who are crackheads—they'll jump you just like anyone else."

While we wait for his daughter, Steve gets to talking politics. And in Louisiana, Steve says, politics always comes back to guns. "Power is who has the guns and who don't have the guns," he says, his voice casual. "That's why Clinton's trying to get all our guns away, because he likes minorities." This, he says with a shrug, makes him feel threatened. "You get all the guns away from the white majority . . . hey, I ain't no fool."

For him, the worst-case scenario is an inevitable consequence of the recent Republican victory. "Monroe will be ablaze, and West Monroe will be a lot of redneck country folk like me with their guns protecting themselves." He believes the flames will be set by Blacks— "carloads of Blacks driving out here to do bodily harm. I'll tell you what's probably going to trigger it: When they cut back on all the welfare stuff, when they start making the immigrants go back, and they ain't going to go back peacefully. They're going to revolt, and there's not enough police force to stop it."

"Do you often think about this?" I ask.

"Every day. I believe in my heart it's coming," he says, "and I know there will be a whole bunch of people who will be prepared like I'm prepared."

II. Pensacola, Florida

In the Florida panhandle, where I traveled next, the commissioners of two counties—Escambia and Santa Rosa—voted last year to enlist every local citizen in county militias. Dozens of other counties are considering forming similar militias. Already, thousands of citizens in at least twenty states—including Michigan, Pennsylvania, California, and Montana—have formed militias to protect their gun rights, citing the Constitution's specific reference to "a well-regulated militia" as their authorization. Militia member Ellis Watson, sixty-seven, who is squiring me around Escambia County's largest city, Pensacola, population seventy-five thousand, believes that "the mere threat of an armed American citizenry has to have some effect on the most hardheaded politician."

The sign outside Jim Barnett's shop in town says, PEPSI and underneath, GUNS. Barnett, forty-five, has brokered a meeting for me with two members of a more militant underground militia in Escambia County. A yellow-dog Democrat known to sing tenor in all-night gospels, Barnett is the de facto leader of the official militia, and his back office is command central. Though Barnett likes to say that the vote is a militia's largest-caliber weapon, he also says, "If I needed firepower, these are two of the guys I would turn to."

They arrive under cover of dark, through the back door, both wearing camouflage gear and carrying assault rifles. The taller one wears a ski mask, and I call him Max, since he won't tell me his real name.

Max is clearly the leader here. His blue eyes and blond mustache are visible under his ski mask. His compatriot's face is wrapped in green cloth, and his eyes are masked with goggles, making him look like Kermit the Frog. His voice is nervous and tight. Both men are twenty-eight. The back room of the gun shop is small, and we all sit about two feet apart. The perimeter of the building is monitored by members of their unit, who periodically phone in to check progress. Kermit has brought a tape recorder, which he puts on a table and clicks on.

When I suggest that in their paramilitary getup, they might be considered a little extreme, Max says, "If you ran into either of us at work or in a restaurant, we don't scream redneck, Klansman, skinhead, or anything like that. We're just normal people who live within city limits. I have a wife and kids. We are frightened of where the government is taking us."

The fear has led them to bury caches of weapons, ammunition, and medical supplies. Most of the buried arsenal is in long guns—World War II-era weapons and inexpensive SKS rifles. I ask if it's fair to characterize this as genuine paranoia.

"If you think they are out to get you," Max says, "and they are, you're not paranoid anymore. We're not trying to overthrow a government. Defend ourselves from a government, yes."

The Branch Davidian standoff at Waco confirmed their fears. "My God," says Max, "they invaded a church."

During the Los Angeles riots, thirty members of the local underground militia and their families retreated to an encampment far outside Pensacola for three days. No fires at night, sentries posted. They maintained that level of vigilance, Max says, until the third night, when "we started having campfire sing-alongs and roasting wienies."

Kermit, whose goggles are fogging, flips his microcassette tape.

Max voted Democratic in the last congressional primary—for Jim Barnett, who lost. "Most of us are college educated," Max says. "We aren't ignorant backwoods savages riding around in monster trucks with scope 30-30s and beer cans rolling out of the back."

The underground militia is organized by county, each split into districts by ZIP code or phone prefix—a command structure, with beepers, faxes, phone trees. There are women in these units, including Max's wife. "She can outshoot me," he says.

Max describes his unit as light infantry, a quick-reaction force. It is divided into basic guerrilla cells; his has eleven members, though five, set up double-blind, is the ideal. Some cells are specialized. "Like demolitions," he says. "I know nothing about demolitions. I don't know if I want to—I still have all my fingers."

Members of his own cell have known one another for years; some grew up together. His own mentor dropped out and sold his guns, but Max continues to believe the conspiracy theories that fuel much of the militia movement—chiefly that UN troops, as part of the new world order, are being trained to disarm all Americans and that concentration camps are being built to imprison all militia members.

"We're not going to just go out and massacre people. We want to keep our families safe." Max picks up his SKS assault rifle, which is equipped with a seventy-five-round drum magazine.

"These guns," Max says, "are designed to kill people. They have no sporting purpose. The Second Amendment is not about hunting ducks; it's about the right to keep state-of-the-art military weapons."

While outsiders might see the underground as "guerrillas, terrorists almost," he says, "they have nothing to fear from the militia as long as you don't try to force us to do something that's unconstitutional, illegal, or immoral." For him, the Brady Law and the federal assault-weapons ban came very close to doing that.

At a training exercise recently, he was surprised at the number of doctors and lawyers "running through the woods, believing what I believe." Since the formation of the official county militias, he says, the local underground has grown to about 150 members. He claims Black membership in his own cell, and like all militia members I talked to in Pensacola, Max insists there is very little racial or religious intolerance in the movement at this time. (One Black member, Alan Ponds, would tell me at lunch a few days later, "The right to bear arms cuts across all color lines"; and while there aren't large numbers of Blacks in the militia, "there are plenty of Black huntsmen who are very concerned about Second Amendment rights.") Others talked about the "great maturing of white people" in this area and said fear of government is helping to do away with racial intolerance.

***

The next night, when I tell my escort, Ellis Watson, about Max and Kermit, he says, echoing the sentiments of most aboveground militiamen, "I'm not the least bit interested in thrashing around in the woods." Ellis and I arrive at the Crossroad Baptist Church for Sunday-evening service. A greeter wearing a shiny pistol tie-clip pumps my hand. Pro-gun articles are on display in the church foyer. Among the church librarian's files is a black folder labeled ASSAULT WEAPONS.

Wearing a plum-colored jacket, Pastor Chuck Baldwin, forty-two, is at the pulpit. "The idea of the defensive pistol," he preaches in a sermon on Christian combat, "is to stop the person from hurting you." He quotes from a gun magazine, an article on adrenaline. "It's very important, if you use a firearm to try and defend yourself, that you hit your target." For these folks, the right to bear arms is not just a constitutional guarantee but an inalienable right granted by God.

Pastor Baldwin is not only the shepherd of this flock, a position he's held for nineteen years, but also a rising star on the Christian Patriot Network, on the air each weekday when Rush Limbaugh breaks from noon to one. Turn your dial to 610 AM, American patriot, Chuck Baldwin, live, taking America back by storm! "Turn off Rush and turn on Baldwin" is his slogan.

"We're talking about citizens' militias, federal government's encroachment on individual rights, new world order, United Nations"—lowering his voice—"gun control, it's all related. Give us a call."

But tonight, at the Crossroad Baptist Church, Baldwin ends his stem-winder with a story about the deer he and his son shot last weekend. The congregation listens with interest to the story of a father and son trying to cross a creek with their 130-pound trophy. Baldwin stops a comic beat, and the audience is laughing as he tells of struggling like crazy, both falling into the creek. Over the years, Baldwin's congregation has bought him two rifles as Christmas or birthday gifts—a 30.06 Remington semiautomatic and a 270 bolt-action Remington, which is his primary hunting rifle.

Over coffee after the service, when asked how many pistols he has, he gets cagey and finally cops to a Colt .45, a .40-caliber Glock, and a .38.

Are there more?

"I don't know," he says, laughing. "I have a few."

More than three?

He laughs again, warily.

Asked why the pistol-ownership question makes him nervous, he says, "Only because I'm talking to a national magazine that has the power to identify me by name and say I own firearms.

"I'm not paranoid," Baldwin adds. When fellow Baptists seek his counsel, saying they are afraid of their government, which he says has been happening with greater frequency, "I certainly don't encourage them to let their fear control every aspect of their lives. But is their fear justifiable? Yes."

As a pastor, he says, "I don't hear so much fear of civil unrest as, Is it going to happen to me next?" The fear, he says, is deeper than fear of crime. The fear is of tyranny. "The fear is, Is my church going to be the next Waco?"

Baldwin, who has taught his sons that "there's no such thing as an unloaded gun," believes that men separated from their guns "become less manly. I think that men who have not been around guns, who aren't around guns, are missing something in their masculinity."

A lot of people in the country, he thinks, will never understand this. Firearms have become stigmatized by the liberal media, which, as Baldwin sees it, stresses firearms and crime rather than firearms and liberty. And while poor Bobby Crabtree may have his sympathy, "the cost of having our liberty," he says, "is that, yes, we might shoot people."

III. Noxon, Montana

To get to this part of Montana, you come off the tar and cross a one-lane steel bridge over a wide, blue stretch of river, the Clark Fork. It's January tundra here—black ice, slick roads, about a three-hour drive up the mountains from Spokane. If John Trochmann, cofounder of the Militia of Montana, had his way, by now you'd have passed a billboard that warns, THIS COUNTY IS PROTECTED BY 5,000 SNIPERS.

Noxon, population 350, sits in the snowy lap of Huckleberry Mountain—two bars, a general store, a restaurant, a gunsmith. If the feds invade, Trochmann says, they can't bring tanks across this narrow bridge. And if they come by helicopter—his wife, Carolyn, fears it's John's destiny—he's got .50-caliber guns in the hills and enough of a cache to fend off a battalion. Trochmann's bedtime reading these days includes *The Ultimate Sniper*, which gives instructions on "how to shoot down choppers."

"Good hunters up here," he says, "can shoot six hundred yards from the hip." If you want to know the story of Americans and our guns, you don't want to miss Noxon. The fear I've been tracking across America seems to be tracking me now. This place is the mother lode not only of the militia movement but also of the deepest, most unsettling paranoia I've felt anywhere in my own country.

Trochmann, fifty-one, gray-bearded, with the sculpted face and deep-set eyes of a prophet, says, "We believe in gun control—in controlling the guns of our government. They've shown themselves to be unworthy of our trust."

If troops invade this valley, he believes they'll come disguised as firefighters. And he's convinced they've targeted him because "we're helping to establish resistance across the country."

Through videos, the American Patriot Fax Network, and national shortwave-radio shows, the Militia of Montana has become an ideological nerve center of the growing militant gun-freedom movement. Trochmann's right-hand man, Bob Fletcher, claims that the group can disseminate an intelligence report to a half-million followers in thirty minutes. In December, when hundreds showed up at militia meetings in Montana, Idaho, and Washington, human-rights monitoring groups were alarmed. Some of the attendees had driven from as far away as Alabama.

Most militias are online and use the internet as a recruiting and information tool (there are more than a dozen active militia bulletin boards), but when I tried from Florida to find my way to Noxon through cyberspace, the Trochmanns didn't answer my email.

Finally, I picked up the phone and called Noxon. Carolyn Trochmann answered and, after warning me that the phone was tapped, said they were staying off the bulletin boards because "you-know-who monitors the internet." Her husband keeps the names of his militia contacts on recipe cards, she said. "He's very protective of that list."

On my first morning in town, Carolyn, forty-one, meets me for breakfast. Wearing handmade, ankle-length bloomers under a print dress, she's an attractive woman with long, dark hair. She's from these parts. Her first gun was a .22 rifle, followed by a 30.06. Her first pistol was a .45. "My mother taught me how to shoot, and my father taught me how to cook."

The night before I arrived, the FBI, responding to a harsh Justice Department report, finally admitted to fatal blunders in the celebrated Randy Weaver shoot-out of 1992. In the case, agents attempting to take Weaver into custody on gun charges laid siege to his house in the Idaho mountains for eleven days and killed his wife and fourteen-year-old son. "The use of four hundred personnel to take out two people in a cabin is more than a blunder," Carolyn says, "it's calculated violence." Carolyn and John knew the Weavers, having met them at an Aryan Nations family day.

"The FBI snipers should be prosecuted for murder. They deliberately shot Vicki Weaver through the neck so she would live and pump out every drop of blood in her.

"The feds were setting the Weavers up to kill them," Carolyn continues. "They were saying he was a neo-Nazi, a white supremacist. They say 'compound' rather than 'house.'"

Sitting in the Landmark Cafe, eating cereal, she tells me, "I've already been written up as a racist and white supremacist." She is worried, she says bluntly, that I will further demonize her family. "And then killing us can be justified to the public. Mister, our blood is on your hands."

***

John Trochmann and I are in a four-wheel-drive truck, and we're heading along a ridge overlooking the Clark Fork River, up the snowy road toward his house. A "rat patrol" guards the perimeter of this property twenty-four hours a day. His militia regulars sleep beside shortwave radios tuned to the same frequency. "We're prepared for war with the federal government," he tells me. "We also have several camps in the mountains where we can go."

Trochmann's first rule of engagement is that you don't stay inside your house when it's under siege—you have an escape plan. Randy Weaver should have known better, he says. He was, after all, a Green Beret. Also, he advises never to bury the best weapons—you might need them quickly. The .50-caliber guns, he explains, will down helicopters. And .50-caliber armor-piercing ammunition will stop an armored personnel carrier.

"Do you have guns bigger than .50 caliber?"

"If I say yes to that, we go to prison."

At the end of the snowy road is a gate. We stop the truck. Trochmann pulls out his .45 Springfield semiautomatic. Trued and chamfered, with a smooth two-pound trigger, it has a stainless, satin finish. It is a work of art, perhaps the most beautiful handgun I've ever seen. Trochmann has a permit to carry the weapon concealed.

Getting out of the truck, we face a geological feature actually called Government Mountain, an icy peak that dominates the valley. We walk a bit on his homestead, ice and snow crackling underfoot. The Cabinet Mountains are behind us, and not so far beyond them, a man named Gordon Sellner has been holed up in his cabin for more than a year after shooting a deputy sheriff. The FBI, says Trochmann, "is handling it with silk gloves. They don't want another Weaver."

There is speculation across the Northwest that John Trochmann will be the next Randy Weaver. But, Trochmann is quick to say, the outcome will be very different. "Next time, we'll throw up fifteen hundred militia on a moment's notice in a circle of protection. And if there's shooting," he adds, "it will be the shot heard round the world."

Trochmann stops and pulls a dog-eared copy of *The Citizen's Rule Book* from his breast pocket. He puts on his wire-rimmed glasses and, standing erect, reads aloud the Second Amendment to the Constitution: "A well-regulated militia being necessary to the security of a free state, the right of the people to keep and bear arms shall not be infringed."

We get back in the truck and start down the mountain to the Noxon Inn, where I'm staying. "I'm not in love with guns," Trochmann says. "I value guns as tools of necessity. I hate the spilling of blood."

"Have you ever shot a man?" I ask.

He draws a breath. "That's a tough question." In the silence that follows, he looks at his hands for a long time, then touches them to his face. I can hear the snowmelt, the runoff down the river far below. Finally, Trochmann says quietly, "I think you should withdraw the question."

***

Tomorrow, I will go up to the shooting range on Huckleberry Mountain, up through the snowy woods, with Clancy, the local gunsmith. I'll take an SKS assault rifle with me; I saw one for sale at Clancy's gun shop, the same kind Steve Redding had, and Max. I know it's a Chinese rip-off, and not so good, but I'd like to try it, if for nothing else than to just keep pressing the trigger to see how it feels to fire off a couple of ten-round clips.

As I sight the rifle on a target, I think of something Bobby Crabtree told me. He said he'd never have another gun, would never even fire one. And after the tragedy by his own hand, who could not understand that? We exercise our right to keep guns, yet we kill one another with staggering regularity. I reload and keep pulling the trigger. I'm unsettled by the feelings in me. Some researchers argue that even more lives are saved because homeowners have guns. I'm not sure I believe that. But I don't think I could make Bobby's pledge. And twenty thousand more guns will be legally purchased tomorrow in the United States. I will not be buying. But I keep pulling the trigger.

Clancy, who has been kind to me even though I am a stranger, brings out the gun his father, also a gunsmith, gave him before he died—a .45 Long Colt pistol. His own name is engraved on the stock, and underneath, in silver, LOVE, DAD.

Esquire, 1995

AT HOME WITH M.O.M.

When the bomb hit, John Trochmann's Militia of Montana went on red alert, called up the FBI, and headed for a strip joint. An intimate week in the bunker with the most dangerous patriots in America.

"Baby killer! Baby killer!" the voice on the phone snarls into the ear of John Trochmann, fifty-one, cofounder of the Militia of Montana, as he picks up the receiver at his headquarters in tiny Noxon, Montana. "We are going to burn you out!" The voice sounds long-distance, but Trochmann can't tell exactly. The man described by *The Washington Post* as the "guru of the American militia movement" looks scared. These calls have been coming in constantly in the four days since the bombing in Oklahoma City which killed 168, including children.

Taped to a wooden drawer underneath Trochmann's desk is a paper labeled, in his neat script, FBI SNITCH LINE, followed by an 800 number. He's going over to that desk and he's going to get Mr. FBI on the phone. He dials. "One of your citizens is threatening me and my family again," he says to the agent in charge of the Missoula, Montana, office. John sounds like Clint Eastwood. And with his heavy brow and patriarch's beard, he looks like a baldish John Brown. The agent says something that makes Trochmann laugh tautly. He'll drive up in a few days. Perhaps they can take a walk in the woods.

Trochmann hangs up the phone. "Ha!" he says. "I'm going to take a walk in the woods with my government."

The FBI and the Bureau of Alcohol, Tobacco, and Firearms are viewed by most militia members as jackboots of the New World Order. Yesterday, Trochmann was informed by his "intelligence network" that the FBI had issued warrants for him and the other cofounders of the Militia of Montana, his brother Dave and Dave's son Randy.

But something unexpected has happened. Just talking to a government agent has the fierce John Trochmann purring like a kitten. "I've known this agent for years," he says. "We have this glitter in our eye for each other and a handshake that about breaks the other's hand off. Of course, I haven't forgotten who he works for."

The rest of the people in the room don't seem to be as charmed with Mr. FBI as John is, but they're not against dialogue. "The more we're a mystery, the more they can justify coming at us," says Randy Trochmann. Randy is twenty-seven and has the look of a rodeo cowboy. Between drags on an American Spirit cigarette, one boot up on a desk, the other on the concrete floor, he says, "Our fear of being arrested is never returning, or being declared psychologically unfit and being shipped off to an institution."

If a federal warrant is delivered, Randy fears the FBI will grandstand—helicopters overhead, troops crouched behind trees. "One false move triggers a shoot-out," he says. He has already sent his wife and baby to stay with relatives.

Bob Fletcher, Trochmann's minister of information, enters the room, hunched and wearing suspenders over a white shirt, a .380 tucked into his flesh-colored belly holster. A former gumshoe for the Noriega defense, he is the latest addition to the Trochmann gang, originally signing on eight months ago as a conspiracy investigator. "*US News & World Report* is saying we're fucking satanic worshipers." His hands are shaking. "Good thing I'm not in New York or you'd see one fucking son of a bitch with his ass fucking kicked."

MOM headquarters is up a dirt road, past tin-roofed houses and empty corrals. It looks like an oversize green machine shed from the outside. This is command central. Locals call it "the compound." John Trochmann has lived in this area for seven years. He came from Minnesota, where he manufactured snowmobile parts with his brother. Until a year ago, he made his living as a master mechanic.

His specialty now is setting up covert guerrilla cells around the country. He calls it "networking," part of a long-range leaderless-resistance strategy. For this reason, Klanwatch regards him as one of the most dangerous forces in the militia movement.

Two afternoons ago, when John heard that Tim McVeigh was being charged with the bombing, he rifled through his membership file, pulling out recipe cards from an old red suitcase, searching for McVeigh's name. He contacted Mark Koernke, head of Michigan's unorganized militia; Randy called Norm Olson, head of Michigan's organized militia. Carolyn, John's wife, talked to survivalist Bo Gritz in Arizona, who'd been quoted that day in the press, saying the bombing was "a Rembrandt." Goddamn, is he one of ours? John received an alert from Michigan's command post; the official spin would be that McVeigh may have attended a meeting or two, but the militia had kicked him out for being "too radical."

Koernke, or "Mark from Michigan," the shortwave voice of the militia movement, spent ten days here in Noxon only a few months ago. The Trochmanns had helped build the covert-cell program in Michigan, and Koernke repaid them by frequently promoting MOM on the air.

Hearing that McVeigh considers himself to be a POW, John tells me, "If he is a good soldier, we'll never know who he is." This is the essence of leaderless resistance. Trochmann and other militia leaders, like men sowing deadly nightshade behind them, drop the seeds of armed resistance on fertile ground and walk away without leaving a trace.

"The government is going to need a scapegoat," he says grimly. Soon, Trochmann knows, the shock troops of the New World Order will land in Noxon.

***

Normally, the first thing you see when entering MOM command central is a color poster of an M-60 machine gun mounted on a tractor that reads, YOU'RE GOING TO REPOSSESS *WHOSE* FARM? This week, as the national press invade, the Trochmanns decide to clean up their image. The poster comes down. The empty spot is filled with a map.

The Trochmann gang's core beliefs are also being sanitized for the press. When I was last here on assignment, before the bombing, John sat in the Landmark Cafe and explained his Christian Identity theology, which he hoped to yoke to the militia movement. "I am following God's law," he said. "Blacks, Jews, are welcome. But when America is the new Israel, they'll need to go back where they came from." His voice grew quieter. "It's just nature's law—kind should go unto kind."

There is no talk of that now. No racial cleansing, no final solutions. And no talk of the caches of guns—enough to hold off a battalion, he'd told me—that are already hidden in the mountains. This week, it's only this land is my land, this land is your land. Strictly Second Amendment, states-rights indignation, with a generous helping of conspiracy. "An interview is a chess match," John tells me, "played flat-out." When the *Nation*'s Marc Cooper, sitting beside me in the Landmark Cafe, asks about international banking, Randy is able to laugh. "You're going to ask me about the Jews next, aren't you?"

"Well, no," Cooper says, "but since you brought it up . . ."

On Wednesday, Ron Haviv, the photographer accompanying me, arrives. He's worried that, being a Jewish kid from New Jersey, he's being thrown to the lions. As he enters the Trochmann compound, I introduce him to John. John says nothing. Instead, he reaches out and touches Ron's curly, coarse hair. "Where'd you'd get that hair?" John laughs, showing his teeth. "What'd you do, get plugged into a light socket? Hope she was a good ride."

He then proceeds to treat Ron like an honored guest, and when Ron leaves a few days later, he says he's "never met a nicer bunch of people."

***

Command Central, to the disappointment of the TV guys, is no bunker. A few old and dusty guns in a corner. Computers, a fax machine, old boots under desks. A regular sales office, or, as Randy says, "a think tank."

Cameramen, some just back from Sarajevo, are desperate for visuals. No one here is running around in camouflage. Cameras pan over the meager collection of hunting rifles and a couple of blow-guns. A TV reporter from Spokane does his stand-up from right here, laughing. "My mom's got more guns."

The ABC crew discover what they think is a bunker in the back-yard, and they want to film it. Randy Trochmann leads the eager reporters to a massive root cellar. "Y'all be careful," he warns. "These are exploding carrots."

The three phone lines at command central are all ringing. Fletcher is on the line to a radio talk show in Connecticut. He blames the government for the bomb. "We predicted this," Fletcher says. "Expect *more* bombs. I'm telling you, the Americans who think this is left field are going to be rudely awakened."

***

Ten days after the bombing, I take Dave Trochmann up on his offer and fly to a gun show in Great Falls, where Dave, forty-nine, has arranged for me to work behind the counter at the MOM booth. This type of show is the high mass of the movement. Dave arrived last night in his old Suburban and has brought enough supplies to stock five tables. With him is his sidekick, Ed Dosh, who calls himself a minister of metaphysics. ("I got my degree in Houston.")

It's a medium-size gun show, with a crowd of five thousand–plus over two days, indoors at the fairground. A fully automatic Uzi can be purchased here, but the trade is generally in semiautomatics, pistols, and hunting rifles.

Here at the Trochmann display, we've got mostly propaganda for sale. Bob Fletcher's *Invasion and Betrayal* video plays on a monitor. Field manuals on incendiaries, sniping, and booby traps are stacked next to chemical-warfare suits. I'm hawking canisters of pepper spray, discounted today by 50 percent.

Transactions are cash-only. Dave, like all the Trochmanns, pays only "lawful" taxes—property and excise. He's not worried about the IRS. "This is incoming," he says, tapping his left pocket, which is bulging with cash. Tapping his right pocket, he says, "This is outgoing. And if someone wants to find out what's in my pockets," he says, pointing to his zipper, "they got to go through here. And there's a mighty ornery son of a bitch inside."

A crew-cut ex-military type walks up behind Dave and seizes him by the elbow. "I've got an intelligence report." As the man whispers, Dave scratches notes in a spiral notebook.

When Crew Cut leaves, Dave flips the pad for me to read: "SWAT team moving from Helena into mountains around Noxon. Are being told to prepare for three days in mountains with cold-weather gear. Being told to be on guard, John Trochmann will come up behind you."

He slips the pad back into his shirt pocket. "We'll send some guys to do recon," he says.

A bespectacled, bald man who says he is a local stockbroker drifts up to the table. "I'm not a competent shot," he announces, "but if there is violence against your militia, I could raise money. If you don't have financing, you can't take your morals anywhere—ask Billy Graham."

Dave introduces himself, and the stockbroker beams. "You're virtually famous."

Everyone stops to watch Fletcher on video in front of an American flag. "After watching this video, you will have absolutely no doubt left in your mind that America has been betrayed by its leaders and invaded by its enemies." Two guys in baseball caps walk by. "There's that dude," one says, seeing Fletcher. "Fucking psychos," says his friend as they walk away, "blowing up things."

***

Dave packs the day's earnings into a briefcase with a decal reading, HAPPINESS IS FOLLOWING GOD'S LAW, and we head to Dave and Ed's hotel room. Dave calls his wife in Noxon. All is well; the SWAT team hasn't landed. Suddenly, Ed breaks into his best Loretta Lynn: *"I'm a Christian, but I'm a woman, too. / Lord, I get these feelings, what am I to do?"* And off we go, unchaperoned in Great Falls, Montana, to the city's premier strip joint, the Playground Lounge, which these two closed down the night before.

Within twenty minutes of taking a front-row seat at the dance stage, during a two-girl act that features whipped cream, the cofounder of the Militia of Montana is leaning forward into the ample breasts of a young stripper who slowly teases a dollar bill from his teeth. He sits back down, grinning, whipped cream smeared on his face. We stay for a couple of hours, and my cowboy hat ends up on the head of a naked woman named Charyne.

A toy convention in town has taken all available hotel rooms, so I am without a bed for the night. Back at Dave and Ed's room, we find all the rollaways are taken. "No problem," Dave says as he plops down on one of the king-size beds. "I insist. It's huge. You take half." Ed showers and takes his diuretics. I sleep in long underwear, socks, and a stocking cap. Dave wears valentine-red Hanes briefs. I stay on my half of the bed.

***

In Noxon the next day, at the tin-roofed church, a couple of dozen townspeople hold a Catholic mass with three guitars, singing "The Battle Belongs to the Lord." On the altar is a red cross from a sister church in Bosnia.

These people hate the dangerous air that's filled their town, especially since the bombing, and they are ashamed that they didn't do something about the militia sooner. "I saw a railroad car on a flatbed pull into the compound," one woman says. "They've got it buried as a bunker."

"John once told me he had plans to blow up dams," says another woman.

Sharon Larkin, whose daughter married the only Black man in the valley, has started an anti-militia support group. "We're afraid," she says, "but, so far, Trochmann hasn't broken any law."

Everyone agrees—the Trochmanns have been good neighbors and have been especially active in the roadkill food bank, which last year gutted and dressed out forty-seven deer and elk for area poor.

"So, what do you want to do," asks Sharon's husband, Larry, pushing away from the table, "walk by and kick their dog?"

***

"You want to see those buried boxcars?" Mike Richter asks, driving me down a rutted path in his old Toyota. Richter was once a Christian Identity confederate of John Trochmann's, but the two had a theological falling-out. "John doesn't believe in Jesus anymore, and I just can't accept that." Four hundred wooded yards from militia headquarters, we crest a small hill. In the meadow ahead sits an old boxcar, forlorn looking. Two cargo carriers are nearby.

Stacked close by are what appear to be small missiles. "Those would be bazooka rounds," Richter confirms. Inert, nonfunctioning—practice rounds, he calls them.

"It's a legal operation," he says. "My son and I work for the owner, and Carolyn Trochmann does his bookkeeping. He deals in surplus ammo, guns, cluster bombs. He just happens to be next door to Trochmann. He bought his property from them. That transaction involved a trade for weaponry."

"He sells cluster bombs?"

"Sure. They're inert."

"Inert cluster bombs can be made noninert, right?"

"Oh, sure. A dealer can sell them if they're inert. What somebody does afterward, that's their business."

Richter continues the dealer's inventory: anti-tank rifles, grenade launchers, vehicular-mount cannons, inert LAW rockets, which you launch off your shoulder. Ammo includes incendiary rounds, armor-piercing bullets, and tracers.

Fifty yards away, a huge piece of lead the size of a Rodin sculpture is anchored into the ground. It is pocked with .308- and .50-caliber ammunition holes.

***

At nightfall, Richter sits at home next to a wood-burning stove, having supper and talking about Identity theology. He stands and walks to the window. "I want to shut this in case they are out there with the Big Ear."

The Big Ear?

"A listening device. You can hear from Dave's to here."

He doesn't fear retribution "from John himself, but by proxy. He has the power to push other people to violence. I was in Bible study with John and Dave," he says. "They talked nonstop about the Holy War."

Outside, Richter's dog starts to bark. The neighborhood dogs join in. The Trochmanns are out on patrol.

Richter removes his wire-rimmed glasses and pulls at his matted gray beard. "John will be in his glory when they are attacked one of these times. He wants to be a martyr."

***

"I know my husband will be killed," says Carolyn Trochmann, "and I have made my peace with that fact." She's wearing a bright-red dress, a sunbonnet, and handmade bloomers. "It's his destiny. I'm proud of my family and what they've done." She turns strident when she talks about the townspeople. "These people are ignorant. If you live according to natural law, you'll be at peace in the universe. They're not at peace. Do I look like I'm at peace? Well, I am."

***

Two weeks after the Oklahoma bombing, John walks in the woods with Mr. FBI. They hike for hours beyond Government Mountain. "We would be shut down," John tells me back at headquarters, "if it wasn't for my relationship with this agent." FBI agents are a tool of the enemy, but he believes they can be "defused so that they can't function properly."

The law has already arrested him once, in March, on charges of inciting others to violence. The charges were dropped, but he knows he may not be so lucky next time. He takes his .45 Springfield semi-automatic, pulls the clip, and hands the gun to me. Scratched into the satin finish are the initials, he says, of the deputy who arrested him. "He stole my gun." John's eyes narrow. "He planned on owning it."

John lifts his hands up to the light, studying them. "They took my fingerprints—my private documents!—and sent them to four different countries, including Interpol. And I was innocent!"

The phones have gone quiet. We are alone, the rest of the media long gone. He packs two metal boxes of militia names, all hand-printed on recipe cards, into the red suitcase. "Oh, boy," he says, lifting the suitcase, "wouldn't the treasonous sons of bitches give their left you-know-what for this?"

He opens the door to the windowless office. Sunlight pours in. He wants to go finish some work on his car engine. He tucks the .45 into his belt. Before shutting the door behind him, he turns to me and says, "Hold down the fort."

Esquire, 1995

HE ONLY COMES OUT AT NIGHT

Billy Bob Thornton is writing, directing, or starring in six movies in the next year—and recording an album with Johnny Cash. He's newly married but hasn't seen his movie-star wife in months. He can't sleep in his own house. Billy Bob has trouble sleeping at all.

2:00 a.m., first night

Billy Bob Thornton is waking up. He's been working a lot, making a lot of movies, so he's real tired. He's been making a record, too, after hours. The voice of Johnny Cash, in duet with Billy Bob's own voice, streams from the speakers. They sound pretty good together. Marty Stuart, the producer, is up from Nashville, and he's burning CDs tonight here at the studio, and it's late, all the girls have gone home, and Marty's switched from champagne to Mountain Dew. This is the first time he's heard the full mix. "This record is tryin' to be something," he says to Jim, the engineer. "It's comin', it's comin', it's comin'. I see its little head."

Billy Bob's been asleep on the couch, which is funny, because normally he needs to be told to go to sleep, and Marty says this is the most rest he's gotten since 1979. "I've wore his ass out," Marty says, even though he's known Billy Bob only a couple years. As Billy Bob's mother says, her boy's been "keeping the roads hot." It's a composed sleep, no more than a half hour or so—his face has not gone slack—and it seems as if he's beginning to stir. His hands are still folded between his knees, his head bowed, chin to his chest. His cap, which reads HENRY SWING CLUB, is pulled low. His skin is amber, the color of whiskey. A short-sleeved bowling shirt covers most of his tattoos, but one peeks out from under his left sleeve. He wears a black leather band on one wrist and black jeans and black tasseled motorcycle boots, which are starting to show signs of life. He is a parched and worn forty-five, but in sleep he has the aspect of a baby. People want to stay around and make sure nothing bad happens to him. A hand goes up to his face, index finger softly rubs the bridge of his nose, and then the hand goes slack as he dissolves again into sleep. He is clean-shaven. He looks like a farmer, not a movie star.

This is Billy Bob's couch, in the recording studio that also belongs to him, in the basement of his new house in Beverly Hills. He's owned the place since June, just after he got married to Angelina Jolie—he calls her Angie—and they paid more than $3 million for it. The house is eleven thousand square feet, and it has this recording studio in the basement, which is a big reason Billy Bob wanted it. Slash, the former guitarist for Guns N' Roses, lived here before. Billy Bob's a Hollywood guy, yes, but his music is important to him, and this is not going to one of those actor-wants-to-be-a-rock-star records, so he doesn't talk about it much. But the studio is a comfortable room, and he likes it. He hasn't really unpacked yet. Boxes are stacked against one wall alongside a framed Pink Floyd poster. There are a couple Oriental rugs, an acoustic guitar, a box labeled BILLY BOB'S DRUM KIT.

Billy Bob lifts his head and squints for a second, and then suddenly he is all awake, as if he had never been asleep. He hears Johnny Cash. "I think his voice is a little hot," he says softly. Marty's sitting at the soundboard. He adjusts a few knobs. Billy Bob wonders if they should get Cash to record his vocals again. Marty says, "It's easier to sing to Mount Rushmore than to have Mount Rushmore sing to you."

Then Marty says, "Time to go, cuz." Okay, enough work for tonight. Time to go to bed.

Billy Bob gets to his feet and heads upstairs. He scrapes his heels when he walks, as if the boots are weighing him down. On the landing, he passes a huge arrow pointing back down to the studio.

There's a sign on it that reads THE SNAKEPIT. Upstairs, the house is a construction zone. Only one room is finished. Newspapers mask the floors. Buckets of paint are stacked along the walls in the foyer. Angie's in London, working—she left in June and will be back in January—so he's in charge of the renovation. The bedrooms on the second floor all have sliding glass doors that overlook a small outdoor pool. Billy Bob likes that it has the feel of a motel and wants to preserve that. "I'll never live a normal life," he says. "But I try to keep bits of it in my life. Just the idea of having a house, of buying one, knowing there's someplace to call home."

He walks over, flips off the big TV, which has been playing on mute all night, and then goes to the front door. "Come on, we're goin'," he says. He steps out, lights a cigarette, and locks the door. He won't be sleeping here.

"*Nooo* sir," he says, heading for his truck. "Not until a guy comes and checks the place out for snake eggs."

The house may have a snake problem. Slash liked snakes and kept them in cages and boxes and pens all over the house. Billy Bob can't abide snakes. He hasn't yet spent the night in the house, and he won't until the snake-egg guy comes. He doesn't live in places easily. He once lived in New York City for ten hours before driving back to Arkansas, defeated and afraid. Tonight he's going to sleep at the Sunset Marquis, the hotel where he's lived off and on for years.

When he gets to the hotel, he'll call his bride, who'll just be starting her day. Well, maybe he'll call her. He's not sure. "It's one of the things I like about this marriage," he says. "I was always afraid in relationships before, but I'm not afraid of her. Well, I am afraid of her; I told her that once. First I told her I wasn't afraid of her, and then twenty minutes later I told her the opposite, that I was afraid of her." So maybe he'll call.

This is an early evening for him. He's got to get up at six to cut hair because he's in a movie. He's playing a barber.

It's a great night out, warm, swimming weather, but all the Beverly Hills mansions on Billy Bob's street, all built during the same few years—late twenties, early thirties—for the first generation of

Hollywood royalty, are dark now. Who could be in bed on a night like this? It's going on 3:00 a.m., and so Billy Bob's boots and his voice echo a little as he shuffles toward his truck. He's looking at the dark houses. "I hate people who go to sleep early," he says.

11:00 p.m., second night

He will never live a normal life.

So he went to work today, made some film, negotiated some deal. All real work in the adult world. A bunch of extras lined up at sunrise for haircuts. "Most nervous extras you ever saw," Billy Bob says. He gave a couple of flattops with antique clippers. It's a Coen brothers film, known currently as *The Untitled Barber Project*. He is, by all accounts, a delight to be around on the set, any set. He is kind, funny, and inspiring to other actors, and reverential about the work, having had a strange sense of hillbilly destiny about it ever since his mother told him not to worry, he'd make it, one day he would work with Burt Reynolds. (He has.) He's got six movies coming out in the next year, four of which he's acting in and two of which he directed, including *All the Pretty Horses*, the $45 million adaptation of Cormac McCarthy's novel, which will be released at Christmas. *The Gift*, which he wrote about his mother, will come out at the same time. He's never been busier and never been more tired; he's got a cough, and there's so very much daytime work to do, so many decisions to make, so many people to take care of, so much writing to get done, so many stories to get out of himself before it's too late. "I've got so much shit backed up that it almost gives me an aneurysm," he says. "I've got at least another twenty movies in me."

But after dark, Billy Bob's mind seems so starved that he won't sleep voluntarily or easily; he never has since he was a kid, and at these times he has been known even to seek out the interesting company of those he doesn't know very well, and he is disappointed when they don't have the stamina for his hours. "Oh, no, come on, you can't leave!" he'll say.

The bar at his hotel is called the Whiskey, and the candlelit patio out front, with its low wrought-iron tables, is Billy Bob's nocturnal office. There's always somebody or somebody's entourage here. Blond, lithe young things everywhere. And lots of musicians; there's a recording studio in the basement here, too. And everybody touches everybody else here. Little touches, lots of hands, which is fine with Billy Bob because he's from the South, and there they drape themselves all over you.

Billy Bob keeps pretty regular hours here, and the Reverend Billy Gibbons from the great ZZ Top drops by sometimes. He's here tonight, and this is cool because it was not very long ago at all that Billy Bob was the completely unfamous drummer of a ZZ tribute band, Tres Hombres, which Gibbons now graciously calls "the best little cover band in Texas." And earlier, Billy Bob jammed in an upstairs room with Chris Robinson of the Black Crowes. And now the Irish director Jim Sheridan pulls up a chair, and Billy Bob talks to him about boxing movies because that's something that Sheridan knows about, and Billy Bob's thinking about directing a boxing movie for Miramax even though he's said no to all studio films forever ("Well, at least with Miramax you know whose ass you're kissing"), and Lord knows how he'll find the time and preserve his health, but he's already seeing scenes in his head, so he figures it's the right thing to do.

This is a night, a few minutes, really, at the Whiskey.

And life at the Sunset Marquis has other rewards. There's a real nice gym that Billy Bob uses when he finds himself in bouts of self-improvement. He sometimes works out in his cowboy-and-Indian pjs, and he'll wear Angie's pink underwear. "Once I was lifting weights, and I thought they were hidden, but some guy kept looking at me strange," he says. "Finally, I said, 'They're my wife's.' I don't think it's strange at all. I wear them to the set some days. I like having her close to me, you know?"

Another good thing about the hotel is that everybody knows him here, and the bartenders at the Whiskey are as much as he'll indulge himself in psychotherapy anymore. Along the way, he's entered therapy a few times and even tried it with a couple of his ex-wives when things started souring. But he doesn't trust it. "People in L.A.

think you learn by therapy. But you learn by living. I mean, if you've got to get over having your puppy run over when you were nine, fine, but you've got to keep living.

"See, I've fucked a lot of things up. I've been wrong. In relationships, I've been, like, not present. Or doing some wrong things. People talk about working on things. I don't like to work on things. I never like working on things. When I write, I don't work on it. I start, and I finish. If it don't come out in one long stream of consciousness, it ain't for me. I don't want to construct when I love, when I write. I don't want to go to couples therapy to solve a relationship. I don't want to work on it. I don't believe in it, never have."

Billy Bob had been with the actress Laura Dern for three years when she went off to make a movie. When she got back, Billy Bob was married to Angie. He knows that lots of people out here are sympathetic to Dern's side of things. "Others may say that you left our girl and married someone else," he says. "But it made me happy and somebody else happy. I'm sorry it caused pain."

As the evening unwinds and the foot traffic slows down, Billy Bob chain-smokes and drinks bottles of water and hangs out with the unfamous Whiskey denizens, talking about *All the Pretty Horses* and his idea of the movies. He finished the film some time ago but continues to edit, tweak, and fight battles over every little thing. He went to test screenings. "Where will people really hate this?" is what they're for, Billy Bob says. "And the studios use those numbers to try and convince you to make the changes they wanted you to make all along."

He knows the audience out there is finicky. "You've got people who only want to see someone screw an apple pie. But some people are sick and tired of it. They want raw stuff again. We did the movie the way they used to do it."

All the Pretty Horses is a modern epic, with "interiors out of *Sling Blade*" and "outdoors that look like John Ford," with a big budget and big stars, directed by a guy who's never been trusted with more than a few million dollars before.

"I think the natural tendency these days is to use one of the big guys to direct. I'm not one of them."

Out of nowhere, someone asks, "When are you going to London?" Billy Bob's fear of flying is famous. Before he gets on a plane, he'll call his mother, who is psychic, to ask her if it's safe. He'll go over there on one condition, he says—if Angie'll take him on the Jack the Ripper tour.

It's quiet for a minute, and then Billy Bob speaks. "You know she won't do anything to hurt me, because she knows it'll hurt her more," he says.

He orders more cigarettes and gets up to go pee. As he's walking back, he's already talking. He seems excited, maybe exercised. "Did you ever look at a woman when she's asleep, and you think, Who the fuck is *that*?" he says, and sits down. "And, like, the moonlight's coming in when you're sleeping next to her at night and you can kind of see her face—and she looks like a fucking *monster*? This might be somebody you've been with for years. And you look at her, and it's like, Who in God's name is that? Why—she's a stranger. What is she doing here? I don't even know her. And much of the daytime, you're like, 'Oh, honey, I love you. Are you okay? How was today?' But when she's asleep, that's how you *really* feel about her."

8:00 p.m., same night

Billy Bob bleeds Cardinal red, but the Dodgers will do for tonight. He got good tickets and decided to catch a game. Back in Malvern, Arkansas, Billy Bob was a hometown baseball hero, the promising kid who got a major league tryout at eighteen, got nailed by a bad throw, and broke his collarbone. "There's nothing in the movies or entertainment that feels like the third pitch that strikes a guy out," he says.

A couple years ago, after *Sling Blade* made him famous, he was invited to throw the first pitch at a St. Louis game. He drove all night from Little Rock in a rented limo after a day of filming. "When I walked out there to the mound with a Cardinals shirt on, it was like a dream," he says. As a surprise for Billy Bob, Bob Gibson was behind the plate, crouched down in his street clothes. Gibson was his boyhood hero. "I learned to throw a slider from his book when I was a kid. So I thought, Shit, I'll try it." He threw his pitch. Gibson walked out to the mound afterward and said, "That was a hell of a slider. Where'd you learn that?"

Billy Bob remembers that his father hung a tire up in the yard so that he could practice his pitching. "It's the one place my dad and I connected every now and then," he says. He looks around Dodger Stadium, shrugs his shoulders, and squints. "Or maybe that's my fantasy."

Billy Bob was not close to his father. Billy Ray Thornton was gone a lot, teaching and coaching at small high schools out of town, mostly basketball. Billy Bob says that every film he does is a reckoning with his father. "In my movies, there's either shitty fathers, absent fathers, fathers that you want their approval. Or the father's just not there. He died or whatever." In *Sling Blade*, when Karl Childers goes back home, his father's only greeting is, "I ain't got no boy. Now, why don'tcha get on outta here and let me be."

At the ballpark, Billy Bob sits next to a suburban lady and her nephew, who is a high school catcher. They're gabbing away about the mechanics of baseball, and Billy Bob focuses significant attention on the pair, giving advice, telling stories. But every time a foul ball is hit up into the stands, Billy Bob's gaze follows the ball. "I worry about people," he tells the lady.

***

At the game, he wears jeans and a plaid shirt unbuttoned and an Animals T-shirt underneath. He is awfully lean.

His weight has been the subject of some speculation that perhaps he's not well. He says he's six feet tall and now weighs 140 pounds, which he says is his natural weight. And he has quick recall of every pound gained or lost during his film career. For *Sling Blade*, he weighed 175, because the backwoods Frankenstein, Karl, needed to be bigger than Billy Bob. For *U-Turn*, 195. *Primary Colors*, 170. *Armageddon*, 155. *A Simple Plan*, 145. And for

Pushing Tin, he was down to 130. He's skinny by nature, but sometimes he just doesn't eat enough, or he forgets to eat at all.

It's good that he's got a cook and assistants around him. During shoots, studios hire trainers for him. Before he had these people, before he got famous, back in the days when he couldn't get hired as Redneck No. 4 (all those jobs went to guys from New Jersey) and he was trying to write in between shifts at Shakey's Pizza, he landed in a Los Angeles hospital, almost dead from a heart condition brought on by malnutrition.

Longevity has not graced the Thornton men. His younger brother Jimmy died at thirty of an infection that inflamed his heart. His father died of lung cancer at forty-four.

***

After the game, Billy Bob's in the car talking on the phone to his most recent ex-wife, Pietra, with whom he has two young sons. "Don't make any plans for Friday night. We can make a dessert like strawberry shortcake or something like that." He's sweet and kind to her now. It's late, but his kids aren't asleep. One of his little boys announces over the phone that he's trying to kill a spider. "Your mom ripped his body off? Wait, what—the spider's on his back, shivering with a chicken bone in his mouth? Well, that's a huge spider. Oh, that's the dog. Okay, honey, did your mom tell you that I'm coming Friday night and we're gonna cook? We're gonna make something, just you and your brother and me and your mom. You sure are, baby, you are the luckiest boy. I love you. Goodnight, baby."

1:00 a.m., first night

The house is rockin', sort of. In the one finished room, Billy Bob's trying to convince Odessa, his young assistant, that he always wanted to "fuck a midget."

"I always wanted to fuck a midget," he tells her in earnest. "I just wanted to see what it was like. I don't anymore. But didn't you ever want to?"

"No!" Odessa yelps in a slurry North Carolina accent. She's twenty-five, pretty, and has worked with Billy Bob for a couple years.

"I always wanted to just pick them up by the ankles," Billy Bob goes on. "Think of all the things you could do with 'em. You can pick 'em up, turn 'em upside down by their ankles." He holds up an imaginary midget, shakes it a little.

Then he's slow dancing, loving the midget up and down. Odessa backs off a bit. Kristin, another assistant, is on the couch with Odessa's pit bull, Percy, giggling.

"I've *seen* midgets fucking," Billy Bob says.

'You've seen it?" Odessa asks.

"Of course!" he says.

"What do you mean, *of course?* Like everybody has?"

"Not like *everybody* else has," he says. "'Of course,' like I have."

"I don't ever want to see that," Odessa says. "It's just wrong."

Marty Stuart comes whistling up from the studio. "More bubbly?" Billy Bob asks, cackling. He's broken out champagne, ecstatic that he wrote a new song tonight. And that's as good a reason as any to make this night the first party in the new house.

"Slash had a room full of iguanas over there." Billy Bob points past the bar. "Man, I can't stand a lizard. I don't like that skin, I don't like the way they look." Percy the pit bull ambles over and rubs against Billy Bob's leg. The dog's got a long, mean scar on his back. Odessa rescued him from somewhere up in the Hollywood Hills. It's one of the things Billy likes about Odessa, that her heart's so big. Another thing is that she genuinely doesn't seem to know or care who's famous and who's not, except for the day she saw Rhea Perlman on the street and just about lost it.

"Marty and I were talking today," Billy Bob says, "about how in the South it's all right to beat a dog."

He and Marty are trying to work each other up.

"It's kind of a way of life," Marty says. Both men are laughing, their shoulders shaking. "There's a place in Nashville," Marty says, "where you could get braces for your dog's teeth. The dog dentist. If your dog had buckteeth, you could get him braces."

"Oh, well, that's just ridiculous," Odessa says.

"Not if you're a buck-toothed dog!" Billy Bob says.

Ime Etuk walks in, a stout, soft-spoken Black man in his twenties. Ime's an assistant director around town and Billy Bob's bowling buddy.

"You got a marijuana cigarette?" Billy Bob asks Ime.

"Not on me," Ime says.

Billy Bob is happy and loose, and he wants to have fun. He wants to have fun like Sinatra did, all night and whatever the hell he wanted. He can't wait for the house to be up and running so that he can get a little of that Southern Rat Pack feeling. A pool table, some Foosball, and a Velcro room of his own design.

"Where are all my bitches?" Billy Bob cries out. "I know I have more bitches than this! Odessa, *call people*! Tell 'em to come over!"

"We tried to call everybody," Kristin says. "We told them it was a pajama party."

"What's wrong with the world?" Billy Bob says.

"Everybody's tired," Kristin says.

"Well, *I'm* tired *too*."

The big-screen TV is on but muted. Bill Clinton's face appears. "When he leaves office, he's going to be tempted," Billy Bob says, pointing at the screen, exhaling a Marlboro. "Chasing pussy is a form of Tourette's syndrome. The same thing that makes you want to drink or kill or build cabinets or whatever. It's an itch that you've got to scratch. And once you've scratched it just right, you form a habit."

They've hung out, Billy Bob and the president. Clinton screened *Sling Blade* at the White House. "I like the guy," Billy Bob says. "If he was asleep right now on that couch, with his socks on and gray pants, he'd start drooling, and you'd look at his socks, some kind of fucking Armani socks, and he'd be laying there, and you'd look at him a little bit the way you look at your son or your daughter or your brother. You'd look at him with pity. I mean that in an endearing way, like he's just one of us."

Alex, Billy Bob's chef, shows up, along with a blond actress and a producer and a guy in a suit. Alex says that during the filming of *All the Pretty Horses*, she had to call Arkansas to "find out from his momma how to make chocolate gravy and biscuits." Billy Bob veers into a story about the night he saw a man barking his ass off in a grocery store. This was in Santa Fe late at night, after a day of shooting *All the Pretty Horses*, when Billy Bob and a couple of the girls were looking for a midnight snack. "We've always been addicted to various kinds of cereal," Billy Bob says.

"Cap'n Crunch!" Odessa says.

"Golden Grahams!" Kristin says.

"There was a guy there barking his ass off, just throwing his head back, doing the whole thing. I love that shit. I *love* that shit!"

***

The party never becomes more than Ime, Marty, a couple girls, and a dog on the couch. It's a work night. The girls want to go home.

Billy Bob's got a joke. Won't they stay to hear it? "So Bubba and Marcel decide they're going to go back to school. . . . " He turns to Odessa. "You know this one, right?"

"No!" Her voice is rising now, a little irritated. "I don't know *whaaaat* you're talking about."

Billy Bob looks at her.

"I'll call you in the morning," she says.

"Will you call me at 5:30?" Billy Bob asks gently. "And again at 6:00? I need like nine wake-up calls."

***

The girls are gone.

"It's a holy day," Billy Bob says softly. "Elvis died today." When Billy Bob was two, his mother took him out to the highway to watch as the King's bus passed by their little town. They stood there by the road, waving.

He stretches out on the couch, his physical depletion starting to show. His enthusiasm is faltering. He seems tamed. "I know I'm compulsive," he says. "I'm hungry for the horrible shit, but I can't do that. Not anymore. I got something good, and I'm not gonna mess it up." It's quite late, going on 2:00 a.m., and he's tired and ruminative all of a sudden. He's thinking about his father. "Some of the things he loved are things I love, even though he and I didn't know each other or get along. And I have some of his traits." He says that when his father got upset, he'd go away, disappear. "That's me, too," he says.

His voice is rasping. Some involuntary twitches. Sometimes he gets so tired that his face starts to twitch. He'll blink his eyes and his whole face seems to blink. He just doesn't have the reserves he had when he was young.

"But my father didn't like music," he says. "At all. He might be the only man I ever met who didn't like music. There were two songs he liked—'Puff the Magic Dragon' and 'Easter Parade.' It seemed incongruous." He's talking so softly now, almost whispering. "One's about the magic and wonder of childhood and the hard, cold facts about loss, and the other one is a celebration with hats." He begins to hum, closing his eyes, and then he sings softly: *"In your Easter bonnet / With all the frills upon it / You'll be the grandest lady / In the Easter Parade."*

***

He wants to go downstairs. He wants Ime to hear the new song he wrote, "Beauty at the Back Door." They follow the arrow down the stairs into Slash's Snakepit, where Marty and Jim, the engineer, are behind the glass. Ime and Billy Bob sit on the little couch.

It's a song about screen doors and myrtle bushes and love, about memory and desire and loss. A little slide guitar, but mostly Billy Bob's voice. It's a spoken-word song, raw, stripped down, a southern-gothic Leonard Cohen.

"My, that's a snappy western shirt you got on," Billy Bob says to Marty faintly. "You goin' to a singin'?"

"Yeah, I'm going to a singin'," Marty says.

And then Billy Bob sings another song, called "Poison Honey." His voice is smoky. *She draws me in like a moth to a flame / And sometimes at night, I call out her name.*

"Albums are supposed to reflect what's going on in your life," Marty says.

Billy Bob laughs. "Then I'm fucked."

There's darkness all around, as the evening shadows fall / Time keeps dragging by, but she ain't coming home at all.

Billy Bob listens to the music, his fingers touching his lips. He likes the song, likes where it's going. He crosses his legs, gets comfortable. His eyelids slip down, shut, open, shut. In a few weeks, he'll have run himself down so bad that he'll be in the hospital. But for now, he's got to be up in a few hours, working. His cough will become bronchitis, and an infection will inflame his heart. But in the morning, the extras will be waiting for haircuts. Angie will rush from London to his side. But for now, he folds his hands, nestles them between his knees. The doctor will tell him, You know, Billy Bob, you don't *have* to starve yourself and not sleep. And Billy Bob, in a burst of light, will promise himself to go on living. But now, his shoulders hunch. The music sounds good, like a dream from childhood. His eyes close.

Billy Bob Thornton is asleep.

Esquire, 2000

THE BEGINNING: ON BECOMING A FATHER

In the delivery room—drinking Guinness, listening to The Rolling Stones, and battling a doctor.

"**B**abies die!" the doctor shouts at me. Our doctor. I don't want to fight with the doctor who is going to deliver my son. Cecilia is in labor and we've just gotten to the hospital. It's Friday, 8:00 p.m., New York City. Misty rain outside. "Are *you* going to deliver this baby, Daniel?" he shouts. "Because you're not letting me do my job. You're trying to take over."

Just this morning, Cecilia was standing in front of the mirror breast-feeding a teddy bear. Her due date was a week away, and I still couldn't believe that I was about to be a father. I wanted everything to slow down. I just wanted her to stand naked in front of the mirror a little longer. Now we're in the labor-and-delivery room and the doctor is yelling at me: "Babies die! Nature is cruel. Not so long ago, babies died routinely. *And* their mothers. I know what's best."

The doctor reaches out to touch Cecilia, but she backs away. He's been her gynecologist since college, but she's angry about this morning's exam. Without Cecilia's consent, he pushed his fingers through her cervix and stripped the membranes. "That *hurts*!" Cecilia yelled out. "You've got to stop!" Sharp contractions began immediately. This procedure, we've just learned, is often done on Friday mornings by doctors who want to get babies out before the weekend.

She whispers in my ear. "I need you to fight for me." All of a sudden, we're deep behind enemy lines. She wants a natural delivery. No C-section. The doctor says she has only a 10 percent chance of that happening. "I know my body," Cecilia says. He claims the baby is overdue. We think he's wrong.

If he wants to cut her open tonight, I tell him, he'll have to cut through me.

We had opted for the benefits of a modern hospital, but all Cecilia wants now is to be left alone. The nurses seem to understand. But what to do about the doctor? "We'll take care of him," one nurse assures us, conspiratorially.

The room where Cecilia will labor and deliver is not such a bad place—wood floors and blond cabinetry. Feels outfitted by Ralph Lauren, except for a large red trash can labeled BLOOD WASTE. I drag that out into the hall. We dim the overhead lights and put on Mozart. I've brought a boom box, a couple cold bottles of Guinness, a toothbrush, and a change of clothes.

The senior resident, a petite, dark-haired woman, comes in to examine Cecilia. She tells us our doctor is asleep down the hall. "Don't worry, my hands are small," she says. "I won't hurt you."

Cecilia's been having contractions every two minutes all day, but she's only now entering active labor. The resident agrees that Cecilia should go without drugs as long as possible. Contractions will help push the baby down. Drugs will slow progress. But, she warns, the next hours will be painful. She's right.

Cecilia rocks back and forth on the bed, breathing hard. She gets up and leans on walls. Between contractions, she can talk until the next one takes her under. I massage her back. She climbs onto the chair and into my lap.

"Am I snorting like a water buffalo?" she asks.

***

Cecilia's parents arrive around ten o'clock, smuggling in soup. We're glad to see them. My own father wasn't allowed in the delivery room when I was born. Cecilia's father has never been in a labor-and-delivery room, either. She sees the concern in his face and tries to hide her pain. A few days ago, he and I were drinking pints in an Irish pub and showing off grainy sonogram pictures to the barmaid. Now we both sit at the end of Cecilia's bed. He massages one foot; I massage the other.

Her father tells us they'll be next door in the waiting room, watching the hospital's breast-feeding channel. He says the breast-feeding channel is quite informative. Women with engorged breasts urging their babies to suck. He offers Cecilia breast-feeding tips, and she laughs for the first time all night.

A nurse puts a monitor on Cecilia's belly, and I hear the beep, beep, beep of our son's heartbeat. I watch the glowing red numbers. Now it's 130 per minute; if it drops below 100, he's in distress.

"Please, just pass over me," Cecilia begs the next contraction. She clings to the side of the bed, her knuckles white.

She's tied to the mast.

This goes on for five more hours.

Cecilia's pain threshold is high, and she's strong from years of yoga, but as the contractions intensify, she's astonished. "This is a whole other universe of pain," she says. At three months pregnant, she was in Texas, shooting a documentary on death row. She's danced with Martha Graham, climbed most of the Swiss Alps. Now she can't talk. Only hand signals. She wants ice chips.

At 3:00 a.m., I roll up my pants and take Cecilia into the shower. "It will give her relief," the nurse promises, and, although I don't understand why, she's right. Something about ions. For half an hour, I nozzle warm water onto Cecilia's back. Afterward, she vomits.

Her work is paying off. At 4:15 a.m., the baby's head is almost in position. Cecilia's been in labor eighteen hours. She finally asks for Demerol to take the edge off. It will slow the contractions, but she needs to rest.

"Danny, don't go to sleep. If you're awake, I'll know everything's going to be okay."

I watch her drift off. I think about my father and how dependent he is on my mother. I have always been afraid to be that helpless. I have never before wanted to be so at the mercy of love. To be a parent, or truly a partner, is to risk being wholly seen. Until now, I have always tried to step back, to leave a margin to move around in, a shadow where I can hide.

I can see the first light outside. The senior resident stops in to say goodbye at the end of her twenty-four-hour shift.

We are handed off to the last of the great combat nurses. Straight out of a MASH unit, she's the nurse I'd hoped for down the stretch. "You're going to have this baby the way you want," she tells Cecilia, sending us back into the shower. "Keep the door locked," she says. "Your doctor is looking for you."

***

Our doctor strolls in at 9:00 a.m. looking well rested. He says that maybe he was wrong about the C-section. The baby's head is engaged and pressing against Cecilia's cervix. But she needs to dilate six more centimeters before giving birth. That means hours more of severe contractions and pain. He suggests an epidural to numb her from the waist down.

"I want to be able to feel when it's time to push," Cecilia says.

"You will," the nurse promises.

We vote for the epidural.

But the anesthesiologist can't get the damn needle into her back. I watch it bend. He tries again, two vertebrae lower. Finally, he gets it right.

Cecilia is fully dilated at 1:00 p.m. The room is buzzing. The nurse flips the surgical light on. The BLOOD WASTE can returns.

Our doctor, in scrubs and a hairnet, looks like a guy behind the counter at Burger King. Cecilia is on her back. Time to push! Time to bring our son into the world! Wait—one last thing. Cecilia wants the Rolling Stones, loud: *Pleased to meet you, hope you guess my name....*

Deep breath.... Now *push*.... Quick breath... *push*.... Quick breath... *push*.... Now rest. This goes on for an hour.

The doctor picks up a pair of scissors. *Scissors.* Shiny scissors. Damn, an episiotomy. He wants to cut her perineum to help bring out the baby. Cecilia doesn't want this; she'd rather risk a small tear.

She's told him this a hundred times. "Prepare the local," he tells the nurse. She ignores him. Gives me a wink. No question who's in charge here. He protests, and she raises a hand: "We're going to give her a chance."

He puts down the scissors.

With the next contraction, the nurse and I help Cecilia squat on the bed. Now gravity is working with her.

"I feel him coming," Cecilia yelps. Five pushes later, his head crowns—dark, wet hair, a pale scalp. "Look into the doctor's glasses," the nurse tells Cecilia. "You can see him coming out." She gives a final push, and now our son's head bursts out, facedown, into the doctor's hands. He sucks a breath, hungry for air. His body emerges, but his skin looks gray, like death, and I have a moment of genuine panic. But with every breath, his skin will pinken.

2:19 p.m. Twenty-eight hours since Cecilia felt the first contraction. And now he is on her chest, his tiny hands reaching toward her face. Her arms around him. His eyes are huge and slate-blue.

I want to thank the doctor, but I can't talk. He seems amazed himself—no stitches, no cuts. Cecilia looks more beautiful than ever. The baby is nursing at her breast. Cecilia's father pours champagne. "A toast," he says, lifting his Styrofoam cup. "To this wonderful boy, a long life, a healthy one, an interesting one, an adventurous one. On the cusp of the new century, we toast this wonderful Harper."

Tonight, Cecilia and I will sleep together in the narrow hospital bed, the baby on my chest: seven pounds, seven ounces, the weight of my entire world.

Esquire, 1999

UNWED DAD: MARRIAGE IS JUST A MAYBE

Why get married when we're having so much fun? To marry or not to marry.

When my girlfriend of only six months pulled me into her bathroom and showed me the telltale second pink line on a home pregnancy test, the last thing either of us thought about was marriage. We were still disentangling ourselves from recent exes, other marriage proposals (hers) and various bad habits (mine). Our thoughts ran toward, Are we even going to have this baby? How can we? Are we ready for this?

Both of us were in our mid-30s. Clocks were ticking, but this was terrifying. What if she took our baby and ran off with her ex? She meanwhile worried whether she could really count on me. Or whether I would take off on my next freelance assignment and be out of touch. I wasn't exactly somebody who had mastered commitment. The longest I had ever lived with anyone was seven months, with a woman in Santa Fe who shot rats with a pistol.

We waited months before telling our parents that we were having a baby. We were surprised at their reaction. Her parents have been married forty-five years, and mine almost as long. Her mom's response: "Your father was just saying that he hopes you don't think you have to wait until you're married to have a baby." My dad is an ordained minister and we were sure we would get the third degree. But the issue of marriage never came up. It still hasn't. Maybe at night they pray for our salvation, I don't know, but so far they've trusted our decisions.

Had my son been born to a woman I didn't love, I might be some other statistic from the 2000 census—a single father, perhaps, sharing custody. But now I am part of an unwed couple living together, one of 5.5 million such households. Our numbers increased by a lot, 72 percent, over the previous decade. The figures include gay and lesbian couples, although most of the increase is believed to be among couples of opposite sexes. Some, like us, have children.

The statistics were interpreted by various conservative "pro-family" groups as further evidence of moral and social decline. We are accused of hastening the death of the American family, of American values. Are we?

I loved my son's mother before Harper was conceived, and I loved her even more after she delivered him, seeing how hard she fought to bring him into the world. I do not wish to imagine my world without her. Even though our boy wasn't planned, he has never felt like an accident. He is a bridge between us, a living vow. Since we're adding another person to the population of the world, we want to raise a child who has curiosity and imagination. Who is capable of love and who feels worthy of being loved. We're trying to get it right. So far that has seemed more important than any ceremony.

While I was watching Harper roll over and sit up and crawl for the first time, his mother and I were also still learning to be a couple. We were testing the boundaries of our worlds, learning what it means to come home. To have a home, a family.

Sometimes we fall. Sometimes it hurts. We knew it would be difficult, but nobody told us it would also be so much fun—that's been our biggest surprise. I was always afraid of needing someone else so much, of being watched so closely. Though we were spending every night in her apartment, I didn't let go of my bachelor loft until my son was almost one. It had become the most expensive doghouse in history.

He has begun to go to a nursery school a couple of hours every few days. I went one day and sat on the sideline, during what they call the separation phase. He looked over at me only once. His mom went away recently, leaving us alone overnight for the first time. We felt self-sufficient. We knew what to do next. Mostly, he would tell me, "Dada, you have to feed me now."

"Sleepytime," he said.

We are teaching each other, Harper and I. He has his mother's eyes. He's lanky, and he talks in full sentences. He has imaginary friends.

Sometime in the second year, his mother and I started to refer to each other in the presence of others as "my wife" and "my husband." At first it was out of convenience, making reservations on the phone or pointing across a room. But naming is a powerful thing. We had begun to think of ourselves as married, and it felt good. We're committed to each other in a way that's as strong as any marriage we know of.

My girlfriend's father now calls me his son-in-law and jokes that these days, by not being married, we are almost conventional. We have been to weddings and felt simultaneous longing and horror. My girlfriend caught a bouquet, and that seemed to give everybody license to demand that we marry, but we usually don't feel any pressure. People around us know we're a real couple.

We have a few friends to whom it seems important that we marry, but when we press them for why, they say stuff like, "Well, you know, just because you should." Without formal vows, would my parents' relationship have unraveled long ago? I don't know. I do know that on both sides of our families, our parents have given us models of commitment.

We are curious about whether taking those vows would make us feel anything we don't already feel, but we can't know the answer to that. Whether we are married or not, I suspect, will not matter so much to our son. In a sense, he has married us. His presence tells us we are no longer single, that we can't be selfish, that it's not all in our control. I feel no obligation, but the idea of marriage makes me happy now. After all, the three of us have lived in two rooms for more than two years. We've bought a used car.

Today, my father will be with us out at our rented shack by the beach. He will hold my mother's hand, and they will go for long walks. He will play the harmonica. They are each other's best friends.

And who knows? One of these nights, around the fire, we all might start talking about a wedding.

The New York Times, 2001

THE PICTURES

Bosnia's Muslim prime minister longs to be in Hollywood development hell.

Haris Silajdzic, the fifty-one-year-old Bosnian Muslim who is co-prime minister of Bosnia-Herzegovina, has a movie to pitch. He had some other chores to take care of when he was in the United States last week—a meeting with Secretary of State Madeleine K. Albright, a speech on religious tolerance to an audience at the Park Avenue Synagogue that included ambassador-that-was Richard Holbrooke and ambassador-that-probably-will-be Felix Rohatyn—but the main thing was the movie. The film he wants to make is about his homeland, and it is a love story, "There are a lot of Romeos and Juliets in Bosnia," he said.

"I like movies," the prime minister said, puffing on a cigar in the library of the Regency Hotel. "And nobody reads books. I want the largest audience to keep seeing Bosnia. If this crisis can happen in Bosnia, it can happen anywhere."

Built like a welterweight boxer, with sharp cheekbones and a cowlick of brown hair, Silajdzic is a heartthrob back home. He earned his political scars the hard way, serving as the sole prime minister during the most intense years of conflict in the Balkans, from 1993 until February 1996.

The prime minister isn't interested in some earnest little documentary. "I want a big movie," said Silajdzic, who plans to hold out for an executive-producer credit. "If we tell a good story about Bosnia, people will sit even for three hours."

Silajdzic is thinking epic, Cecil B. De Mille style. He wants us to see Bosnia as a home to refugees since the Inquisition, a place where love gets tested. His movie covers five hundred years. "It begins with the expulsion of Jews from Spain in 1492 and their arrival in Bosnia," he said. "I can see the scene. I can hear the Bosnian folk music. The ships with the Jewish refugees heading for Bosnia will cross paths with Columbus's ships on their way to discover America."

Cut to a half millennium later, to a scene in which Silajdzic's current ambassador to United States, a descendant of those Spanish Jews, meets with the American president and "pleads to help end the genocide in Bosnia."

Fluent in English, French, and Arabic, Silajdzic is still not so sure how to speak Hollywood. He has written a three-page treatment, but it has the unsnappy title "The Exodus: A Brief Elaboration of an Idea." A scholar of Islamic history, he has written short stories and poetry, but he has never written a movie. He knows he needs help. He recently took a long meeting in Sarajevo with Branko Lustig, a Croatian-born Holocaust survivor, who produced "Schindler's List." The meeting was friendly, if not terribly successful. "If I go to Spielberg," Lusting told Silajdzic, "I must tell him the story in three words. If I tell him it starts in 1492 and ends now, he will think I'm crazy."

The prime minister isn't worried—at least not about the viability of his movie project. "I hear there are sharks in Hollywood," he whispered, leaning forward. "Do you think they'll steal my idea?"

The New Yorker, Talk of The Town, 1997

EDWARD TELLER— FATHER OF THE BOMB: WHAT I'VE LEARNED

Edward Teller helped build the hydrogen bomb—the most powerful bomb ever invented. He believes he saved the world. Interviewed at 93, in Palo Alto, California.

'm proud to be called the father of the H-bomb. It was necessary.

If not for me, the H-bomb would have been developed in Russia first. In the US, we would now be speaking Russian.

That I spent my life working on weapons, I have not the least regret. I succeeded. I believe that by building the H-bomb, I contributed to winning the Cold War without bloodshed. I am not overly modest.

We now have more than enough nuclear weapons.

Anything connected to war is wrong in some people's opinion. But there is a Latin statement: If you wish for peace, prepare for war.

What makes me angry is danger. When I see something coming and I don't know what to do about it, that makes me angry.

In wartime, things are permitted that otherwise are not permitted.

I was at the Trinity test in New Mexico on 16 July 1945. I was twenty miles away, lying down in the sand with my face turned illegally toward the bomb. I put some suntan lotion on my face and very dark glasses. A spot lit up in the distance. The luminous region spread, more sideways than upwards, and then began to rise, and within a minute it reached the atmosphere—with some imagination you could claim it looked like a question mark—and then the bang arrived half a minute after the explosion. About twenty of us were there on the sand. This was at 6:00 a.m. When I got home, I went back to bed, but I couldn't sleep. I wasn't allowed to tell my wife, and I didn't. She told me what she'd heard on the news—that an ammunition barn had blown up and nobody was hurt. She knew, I guess, and I knew, but we never told each other.

Oppenheimer was against the hydrogen bomb. He said we were making the god of destruction. I thought it was absolutely necessary. At the hearing, they pushed me to answer if Oppenheimer was a communist. I said he was a complicated man, and that I did not always understand his actions, and that I felt safer without him being in the loop. I was one of many witnesses. He lost his high-level security clearance thereafter. I did not label him a communist. I certainly did not. That assertion came from others.

I am the opposite of a warmonger. I've tried to protect us.

President Kennedy called me to the White House. As he said goodbye, he asked me, "After 1945, for a few years we had an atomic weapon and the Soviets didn't. Why didn't we use it?" I found the question scandalous. My answer: I think under no conditions should we use atomic weapons first. I said that to the president.

I told Ronald Reagan my idea about a missile defense system. He liked it.

How well will a missile defense system work? I don't know, but I'm absolutely sure that if we don't work on it, it won't work.

The first atomic bombs had about thirty thousand tons of TNT. The bombs we now have stockpiled are ten times bigger, but they could be easily a thousand times bigger. Bigger bombs are not better. The kind of weapon we now have will blow away the atmosphere into outer space. You make the explosion bigger, you blow away the atmosphere quicker.

There is nothing called nuclear waste, only nuclear materials that we haven't found a use for.

Recently I dreamed of Heisenberg. He was my teacher. He is young in my dreams, at the height of his intellectual power. In my dream we were playing Ping-Pong. We used to play every Tuesday night. I beat him. He went off to Japan. When he came back, he could beat me.

Tarzan is the last movie I recall watching. I didn't see *Apocalypse Now*. Nor did I see *Dr. Strangelove*, but I heard that it's a satire. A character rides a bomb to earth and loves it. I assure you that I would not love it.

Radiation has been overblown by the media.

For a nonbeliever like myself, I'd like to ask the pope: Why didn't you make your God in the Bible a little more credible? Why did you have to say so literally that God made the world in six days? A vague notion of God would be acceptable to me. Why the devil did He not say, "This world is wonderful, what you see is remarkable, and there are many other remarkable things you have not yet seen. And I've done all of them!"

I have regret connected to Hiroshima. We should have dropped the bombs not on Hiroshima but in Tokyo Bay. Ten million Japanese would have seen the blast and nobody would have been hurt. With the Japanese seeing that, we could have ended the war without killing. Or we could have dropped the atomic bomb over Tokyo at an altitude of twenty to thirty thousand feet, at eight o'clock in the evening, so they would have seen it and felt the shock. Hirohito would have seen the bomb and used it to surrender.

Esquire, 2002

THE DEVIL & ARTHUR MILLER

With filming just wrapped on a Hollywood version of The Crucible, Arthur Miller, at eighty, talks witches and Marilyn Monroe.

"**A** witch phoned the film company," Arthur Miller says, pulling a baseball cap low over his forehead. We are just down the road from Salem, Massachusetts, on a drizzly, cold day, walking through the cavernous hallways of an old shoe factory. Actors in overfrocks and leather boots pass by through the hushed rooms in which *The Crucible*, Miller's classic play about the witchcraft trial of 1692, is being turned into a Hollywood film starring Daniel Day-Lewis and Winona Ryder.

"A real witch?"

"Well, she claimed she belonged to some association of witches," Miller says, tilting back his cap, a bemused smile cracking his Mount Rushmore face. "She was concerned about how the witches would be portrayed in the movie; she hoped they wouldn't be maligned." Miller begins to chuckle, a low rumble of unexpected mirth. "When we told her there were no witches in the movie, she said with a rather indignant flourish, 'No witches? But this is *The Crucible*, right?'"

Apparently the witch never read Miller's urtext on paranoia and betrayal, written at the height of Senator Joseph McCarthy's anti-communist crusade in the 1950s. For the record, there are no witches in *The Crucible*, only citizens falsely accused of witchcraft, a crime punishable—in 1692—by death. And that, of course, is the point.

After decades of turning aside offers, Arthur Miller, at age eighty, has finally forged his own screenplay, daring in its sexual candor and moral vision. Nicholas Hytner, who directed *The Madness of King George* with what Miller calls "an operatic panache" that won his confidence, helms the $20 million picture.

Visiting the set with the writer is like entering a Miller family reunion. Robert Miller, 48, a son by the playwright's first wife, is one of the film's producers, and has fought from the start to protect his father's artistic vision; Miller's granddaughter is an extra; and Inge Morath—Miller's spirited wife of the past thirty-four years and an accomplished photographer—is down the hall with her Leica, shooting stills of the cast for an upcoming book.

Surprising Miller yesterday with a cake and a rousing ovation, the cast of nearly 300—some with tears in their eyes—celebrated his recent birthday. It has been a season of festive adulation for Miller. Two weeks ago, he was presented with an honorary degree from Oxford University, and just four nights ago, before a capacity audience at New York City's Town Hall, some of America's leading dramatists paid tribute. Among those offering praise were Edward Albee, John Guare, and David Mamet, who called Miller's work "drama informed by, and always superior to, the political."

To another artist, wearied from the years and softened by the praise, the Hollywood project might have become just a peripheral amusement. But Miller has maintained a regular pilgrimage to the set, a three-hour drive from home. During the first weeks of shooting, he was ferried to the pristine, uninhabited Hog Island, off the coast of Massachusetts, where the town of Salem has been recreated. Fidelity to Miller's screenplay is absolute. There are no last-minute rescues in *The Crucible*. "Other studios asked if we'd consider changing the ending," recalls Robert Miller, "but the deal was, they either shoot the film Arthur wrote or not at all." True to the historical record, by the film's end, nineteen men and women falsely accused of witchcraft will be condemned to hang.

Miller has never disputed that witches existed in Salem. But it wasn't witches or a pact with the devil that led the young girls to strip off their clothes and dance naked in the woods, triggering the hysteria. "Nobody wanted to accept the sexual imagination of these girls. Rather than seeing it as a normal thing for kids, they blamed the devil," Miller says. "And even now we're not that far removed from Salem. The Other is still considered the devil; forced confessions are more common than we want to believe. Too often what we regard as the devil is merely our desires, fears, and guilt—our humanity." Miller sees at the root of the recent conflict in Bosnia the same human desire for purity and cleansing that destroyed Salem. And in the latest headlines from Wenatchee, Washington, where several children accused nearly one hundred local citizens of forcing them into ritualistic orgies in homes and a church, Miller fears the repetition of Salem's false condemnations. In art and politics, Miller has never stopped fighting to protect others from such attacks. His radicalism is legendary and, Miller insists, largely conservative, "in the sense that I'm trying to defend and protect the most progressive human charter I know of, which is the Bill of Rights." To his mind, only adherence to that document prevents citizens from being ruled by fear and helps them maintain the challenge contained in *The Crucible*'s most disturbing question: Is the accuser always holy?

***

With the broad-shouldered ease and measured gait of a rangy, laconic sheriff, Miller strolls across the movie set and into a life-size replica of the interior of the original Salem meeting house, constructed by local carpenters. The towering Miller, with his strong, corded neck, seems no less vigorous now than when actor Dustin Hoffman first saw him thirty years ago as "bigger than life—he looked like a California redwood and sounded like a New York taxi driver."

"The wood is real," Miller says, rapping one of the hewn logs of the massive, balconied room, the original of which doubled as the community church. This is where the 1692 inquisition took place, the audience gripped by frenzy. "It's a reminder of how little is holding us back from chaos. Mankind is prone to that kind of passion, that exaltation with a false idea." Miller sits on one of the benches, shaking his head. His vigilance is fed not by pure pessimism but by a recognition of society's power—good or evil. Influenced by the Bible and Greek classics, Miller was convinced early on of the need for human cooperation. "This whole idea of society is deeply impregnated in my plays," he said in a recent lecture. "It's the same with the Greeks—they couldn't conceive of the individual apart from the city-state. Think of that little political union on the shores of the Aegean. It was very delicate—it could be wiped out overnight by invasion, by disease, by misgovernment. So all those ancient plays are attempts to feel their way into some kind of politics which could save them from destruction."

Miller was born, in 1915, into a strong, ethnically mixed community at the edge of Harlem. His parents were both Jewish. "Growing up during a time of dangerous anti-Semitism," says Miller, shaped his politics, "in the sense that it made me think of the outsiders, the sense of growing up isolated and helpless."

When Miller was a boy, his father owned a prosperous factory that manufactured women's coats, but the Depression hit by the time he was fourteen. His father lost the factory and became a salesman; Miller himself went to work, delivering bread before sunrise. "After the collapse of the banks, if the government had remained above it all—helpless—a lot of people thought there would be a revolution or social dissolution," Miller has said, recalling the early '30s. "The government, at that point in our history, seemed to be the sole hope for reordering our system—Social Security was created so old people wouldn't be dying of hunger; programs were created so that families like mine, which had mortgages that they suddenly couldn't pay, wouldn't be thrown in the street."

As an adult, Miller watched America go through a sudden "breaking of charity," as he calls it. Anti-communist hysteria, fueled by McCarthy and the House Committee on Un-American Activities, was sweeping the country. In editorials and petitions, Miller and others had denounced the hearings—in which leftist sympathizers were hounded about their "anti-American" reading habits and their sexual behavior. But for many, McCarthy was justified by the Communist victory in China and Russia's first successful atomic test: The Reds were aiming to overthrow America. By 1954, 73 percent of Americans polled said they would turn in neighbors or friends "whom they suspected of being Communists."

Miller had already felt the blow of McCarthyism when his play *Death of a Salesman*, despite winning international acclaim and the 1949 Pulitzer prize, was picketed by the American Legion, forcing a Midwest tour to shut down. Miller and his play were condemned as subversive for showing the baffled salesman Willy Loman believing in the capitalist system and yet ending up a suicide; meanwhile, from the radical left, Miller was rebuked for the play's failure to advance a Marxist political agenda. Miller knew that comparing the anti-communist hearings to the witchcraft trials would earn him more enemies. "As an artist, writing a play was the only way I knew to fight back," he now says.

He had first heard about the witchcraft trials while in college, "when I had the demented idea that I'd be a historian." But it wasn't until 1952, when he was thirty-six, that Miller walked into the Salem courthouse and asked for the court transcripts. There Miller found his flawed, tragic hero, a local farmer named John Proctor. Based on "hints of scenes, offstage" in the transcripts, Miller imagined Proctor, after sleeping with his teenage servant girl, Abigail, watching with guilty horror as she goes on to lead the mob of witch-hunters; in an attempt to win him for herself, Abigail accuses Proctor's own wife, who is then jailed as a witch. Finally, condemned as a wizard himself, Proctor refuses to speak out against others to save his own life, with words inspired by the court transcript: "I like not to spoil their names. . . . I speak my own sins; I cannot judge another. I have no tongue for it."

Driving home from Salem in 1952 after a week of research, Miller heard on the car radio that his friend, the director Elia Kazan, had that day gone before the House committee and named names. The next month, it was Miller's onetime hero, the radical playwright Clifford Odets. Lee J. Cobb, who originated the role of Willy Loman on Broadway, followed a year later.

What outraged Miller was not that his colleagues, most fearing blacklisting, had capitulated, but that the "state had required its citizens to get down on their knees, having committed no known crime. The government knew the American Communist party was no threat, and their few members might as well be praying somewhere in the Himalayas for all the relevance they had."

The Crucible was produced on Broadway in 1953, and on opening night Miller felt "the sheet of ice come over the audience as they realized what they were watching—an indictment of the hearings and of our failure to challenge their authority." Despite winning a Tony award for best drama, the play couldn't find a Broadway audience, and the cast took drastic pay cuts to keep the show running. The problem was not just politics. "The director had staged the play as a kind of Dutch painting," Miller now says, laughing, "you know, like the picture on the cigar box." Within a year, *The Crucible* had its first European production in Brussels, but the State Department refused to renew Miller's passport to travel there. Less than two years later, the play opened Off Broadway in New York, with a young, largely unknown cast performing the play as Miller had written it, "desperate and hot." It was a success, running for nearly two years.

***

Three years after *The Crucible* opened, Miller himself was summoned before the House committee. He had been in Nevada, awaiting a divorce from his first wife, when he received his subpoena; it was already public knowledge that Miller would wed Marilyn Monroe, whom he had met years earlier when she was an unknown actress. The committee claimed it was searching for "communist infiltration" in the Broadway theater, but the chairman of the House hearings, Representative Francis Walter, offered Miller an out: If Monroe would pose shaking hands with the chairman, Miller would not have to testify.

I approached the subject of Monroe heedfully, since the very morning of our interview the *New York Post* had reported under the headline "Miller Goes Punchy Over Marilyn"—that Miller had slugged a journalist at Sardi's, after he was asked: "Do you ever have dreams about Marilyn Monroe?" Miller, who once said he doesn't talk about her "unless some stupid jerk says something about it," then reportedly returned quietly to his meal, "seemingly buoyed by his bravado." (Miller later told me his version: "I just told him to get the hell out of there. I walked him backward about four steps.")

But when I bring up Monroe, as we sit in the movie's production office, Miller's voice is relaxed and unguarded. "She was against the committee. Like most actors, she felt Hollywood was being persecuted unfairly," he tells me, "but nobody around her was being assaulted. It was just in the air. And don't forget, there was a strong contingent in Hollywood—like Gary Cooper and a fellow named Reagan—who were very cooperative with the committee."

What was her response to the chairman's offer? "Absolutely no deal," Miller says. "Marilyn wasn't political, but she'd battled censors before. She was adamant that I stand my ground."

The day after they rebuffed his offer, the chairman grilled Miller, he remembers, "as if I were an espionage spy of the highest level." Miller was apprehensive, knowing that he might be jailed. He admitted to the committee that he attended "four or five" meetings of communist writers in order to "locate my ideas in relation to Marxism . . . I went there to discover where I stood finally and completely. I listened and said very little."

But his reply, when asked to betray others who had also attended a Communist party meeting, was a virtual paraphrase of Proctor's: "I am trying to, and I will, protect my sense of myself. I could not use the name of another person and bring trouble on him." For his refusal, Miller was convicted of contempt by a federal judge and sentenced to one month in prison and a $500 fine. His conviction was overturned a year later on appeal.

Though the committee was clearly publicity-giddy, they never subpoenaed Monroe, who wisely stayed away from the hearing room. "They didn't want to be seen as the committee that was hounding Marilyn Monroe," Miller says. "The public would have been outraged. Marilyn, a communist? It was okay for them to go after me—"

"The egghead?"

"Exactly. What did they have to lose?"

Among the reasons Monroe was never called, Miller adds, "was the committee's own puritanical blinders. They didn't believe you could have a tight skirt and an intellect. They just saw her as a dumb blond. She was a walking scandal to the provincial, conservative mentality of the McCarthy era, because of her frankness about sexuality." Miller leans back on the sofa, hands clasped behind his head, clearly delighted at the memory. "Remember when she was asked by the press, 'What do you wear when you sleep?' and she answered, 'Chanel No. 5'? It was outrageous!"

***

At lunch, cast members approach Miller and ask him to sign copies of the screenplay.

"This and a dollar fifty," he laughs, "will get them a subway token." But sign he does, a small gesture of thanks. He goes on to laud his actors. "Daniel Day-Lewis is perfect for the part. If he'd been around at the time, I would have cast him in the original stage production," Miller says.

Lurking always, insistently at times, under Miller's social grace is his fierce self-confidence. Morath says of their thirty-four-year marriage, "In Arthur's life, Arthur is the one who is important. He's marvelous, wonderful to be with, and we keep each other amused, but you'd better be strong."

His friend Robert Whitehead, who originally coproduced Miller's *A View From the Bridge* and produced *After the Fall*, concurs. "What Arthur always felt, deeper even than his pain or anger, was that he was a great writer, and that was the most important thing in the world. Writing, by its nature, is a selfish, spooky thing. Life is reduced to how it can be grist for the creative process."

Miller needed such confidence over the years to withstand the vicissitude of critics. Whitehead observes, "Of course, as Willy Loman knew best, the making of money is what counts as success in America. *Salesman* put Miller in a category where he was always compared to himself. And if he came up lacking, in the critics' eyes, it's because Arthur had moved on."

When a critic dismissed a recent Miller play for having been "made to last," Miller could only laugh wryly. "Anything that's thought through is suspect of not being true. It's as though *Hamlet* was done off-the-cuff." Such self-assurance in his art and activism may strike some as hubris, but Miller balances it with unsparing candor about the contradicting impulses of his own psyche. Reflecting on his adaptation of Henrik Ibsen's *An Enemy of the People*, Miller says he had no problem relating to the title character, Dr. Thomas Stockmann, who, expecting praise when he finds a contagion in the town's mineral springs, is instead condemned by the townspeople, who rely on the springs for tourist income. "The town did not want to be saved," Miller says, "but Stockmann wants to be perceived as heroic. As a metaphor, it's perfect—all that self-aggrandizement, I understand it completely."

Miller must have realized that such aspirations toward heroism might be fed when, in 1965, he accepted a four-year term as president of International PEN, a worldwide association of writers committed to bringing attention to human rights and free-speech abuses. Miller was reluctant to accept, until he was told it "might actually save lives."

Over the next thirty years, long after his presidency ended, Miller would petition government leaders and travel to support writers in need, making trips to Turkey with Harold Pinter and to Pinochet-era Chile with William Styron. Says Karen Kennerly, executive director of PEN American Center, "I don't know of any other American writer who has devoted so much of his life to these issues."

Indeed, Wole Soyinka, the Nigerian writer, credits Miller with saving his life in the 1960s when he was imprisoned during the Biafran civil war. A letter Miller sent, pleading for Soyinka's release, claimed he was an important writer and a good friend. The message was given to Soyinka's captor, General Yakubu Gowon, then head of the military government in Nigeria ("Of course it was a lie," Miller now says. "I didn't know Soyinka's work, had never met him.")

"Is this from the man who was married to Marilyn Monroe?" the general asked the messenger. The messenger said yes, and the sufficiently impressed general subsequently released the writer, who went on to win the 1986 Nobel Prize for Literature.

Such good news is rare, Miller knows only too well. Days after Miller and I first met, the Nigerian playwright and human rights activist Ken Saro-Wiwa was executed, despite protests from around the world. "Had the campaign started a week earlier," Miller asserts, "it might have saved him."

That regimes imprison and torture writers, Miller says, is "a perverted form of respect. The writer is the soul of the people. You kill the spirit of the people, that's the idea. Paradoxically, leaders want desperately to be celebrated by artists. [Former Israeli foreign minister] Moshe Dayan used to suck up to writers all the time. He openly said, 'In the end, what the artists say about a politician is what sticks.' You just have to look at what Shakespeare did to Richard II."

Though he jealously guards his writing time, Miller has not relinquished his activism. In Connecticut, last September, at a gathering of legal experts and reporters studying the problem of forced confessions, Peter Reilly, a forty-year-old musician, introduced Miller as the man "without whose help I might have spent the better part of the last twenty years in a jail cell." In 1973, when Reilly was eighteen and a high school senior, he was arrested for allegedly butchering his mother. After an eight-hour interrogation, with no physical evidence linking him to the crime, Reilly, in an exhausted state, signed a confession. He was convicted of manslaughter and sentenced to six to sixteen years in prison. Refusing to believe that Reilly had committed the murder, neighbors mortgaged their houses to raise bail and defense funds. The interrogation had been tape-recorded, and Reilly's supporters sent Miller, who lived only a half hour away, transcribed portions. They hoped that the author of *The Crucible* might be interested in such a case.

Reading the transcripts, Miller became convinced of Reilly's possible innocence. "After four decades of writing dialogue," Miller said, "I could not help seeing that Reilly's responses to questions were not his own but were being steered by his questioner." He added at the September gathering: "After Peter had kept repeating that he had no memory of having attacked his mother, the police interrogator happily assured the boy that in fact he most likely would have wiped out the memory if he had done it, but remembering it or not, it was perfectly all right to confess to killing her anyway."

"Miller didn't just sign his name to a petition," says Donald Connery, who wrote a book on the case, and who edited an examination of wrongful imprisonment, *Convicting the Innocent*. "Miller got him a private detective, professional forensic help, and actively investigated the case himself. He recruited top legal and media assistance, which led to developing new evidence about other suspects, and he got *60 Minutes* involved. He was vital to the correction of a very serious injustice."

The verdict was overturned. "It was a completely cooked-up case," Miller now says. "There are a lot of people—young, backward, or frightened—who, to get out of an immediate problem, will confess. Most of these pass in the dark, and we never know. False confessions are a big industry in this country. It's the same procedure under any regime. They want a confession. We all feel better if we say we've locked somebody away."

Now Miller finds himself fighting another case in his home state involving a possible false confession, this time by Richard Lapointe, fifty, who suffers from a brain disorder called Dandy-Walker Malformation. "He's childish," Miller says. "He's got a reasonable IQ, about 90. But he's a baby. This guy has trouble standing on his own feet. He's charged with raping and garroting his wife's eighty-eight-year-old grandmother. Two years after the crime they arrested him and got him to confess. The confession includes details that never happened." With no direct evidence linking him to the crime, Lapointe was convicted and sentenced to life without parole plus sixty years.

Invited by the Connecticut Bar Association in June 1994 to accept an award for public service, Miller chose to plead Lapointe's case before the ballroom of three hundred judges, prosecutors, and attorneys. Miller called for Connecticut to follow the lead of those states—Alaska, Texas, and Minnesota—that require the videotaping of all interrogations and confessions. An appeal to the state Supreme Court is now in progress, arguing that since there was no recording made of Lapointe's interrogation, it was a violation of due process.

Miller bristles when I suggest that some might regard his political activities, including his globetrotting human rights work, as radical chic. "The alternative is silence in the face of possible injustice," Miller says. "We live in a time when radical attempts to right injustices have become objectionable. The new conservatism tends to celebrate this view. I've had too many experiences where, in fact, protests did save people who would have been killed. Are you going to call that radical chic?"

This gets to the heart of Miller's core belief: the need for engagement in society, whether artistic or political. Standing up to the hysteria in Salem cost Proctor his life, "but to have stayed silent," Miller says, "would have cost Proctor his life also—his sense of himself, his truth. Why didn't Hamlet say, 'The hell with it, so he killed my father, so what?' It was his fate. Proctor had to go forward. That's the unstoppable action. That's what drama is."

***

Last May, Miller refused to stay silent when he found himself the subject of one of Newt Gingrich's political parables. In a speech to a group of artists—including Wendy Wasserstein, Walter Mosley, Melanie Griffith, and Joanne Woodward—assembled on Capitol Hill to lobby for continued congressional support of the arts, Gingrich told them: Look at Arthur Miller; he wrote all those plays and never got any money from the government.

Upon learning that he had been used as an argument to deny funds to other artists, Miller fired off a missive to the House speaker, naming himself as a recipient of government support at two "brief but crucial" times. Miller pointed out that he had earned $15 a month feeding laboratory mice during college; without that money, paid through the National Youth Administration, he wrote, "I couldn't have paid my room rent and would no doubt have had to leave school." Upon graduation, having won a playwriting award and already committed to a theater career, he got into the WPA Writers Project—$22.77 a week for six months, during which time he wrote a play about the conquest of Mexico.

Many of the subsidized writers, Miller now believes—apart from Orson Welles—were "second-rate talent writing inferior scripts." But for Miller the issue is more fundamental than money for individual artists—he knows they will survive regardless, like weeds in the sidewalk. "The real question," he wrote Gingrich, "is whether the American artist is to be alienated from his government or encouraged by it to express the nature and genius of his people." Miller never got an answer.

Miller doesn't expect any American politician—"pygmies in the hall of giants"—to follow Proctor to the gallows for an idea. "Power is their business, not truth. Politicians always have a way out," he says. In a *New York Times* op-ed piece last year, Miller satirically endorsed buying senators, preferring "legalized corruption" to hypocrisy.

Not since the sectarian fights within the radical left in the '30s, Miller says, has he seen "such violent hatred and paranoid suspicion as those ruling mainstream politics in America today." Then Miller laughs. He's not above venting a little gratuitous annoyance. "Phil Gramm reminds me of the mayor on *The Dukes of Hazzard*," he says, smiling icily. "You know the one, he only had one line—'Follow that car.'"

The Crucible remains Miller's most produced play, and it seems not a day goes by when it is not onstage somewhere. "I can almost tell what the political situation in a country is when the play is suddenly a hit there," Miller wrote in *Timebends*. "It's either a warning of tyranny on the way or a reminder of tyranny just past."

When the Chinese writer Nien Cheng, after spending six and a half years in solitary confinement, saw a production of *The Crucible* in Shanghai, she could not believe that a non-Chinese had written the play. "Some of the interrogations," she reported, "were precisely the same ones used on us in the Cultural Revolution."

***

What accounts for *The Crucible*'s endurance, "apart from its being a good play," Miller believes, "is that the paranoid streak is just below the surface in the world. Audiences recognize it in the play, and it's resolved by a moral statement: John Proctor is tarnished, but he arrives at a decision. I think the human race wants to hear that—it must be."

When I last see Miller on *The Crucible* set, he has just watched a rough cut from the first weeks of filming, including the highly charged sexual scene in which the young girls of Salem are caught dancing naked in the woods, trying to conjure their sweethearts. He first imagined the scene more than forty years ago, but never dramatized it until he wrote the screenplay. Now, having seen the footage, he sits quietly, and, finally, in a hushed, low rasp, says, "It's just overwhelming, absolutely beautiful." Weeks of shooting remain, including the gallows scenes, but this is Miller's final visit to the set.

Miller believes the role of the artist is "to push the edge—not just dancing naked on the stage, but the edge of what we regard as holy." When theater is memorable, says Miller, "it has a strong civic side. For most of history, theater was involved with the fate of the kingdom, and the importance of power—it's . . . essential to the Greeks, who regarded people who were nonpolitical as idiots." Though Miller calls playwriting "a young man's game," only last year his play *Broken Glass* was awarded England's Olivier Award for best play. Tomorrow he'll be back at work on his next play—he's already sixty pages into it. There's also a libretto to oversee for an opera adaptation of A *View From the Bridge*, which will premiere at the Chicago Lyric. The new play is "manifestly in search of itself," says Miller. "I may leave it that way. It's a comedy." He pulls on his thick overcoat, readying for the long drive home from Salem. "You live long enough, it all seems like a comedy."

George, 1996

SOUL SEARCHING WITH FRANCIS CRICK

The Nobel Prize winner wants to open your brain, literally. Francis Crick on free will, artificial intelligence, and his hunt for the human soul.

Forty years ago, the Nobel laureate, Francis Crick, co-discovered the double-helix structure of DNA—the master molecule that contains the genetic code. Today, in his office overlooking the Pacific at the Salk Institute in La Jolla, California, Crick is studying a copy of William Blake's etching of Isaac Newton depicted naked, sitting in a cleft of rock. Newton is bent with his compass in hand, trying to decipher the mysteries of our universe.

It was Blake, the eighteenth-century poet and artist, who warned that scientists, in trying to decipher that which should remain indecipherable, would "turn that which is Soul & Life into a Mill or Machine."

If Blake were alive today, it seems a fair bet that Crick, and his new book *The Scientific Search for the Soul*, would provoke his ire. In the book, Crick, now seventy-seven, sets out to discover whether what we commonly regard as soul or consciousness is actually a machine, a neural machine. And he implores fellow scientists to tackle "the experimental study of consciousness and its relationship, if any, to the hypothetical immortal soul."

Crick's "astonishing hypothesis" declares that all of our interior states, joys and sorrows, our memories and ambitions, even our personal identity and the cherished notion of free will, are "no more than the behavior of a vast assembly of nerve cells." And with an audacity that Blake would have found heretical, Crick also claims to have located the seat of free will inside the brain.

The desire to map what we call consciousness—what Crick also calls awareness—is not new. But with the publication of his book, Crick has joined one of the hottest scientific debates of the decade. And his views, he admits, are a "head-on contradiction to the religious beliefs of billions of human beings alive today."

Crick comes to the consciousness wars armed, of course, with impressive credentials. However, at the age of thirty-one, when Crick, having spent the war years designing mines to blow up German merchant ships, took stock of his scientific credentials, he found himself with a "not-very-good degree," redeemed somewhat by his achievements at the Admiralty. "No published papers at all," he says.

Determined to get work in England's postwar science boom, he applied his "gossip test" to his own life. Crick's gossip test says that the things you are talking and thinking about, you should go to work on. The two subjects which he settled on in 1947 for his life's work touched on problems which, in many circles, seemed beyond the power of science to explain. "What attracted me to them was that each contained a major mystery—the mystery of life and the mystery of consciousness. I wanted to know what, in scientific terms, those mysteries were." Six years later, he and James Watson had discovered the structure of DNA, widely regarded as the most important biological discovery of the twentieth century, earning them both a share of the prestigious Nobel Prize in medicine. Fifteen years ago, after arriving at the Salk Institute, Crick turned his attention to the study of the second subject which he had chosen to investigate in 1947, the mystery of consciousness.

"What is the neural basis of consciousness?" he asks. "That's the problem. Obviously, it's very mysterious." But people have forgotten, Crick reminds us, how mysterious the nature of genes appeared as late as 1943. Molecular biology, at the time, was considered a sloppy field. "The phrase Watson uses is 'intellectual chaos.' That is exactly the state of our ideas of the brain—intellectual chaos. Lots of ideas rumbling around but nothing very clear. People arguing about things that will probably turn out to be pretty fatuous eventually—it's just chaotic."

To Crick, the key to understanding the mystery we call the soul does not lie in religion, philosophy, or psychology, but in neurons. Most current ideas about the brain, he argues, will not survive a detailed understanding of how it works; the idea of a soul or mind separate from the brain and not penetrable by our known scientific laws is probably an outdated myth, he says. Looked at in the perspective of human history, he argues, the main object of scientific research on the brain is not merely to understand and cure what may afflict us, but "to grasp the nature of the human soul." Whether this term is metaphorical or literal is what Crick is trying to discover.

Unlike dualists, such as neuroscientist Sir John Eccles, who believe in the "ghost in the machine," Crick doubts whether there is any need for a spiritual concept of a soul to explain behavior. Religion, he claims, is "based on evidence which by scientific standards is so flimsy that only an act of blind faith makes it acceptable." In fact, he suggests, raising his white, prominent eyebrows that give him a devilish air, "if the members of a church really believe in a life after death, why do they not conduct sound experiments to establish it?"

The only way to understand what we regard as the soul, Crick argues, is to understand how nerve cells in the brain behave and interact. But with one hundred thousand neurons beneath every square millimeter of the brain's cortical sheet, and with the human cortex containing some tens of billions of neurons—comparable to all the stars in our galaxy—how does Crick suggest scientists go about this?

***

Experimentation on the living human brain is limited by ethical considerations. "Most people do not object to an experimenter fixing electrodes to their scalp in order to study their brain waves," Crick says, "but they do object to having a portion of their skull removed, even temporarily, so that electrodes can be stuck directly into living brain tissue." Crick suggests an alternative strategy, which seems, at first glance, deceptively simple. If you want to learn how consciousness works, concentrate your research on the visual system—on how we see. That our eyes are the windows to our soul is not just an aphorism to Crick.

"Visual awareness is an example of consciousness," Crick says. A yellow-and-blue hang glider drifts into view outside his office window, swooping and diving above the Pacific. He leans forward. "We have a very vivid picture of the world. The question is how that is produced in the brain."

Visual perception combines attention with short-term memory, but by standards of exact sciences, Crick points out, we don't know how our brains produce the visual awareness that we take so much for granted. We can glimpse fragments of the processes involved— the way the eye responds to light—but we lack both the detailed information and the ideas to answer the most basic questions: How do we see color? What is happening when we recall the image of a familiar face?

Although the main function of the visual system is to perceive objects and events around us, the information available to our eyes "is not sufficient by itself to provide the brain with its unique interpretation of the visual world." In a recent special issue of *Scientific American* devoted to the mind and brain, Crick and his collaborator for the past several years, Christof Koch, a computation and neural-systems specialist from the California Institute of Technology, speculated on how the brain uses past experience —"either its own or that of our distant ancestors, which is embedded in our genes"—to help interpret the information coming into our eyes. "Your eyes—or we will say—your brain," they wrote, "must find the best interpretation of visual symbols in the light of its past experience. Thus, what the brain has to build up is a many-level interpretation of the visual scene, usually in terms of objects and events and their meaning to us."

Crick suspects that visual awareness—and perhaps consciousness itself—involves the cortex and also the thalamus, which he calls the "organ of attention." All senses (except smell) have to pass through the thalamus, the gateway to the cortex. Consciousness, Crick says, depends "crucially on thalamic connections with the cortex."

The cortex consists of two separate sheets of nerve cells, one on each side on the head. These cortical sheets are, in Crick's words, "about the size of a man's handkerchief" and are folded so as to fit on either side of the skull. Often referred to as gray matter, the cortex consists mainly of neurons or nerve cells, which are electrical and chemical signalers.

The job of a neuron is to receive information, usually in the form of electrical pulses, from other neurons. Some of these connections are local—they only go a fraction of a millimeter, or at best, a few millimeters—but others leave the cortical sheet and travel some distance before entering another part of the sheet or going elsewhere, for example to the thalamus or the spinal cord. These longer connections are often covered by a fatty sheath, which enables the signal to travel faster and which gives this tissue a somewhat white, glistening appearance. Forty percent of our brain is made of this "white matter," and this is crucial to Crick's notion of just how much communication there is within the brain. This communication system handles both explicit and implicit representations of the visual world. The explicit representation is symbolized without further extensive processing. An implicit one contains information but needs further processing to make it explicit. Crick hypothesizes that our brain must produce an explicit multilevel symbolic interpretation of the visual scene in order for us to "see" it.

Some people, Crick says, may find it difficult to accept that what we see is only a symbolic interpretation of the world—it all seems so like the "real thing." Unlike, for example, the Hindu belief that what we see is "maya," or illusion, and that nothing we see actually exists, Crick argues that the world does exist but that "we have no direct knowledge of objects in the world."

And though Crick believes that visual consciousness is, in part at least, about the very route information takes through the brain, and most importantly, where it gets to and which neurons are firing, he confesses, "I myself find it difficult at times to avoid the idea of the homunculus—a little man in our head directing it all. One slips into it so easily." And if all this sounds a bit complex, Crick sums it up neatly, grinning, "As Lewis Carroll's Alice might have phrased it, 'You're nothing but a pack of neurons.'"

Some of Crick's colleagues at the Salk Institute may have wondered if Crick himself had gone through the looking glass last year when he bounded into an afternoon faculty tea announcing that he'd located the seat of free will in the human brain. Crick describes free will as the "feeling that one is free to make personal choices."

What prompted this announcement was an account he'd read by his colleague, the neuroscientist, Antonio Damasio, of a woman who prior to recovery from brain damage had suffered a loss of will. The importance of studying cases of brain damage, Crick says, is that they show which parts of the brain are necessary for functions such as consciousness or free will. For a month the woman appeared unresponsive, lying in bed but with an alert expression. She could follow people with her eyes but did not speak spontaneously. She gave no verbal reply to any question put to her, though she appeared to understand because of the way she nodded in reply. When the woman recovered, she said she had not been upset by her inability to communicate even though she'd been able to follow conversations; she hadn't talked because she had had "nothing to say." Her mind had been "empty."

Crick was intrigued. "I immediately thought she'd lost her will and wondered where the damage was." The damage turned out to be in or near the anterior cingulate sulcus, a region Crick was delighted to learn receives many inputs from higher sensory regions, and, as he had guessed, is at or near the higher levels of the motor system where movements are planned. "Take the complex act of swimming," he says. "How does the brain plan it all?" According to Crick, one of the functions of visual awareness is to plan movements. "What is the connection between seeing something and the part of the brain that plans and executes movements?" he asks. "Clearly, it's about neurons firing."

Reading more case histories, Crick stumbled upon the "alien hand" syndrome, a kind of brain damage in which one of the patient's hands makes simple movements, which the patient denies he or she willed. A patient's left hand, for example, might spontaneously grasp some object put near it, though the patient denies that he or she is responsible for the movement. In some cases, the patient is unable to get the hand to let go and has to use the right hand to detach the left hand from the object. One patient found that he couldn't make his "alien" hand let go by his own willpower, but he could make it release its grasp by saying, "Let go!" in a loud voice. These cases fascinated Crick, especially when he learned that the damage was again in or near the anterior cingulate sulcus, substantiating his theory that this is the seat of free will.

Some scientists have speculated that the seat of consciousness is located in the hippocampus, a small, seahorse-shaped part of the brain that stores for a few weeks or more the codes for new long-term, episodic memories before the information is conveyed to the neocortex. Crick disagrees, citing the case of a patient who had his hippocampus system on both sides knocked out after an injury. While the patient couldn't remember anything that happened more than a minute before, he could see and talk perfectly well, which convinced Crick to rule out the hippocampus system as the seat of consciousness.

The trouble with speculation about consciousness, Crick admits, "is that the damage is rather crude. If we could make nicely controlled brain damage on people, we could find out how the brain works, but we're not allowed to do that—quite rightly."

A plastic model of the human brain is on a shelf nearby. When I asked Crick to show me the location of free will, he cautioned, back-pedaling a bit, "Now, this is still highly speculative." From the walls of his office, portraits of Einstein and Darwin stare down at us. He cradles the brain in his hands and says, rubbing the anterior cingulate sulcus with his forefinger, "Free will is most likely located here, but we think there probably is a frontal component as well. It certainly isn't at the back of the brain." He lays his thumb against the primarily motor area: "Yes it's definitely near here, but it may depend on interactions with this frontal region."

When reminded of the widespread belief in the existence of the soul separate from the body, he pauses, looks up from the model. "Surely, if almost everyone believed it, that is itself prima facie evidence for it. But then some four thousand years ago, almost everyone believed the earth was flat."

Smiling now, Crick reminds me that his friend, the evolutionary biochemist Leslie Orgel has teasingly suggested that there may be a religious peptide in the brain. Seeing that this speculation is going on the record, he settles back in his chair. "Oh, I don't think there is quite a religious peptide, but there is probably something in people's brains that makes some of them more susceptible to religion than others. Whether it's inherited or not or whether it's something produced by early training is like the question about homosexuality. There's no reason why all that shouldn't be found out."

***

Eight paintings of nude women line Crick's office at his quiet, airy home in La Jolla. They were painted by his wife, Odile, whose studio adjoins his office. It was Odile's drawing of a double helix that accompanied the now legendary seven hundred-word article in *Nature*, the British science magazine, announcing the 1953 discovery of the molecular structure of DNA.

The Cricks have been married forty-four years. Odile with bright hazel eyes and a quick laugh says of their courtship, which began when she was translating captured German documents in London, "I'd never been with a scientist; it took some getting used to. When we went on our first picnic one very romantic afternoon, Francis gave me a lecture on gravity." They are both laughing now. "I simply asked," Crick says, "if she knew how far up gravity went."

On Crick's desk is a home computer—nothing fancy, a simple workstation. Mostly he uses it for accounting and domestic func-tions. He finds computers, he says, "a bit obsessional" and prefers to work out his science theories in longhand. When the discussion turns to the comparison of the brain to a computer, Crick cautions that this parallel, if carried too far, leads to unrealistic theories. In the first place, he explains, a computer works much more quickly than the human brain. And while the operations in a computer are largely serial—one after another—the arrangements in the brain "are usually massively parallel. For example, about a million axons go from each eye to the brain, all working simultaneously."

The loss of a few neurons is unlikely to alter the brain's behavior appreciably. "In technical jargon," Crick says, "the brain is said to 'degrade gracefully.' A computer degrades catastrophically—even small damage may cause havoc. A typical neuron in the brain can have anywhere from a few hundred to many tens of thousands of inputs, but a transistor—a basic unit in a computer—has only a few inputs and outputs. Yes, Crick argues, computers can be programmed for extensive number crunching, rigid logic, and playing chess, but when faced with tasks that ordinary humans can do in a rapid and effortless way, such as seeing objects and understanding their significance, even the most modern computers fail. And yet in the storage and retrieval of information, the computer is much more precise, and it's clear that memory is stored in a computer in a different way. But for Crick, the fundamental difference is that while a computer has been deliberately designed by engineers, the "brain has evolved over many generations of animals under the pressures of natural selection."

The mysterious aspects of consciousness might disappear if we could build machines that had the "astonishing characteristics of the brain and if we could follow exactly how they worked," Crick says, but he does not hold much hope that in the near future such a machine will be built. "Perhaps they will be more like the brain of a frog or even that of a humble fruit fly. Until we understand what makes us conscious, we are not likely to be able to design the right sort of artificial machine nor to arrive at firm conclusions about consciousness in lower animals."

The problem of consciousness, Crick believes, will be far more difficult to solve than DNA. "But you have to remember," he says, "that we didn't know how simple DNA was. For all we know there may be a simple answer to this one, but it doesn't seem likely. The brain is a more complex system. DNA was much earlier in evolution—the answer had to be simpler or it wouldn't have got started. DNA has been there for three-and-a-half billion years. Consciousness is relatively late. Don't forget, modern man has been here for only a hundred thousand years or so."

For Crick, the image of the brain as an impenetrable black box is outdated and self-defeating. "Most of the mysteries of life are not seeable—all of science depends on roundabout methods. If it were straightforward, it would be done straightway." Our secret weapon in brain research, Crick suggests, may not be theorists and computation experts, but people who are using computers to solve practical problems. In the workplace, "people have to produce gadgets that work, which is what evolution has to do." For example, the post office had to produce a machine that can read handwritten zip codes. Gadgets like this "probably, will give us ideas of what happens in the brain, because evolution tends to produce gadgets as well. In that sense, evolution knows nothing about theory; it only knows how to build gadgets."

***

From San Diego, it's two hours over the mountains to the house Francis and Odile Crick have recently built in the Anza Borrego desert. Driving down Montezuma's Grade toward the desert floor, the steep, boulder-strewn descent is reminiscent of the barren, atavistic landscape at the start of *2001: A Space Odyssey*. In the distance is the dying Salton Sea, which historian Bill deBuys calls a "place where consequences collect."

This is where Crick goes to get away, his hermitage. And like his work in neurobiology, which he turned to after decades of pioneering work in molecular and developmental biology, he is slowly mapping the territory out there as well, walking trails each twilight through the desert with his wife, learning the names of wildlife and vegetation: creosote bush, ocotillo, elephant tree. It is to this desert in blistering afternoon sun that we have come to talk about the culture that Crick foresees if indeed scientists find that the soul is simply a machine.

He says he will be very surprised if developments in science "don't make radical changes in the way educated people think of themselves." And still, he knows, like the debate over evolution, vast numbers won't be influenced—"usually for religious reasons."

In Crick's culture, psychology will be a hard science, and philosophy departments will house researchers who also have degrees in biology or neurobiology. And words like conscious and unconscious, he suggests, may be replaced by processing unit or awareness unit. (Already, Patricia Churchland, one of the few philosophers in the world with a detailed knowledge of neurons and the brain and also of neural networks has, at Crick's urging, an adjunct appointment at the Salk Institute.)

"Many people think all things can't be explained by chemistry and physics, that it's explainable only as something outside science— a life force. That was also the view about our genetic inheritance before we knew about DNA. Most scientists believe there isn't anything else." But, he admits, "that's still a hypothesis." He knows at this point, based on the scientific data, that he couldn't convince a skeptic. "They would just say, 'That is just your prejudice.'" He adds, with a chuckle, "Which is not to say that your prejudice may not turn out to be right."

He admits that some people will be disturbed by the religious implications of the book, especially those who believe there is life after death. "The implication that it might not be true and that we might be able to show it scientifically will be disturbing." The others who will be disturbed, he says, are those "who don't actually believe in life after death but who haven't faced up to the implications of it yet." Though beliefs change slowly, the church in Crick's culture will increasingly have to reckon with science. "Scientifically, we know if you are out in a thunderstorm, the chances are increased that you may be struck by lightning. We no longer think that it's because we didn't sacrifice ox recently to Jove. Look at the beliefs people had in the past. Do you really think it was sensible to look at the entrails of a chicken to predict what was going to happen in the future?"

He predicts that while scientists "are basically tolerant of religion, that may not last. There eventually will be conflict. We might even see religious science wars. One would hope that could be avoided." People outside the scientific culture, Crick says, "are naturally beginning to feel threatened by scientists. And they are wise to feel that. They will be threatened."

I ventured to ask if Blake was right to warn of scientists turning that which is soul into machine? Are there some things that should remain undeciphered? Crick is smiling now—a mischievous, ironic smile. "You know," he says, "Blake used to sit outside naked in the garden with his wife and talk to angels. Now I've got nothing against sitting naked in the garden, but talking to angels—don't you find that a bit odd?"

The desert sun has begun to sink behind the San Ysidro Mountains, its nearly autumnal colors settling over Crick's face, softening his angular features. I wonder if, in his scientific view, there is room for mystery. "Well, what do you mean by mystery?" he asks. "It's a mystery how the darn thing behaves, whether it's in the activities of neurons or not." And as if he implicitly understands what the next question must be, for it is the universal question of an anxious and God-yearning people—If soul is only a metaphor, a story we tell to comfort ourselves, and if there is no ghost in the machine, then what does that leave us with?—Crick leans forward, his face reflecting the last light of this fading day, and says, "Think about the size of the universe. In Shakespeare's time they had no idea how big the universe was. Does your knowledge today remove the mystery of it? It seems to me what you lose in mystery you gain in awe."

Omni, 1994

INSIDE SOUTH AFRICA

Novelist Nadine Gordimer and poet Jeremy Cronin were born into South Africa's "big white country club." Cronin spent seven years inside maximum-security prisons for his underground work with the ANC. Gordimer wrote to him in prison, and a friendship formed. In a country now under emergency rule, both writers keep fighting to dismantle the apartheid regime.

This morning I learn that one more Black man has been hanged in South Africa; this one was a poet, Benjamin Moloise. At noon my radio will report shops looted, whites attacked, cars burned. This evening, my television will flash pictures of every white man's nightmare—police firing shotguns at Blacks marching on white suburbs, killing Black children who'll be buried as martyrs, seeding endless generations of replacements. The reporter will inevitably say, *South Africa is in flames.* Then I'll turn off the set and the flames will die until tomorrow.

A year ago, I visited South Africa. A white middle-class Midwesterner, fresh from college, I imagined South Africa as a testing ground—an embattled land confronting one of the most explosive dilemmas of our time. I spent seven months driving across the country, seeking out ostrich farmers, revolutionaries, Communists—anyone, Black or white, who would talk. My most rewarding days were spent with writers.

Though ruled for nearly forty years by one of the most hated regimes in modern times—one that has placed all but intolerable pressure on dissenters—South Africa has not produced an influential literature of white exiles in Paris, London, or New York. Instead, extraordinary work—fiction, plays, and poetry—has been written *inside* South Africa by white writers who remain in their beautiful, tormented land, fighting the enemy at close range. Some are bomb-planting revolutionaries; others settle for the quiet but inexorable language of revolt.

Nadine Gordimer—sixty-two, the author of sixteen books—is South Africa's major international literary voice and an unrelenting critic of the white regime. Jeremy Cronin, thirty-six, is an important new voice in South African poetry. He has spent seven years in prison for supporting Black revolution. His award-winning collection of poems, *Inside*, was published after his release. Both writers remain in South Africa, continuing the fierce logic of their battle against government tyranny.

***

The day I visited Nadine Gordimer in her quiet, sylvan neighborhood in Johannesburg, the Black townships that ring the city were in flames. Police, moving in with tear gas and rubber bullets, were calling it a "revolutionary situation." It was the start of the bloodiest year in South Africa since 1976, when hundreds of Black children were killed by government forces in Soweto, the notorious township ten miles from Gordimer's home.

The two-story house sits behind a high white wall on a street lined with lavender-petaled jacarandas. I was escorted from the front gate by a gardener, who showed me past neat flower beds to the house, where Gordimer's husband, a cordial man trailing a glossy hunting dog, ushered me into a museum-size front room. Bookshelves lined one wall, art magazines lay on small tables, steady winter light streamed through tall windows. It seemed an eerily perfect place from which to bear witness to the final years of a dying white order. When Gordimer entered smiling, in taupe cords and a sweater, I was surprised: I had prepared for a rapt bird. (Alan Paton, author of *Cry, the Beloved Country*, told me that when he wrote Gordimer that her novel *Burger's*

Daughter "expressed warmth," she responded, "It is not warmth that makes a good novel.") But I find her lithe and hospitable, with the dark, intent eyes of an affable llama. Before starting the interview, I present her with a gift—a Polaroid of Eudora Welty celebrating her seventy-fifth birthday at Bill's Burger House in Jackson, Mississippi (a friend has sent me the picture). "Goodness," Gordimer says, "I first went to see Eudora in Jackson back in 1959. I've always admired her work. You know, I've just finished that book on her childhood." Standing near the window, Gordimer reads the inscription on the cake: "God Bless America and Eudora on Her 75th Birthday." Then, eyebrows arched in elegant reproach, she says, "I would have put Eudora first."

Gordimer serves tea, then perches in her chair, knees hugged to her chin, and talks about the similarities between growing up in the old American South and in South Africa. "There was some kind of relationship—there still is—between white people and Black people in the South that doesn't exist in New York even today. Many of my friends in New York, they just don't know any Black people." She takes a quick breath, then states firmly, "But I don't think that's important. I think it's much more important for people to have their rights than to have white friends."

Such talk about rights is not just easy talk. Not here in South Africa, where the white Nationalist regime has promised to use whatever force necessary to keep twenty-four million Blacks from sharing equal political and cultural rights with the country's five million whites. So far that promise has been kept with brutal efficiency: the morning of my meeting with Gordimer, three more Blacks died in clashes with government forces near a small gold-mining town thirty miles away, where as a young girl Gordimer wrote her first stories.

"The problem in South Africa," she says, "is that we're still one big white country club. I should know. I'm a member, perforce born into it." There is none of the moral evasion in her voice that I've heard from other, less honest South Africans—liberal politicians, Afrikaner farmers, assorted businessmen. She confronts her complicity, exposes her cowardice; and in life and work, she prepares for the day when there will no longer be an exclusive country club.

"The terrible thing is," she says, "that you become accustomed to living in this permanent state of violence being done to people all the time. In that way apartheid has been so very successful, terribly successful."

"Can you imagine a day of political judgment—for whites?" I ask.

"'What did you do in the Great War, Daddy?' I think there is a kind of death-wish longing in many of us, for something to be as clear-cut as that. Just as people talk about a night of long knives—that it will all happen with fear and horror, perhaps, and with great relief, that our struggle will be over."

Gordimer does not see herself as particularly heroic for staying. "Exile as a mode of genius no longer exists," she said in a recent lecture. "In place of Joyce we have the fragments of works appearing in *Index on Censorship*. These are the rags of suppressed literatures, translated from a babel of languages; the broken cries of real exiles, not those who have rejected their homeland but who have been forced out—of their language, their culture, their society."

White writers in South Africa, she stresses, do not face the pressure that her friend Milan Kundera, the exiled Czech novelist, faced in his native land, where he was banned from publishing anything. "It's so wrong," she says sternly, "to say to Athol Fugard or Nadine Gordimer, 'You're so brave.' We're not brave at all. They tolerate us because we're white. We're disliked, and we're a thorn in the flesh, but we have a certain liberty."

Three of Gordimer's books have been banned in South Africa; her novel *The Late Bourgeois World* was banned for ten years. The bans are now lifted, largely because of her international reputation, but censorship laws remain in active force. She is a fierce champion of Black writers in South Africa, many of whom have suffered detention, frequent bannings, and exile.

Long an admirer of Bishop Desmond Tutu, winner of the 1984 Nobel Peace Prize, Gordimer supports the United Democratic Front, the liberation movement, much of whose leadership is in jail, charged with treason against the state. With her son, a graduate of Columbia University's film school, she recently completed a documentary on resistance in South Africa. The film was shown at the United Nations, and has been distributed worldwide. "There are things a writer can do, between writing and going to jail," she says. "I feel you should do what you are particularly fitted to do. I just felt, since I'm a writer and my son is a filmmaker, here was something I could do."

Being a dissident, she admits, gives her life a schizophrenic quality. "There I am spending a Sunday afternoon at a political meeting in Lenasia, one of the townships—which I do often—and then, coming back, I'm invited to some white friends' for supper. And you feel quite disoriented: you don't know where you are the tourist. Sometimes it's possible to feel like the tourist at the white supper."

In America recently, Gordimer noted that she is often asked how she has avoided jail in South Africa, and whether this means she has not written the book she should have written. "Can you imagine this kind of self-righteous inquisition being directed against a John Updike for not having made the trauma of America's Vietnam War the theme of his work?"

"Art," she declares unabashedly, "is on the side of the oppressed." But she refuses to turn her art into propaganda—for any side. "There are some writers who became writers because they became so indignant and were stirred to creativity. I began writing out of a sense of wonder about life, a sense of its mystery, and also out of a sense of its chaos."

Having kept that sense of wonder, despite the entanglements of white privilege and liberation politics, is Gordimer's brilliant advantage as a writer. In the novel *The Conservationist* she sympathetically portrays a shameless white South African capitalist. In *Burger's Daughter* she explores the radical legacy of a white Communist's daughter after her father dies in a political prison. In her 1982 story "A City of the Living, a City of the Dead," a Black woman betrays a Black revolutionary. How does a white woman write of this?

She crosses to the bookshelves. "One of my very first stories concerned a man who'd lost his leg. Now, what do I know about what it feels like to lose a leg? From an early age, I simply accepted that writers are very strange creatures," she says, reaching into the shelves. "How did Faulkner know so much about Blacks in the American South?" She pulls out an early volume of Eudora Welty's stories, opening it with great affection. "How did Eudora know so much about that traveling salesman? You see, writers have this queer extra faculty, or we wouldn't be writers—we could only sit down and write autobiography."

When I ask if there is a chance of peace in South Africa, she listens to my earnest question, and then, like all great storytellers, she tells a story from her own day, her own people, and allows her listener to draw his conclusion. "I was talking by chance to someone yesterday—in fact, he was cutting my hair. He recently became very religious. Having been a wild man-about-town, he now spends every evening poring over the Bible; it's the most wonderful book in the world, and he's now learning it backwards. He's so full of a sense of sin, wanting to be a better person, going through self-doubt and self-examination. But he stops absolutely short of anything outside his behavior toward his own personal circle. Which I find very interesting. I said to him, 'Have you read anything in Black liberation theology?' He'd never heard of it!"

***

Jeremy Cronin personifies the unsleeping vigilance of the young and radicalized white in South Africa. The first time I met Cronin was in a Black ghetto outside Cape Town. It was a bright Sunday afternoon. Table Mountain, four miles away, was wreathed in clouds. Yachts sailing the turquoise Atlantic were visible on the horizon. The ghetto was just off the airport highway, in an area known as the Flats. According to apartheid laws, whites were not allowed in without police permission. But there were no police present as hundreds of Blacks, and maybe two dozen whites, gathered for a political rally in a gymnasium. When I arrive, banners reading RELEASE THE PRISONERS OF APARTHEID and TAKE FORWARD THEIR FIGHT are pinned to the door. Onstage, a Black woman wearing a purple beret is leading the swaying crowd in a familiar song. Though the words are in Xhosa, one of the dozen languages spoken in South Africa, the tune is familiar.

> *This land is your land*
> *This land is my land*
> *From the Great Limpopo*
> *To Robben Island*
> *From the Indian Ocean*
> *To the Kalahari*
> *This land was made for you and me.*

After three hours of songs and speeches by Black leaders just released from prison, and by mothers with sons in prison, and by union leaders who know they'll soon be going to prison, Cronin is introduced. The woman in the beret calls him "comrade" and informs us that Cronin has just spent seven years in prison for operating underground in the African National Congress, the outlawed Black liberation movement. There is a reverent hush in the gym. We all lean forward as Cronin, with jug ears, cleft chin, and hair banged short as a monk's, reads his prison poems. But he doesn't just read; it's a cajoling, stalking performance. Perhaps it's his stark looks, or his need to bring his art to the ghetto, which remind me of Brecht acting in his own epic theater.

He tells of staying in Pretoria's hanging prison with death-row prisoners. "On Wednesday mornings, you'd hear the *woosh, woosh, woosh* as the trapdoors below the gallows were opened and three more were gone. One day I heard the voices of three Black political prisoners singing militant freedom songs as they waited for the gallows. The guards called them '*fokken* terrorists,' not realizing what I was. Those heroic voices challenged me to learn how to speak with the voices of this land." His final poem, "Death Row," pays homage to those prisoners. When he finishes, the crowd, hands clasped high, surges into an anthem.

Later, when Cronin and I talk, his voice is quiet and measured, distinctly South African, with its long *a's* and clipped *i's*. The son of an officer in the South African navy, Cronin had been writing poetry before his imprisonment under the Terrorism Act. "At first I adopted a poetic distance from white society, letting my poems speak for themselves. I had yet to find a way to link my lyrical interests to my growing need to become more politically responsible in the South African situation. The poetry became more difficult, and I became much more serious about my politics."

In 1971 Cronin left South Africa for Paris with his wife to earn a master's degree in philosophy. Instead of exiling himself, he secretly joined the African National Congress, trained for underground work, and returned to South Africa to start a clandestine propaganda cell. "I was very aware that the likelihood of ending up in jail, at best—if not dying in some torture chamber—was in the cards. But it was the path that needed to be followed if one wanted to stand shoulder to shoulder with Blacks in the liberation struggle."

Back in Cape Town, Cronin worked at night in a rented garage with two other activists. "We had several typewriters and an old duplicating machine. Everything had to be done very carefully— rubber gloves, illegal names, mailing thousands of anti-apartheid letters while police were watching the mailboxes to track us down. Our function was to prepare, politically, the people, to steel them for more resistance."

Pamphlet bombs, made by attaching explosive charges to buckets, were also used. "We'd leave these at bus stations, timed to go off at rush hour, when many Blacks had to catch buses to the ghettos. The buckets would explode into the air, hundreds of pamphlets scattering all over. It was a spectacular way to distribute literature—people rushing and grabbing the pamphlets quickly and distributing them on the buses before the police arrived," he explains, smiling.

In July 1976, Cronin was arrested by security police. A month earlier, the police killing of the Soweto schoolchildren had sparked nationwide riots, leaving approximately one thousand Blacks dead. At Cronin's trial, he and other "white Communist agitators" were blamed for causing the riots. "I honestly think the government was surprised to see huge mass hatred for apartheid," he remembers.

"They felt that the stirring amongst Blacks could not be a result of Black leadership, let alone Black anger or unhappiness."

Six months after he was sent to prison, Cronin's twenty-six-year-old wife died. "I had been able to see my wife for a half-hour through a little glass plate once a month while in prison. Something was wrong—she was getting very thin and having severe headaches. One Saturday she didn't arrive. She had collapsed on the plane coming to visit me. At the hospital a huge tumor was found on her brain, requiring an operation."

After the operation, his wife's mother came to see him in prison. Through a plate-glass window with two guards present, Cronin learned that his wife had died. "My mother-in-law was weeping and couldn't get the words out. She just held up her finger and showed me the wedding band."

He was not allowed to attend her funeral. Kept in solitary confinement, he began writing poetry again, which, he says, "allowed me to locate my suffering in a world in which other people suffer as well."

According to prison regulations, all poetry was forbidden unless submitted to prison authorities. "Those were conditions I was not prepared to comply with," Cronin says. "I composed mostly in my head, whispering and memorizing, walking three steps up, three steps down my cell. It gives many of my poems a three-step rhythm. Once out of prison, it was really a process of getting the poems down on paper."

He talks quietly, a knuckle in the cleft of his chin. There is no self-pity in his voice. I ask why, and he explains, "For someone as political as I am, it's hard to feel self-pity. There is the magnificent heroic example from millions of ordinary South Africans who don't allow the frightening conditions of the country to beat them down."

When Cronin was in prison, he had an extensive correspondence with Gordimer. In 1981, two years before Cronin was released, Gordimer published in *The New Yorker* "A Correspondence Course," a story inspired by those letters. "Jeremy taught me the art of writing prison letters, and it really is an art," Gordimer recalls. Cronin says,

"We weren't allowed to write about politics, or the prison, only about family matters. To fool the censors we created imaginary uncles and told fables." The letters were checked by censors for hidden meanings, encoded messages, and invisible ink. Two of Gordimer's letters did not pass the censors, and were cut to ribbons. "Nadine's writings have never been submitted to such perusal—not even by the most analytical of literary critics," Cronin says.

Now that Cronin is out of prison, he is back in the liberation movement. He has also married again. "I regard myself as an ordinary foot soldier in the African national struggle," he says. "Sometimes," he admits, "I slip away from my comrades for a few hours to write. With the boycotts, the strikes, there is so much to do, and just finding the time to write is a form of exile.

"I'm concerned," he says, "that our literature does not simply become a kind of export business, like the old ivory trade. We must ask ourselves what it means to the people here if our theater simply becomes the latest rave on Broadway, or our literature gets front-page reviews overseas. The most important audience is here.

"Some of my poetry belongs to a white poetic tradition. But if you're performing in a fairly noisy hall where the people have just listened to a fiery political speech, you have a problem with the white poetic tradition."

Cronin knows that freedom is not around the corner. As sunlight plays across his face, he looks toward Table Mountain. "The regime remains vigorous in its racist policies. But there is a place for writers in that struggle. We must move beyond simply smashing idols. We are faced with the aesthetic task of assisting and strengthening an emergent national culture. The talent is there—we see it each day in the poetry and drama of the Black townships. Under apartheid that culture will not flourish. The struggle for political and social freedom is also, of course, a cultural struggle."

When I last see Jeremy Cronin he is dressed in a turtleneck, keeping a vigil from the sidelines of a trade-union rally in another Black township. He is not here just to read; he is here to help organize. Thousands of Blacks are seated in rows in front of him. In three weeks they will go on strike, igniting South Africa once again. I feel I'm watching the poet at the edge of his poem "A Naming of Matches."

"Row upon row in closed ranks they wait for their baptism of fire.
This one, *Single.*
This one, *Spark.*
This one, *Prairie Fire.*"

Vanity Fair, February 1986

ACKNOWLEDGMENTS

I am indebted to Mark Warren. His story instincts are nonpareil, as all his lucky writers at *Esquire* and later at Random House know. A life-changing editor and friend, his talent is rivaled only by his compassion and generosity.

My thanks to John Sack for pointing the way.

Tina Brown gave me a first shot as a journalist at *Vanity Fair*. Murray Cox at *Omni* let me go soul-searching with Francis Crick. My thanks to: Trip Gabriel at *The New York Times*; Susan Morrison at *The New Yorker*; John F. Kennedy Jr. and Biz Mitchell at *George*. Freelance gamblers all.

Most of these stories were reported during my years as a Contributing Editor at *Esquire*. My gratitude to *Esquire*'s editorial and production team, including David Granger, Ed Kosner, David Hirshey, Peter Griffin, John Kenney, Bob Scheffler, Kevin McDonnell, Andrew Chaikivsky, John Hendrickson, and Lisa Hintelmann.

My thanks to the *Esquire* photographers, who often guided me into stories, and whose images lived so vividly beside my words—Kevin Carter, David Goldblatt, Greg Marinovich, Margaret Sartor, Ron Haviv, Antonin Kratochvil, Mark Peterson, Brian Smale, Frank Ockenfels, Larry Sultan, and Al Silfen.

There was no greater champion of the written word than Reynolds Price. Godfather to my son, he watches over us all.

Robert Coles and Bruce Payne introduced me to Nadine Gordimer's astonishing novel, *Burger's Daughter*, which, along with Athol Fugard's plays and friendship, helped steer me toward South Africa. Those journeys were further informed by the counsel of Kevin Sack, Joseph Lelyveld, and Marsh Clark.

Terry Sanford and Joel Fleishman at Duke University believed in the power of journalism and made sure working reporters had a home on campus—it made all the difference.

My gratitude to Cormac McCarthy for loaning me his agent, Binky Urban, who negotiated my first *Esquire* contract in 1994, which included, at Cormac's insistence, the cost of a flak jacket and helmet.

My ongoing thanks to Lenny & Joyce Berkman, Terry McDermott, Marc Levin, Robert Leaver, Bone Sloan, Mike Marangu, Shawn Ryan, Alex Harris, Jeff and Lettie Anderson, Lizzie Mickery & Mike Harding, Tim Clemente, Angela Dallas, Rob Kenneally, Jessica Weigmann, Heather Schroder, Maggie Gwinn, Danielle Epstein, and Justine Amodeo.

My Rockford crew of fifty years, you keep it real: Per Brodin, Tim Sutton, Paul & Barb Osborn, Sue McClellan, Barb Bell, also Dan Cooper, Lars, Lew, Mark, Keith, Brad, and Vinnie.

My thanks to Ben Harper, beloved friend, a reporter at heart.

For eagle-eyed proofreading of this collection, I thank Ciela Courtright and Susan Mee. Praise to Alex Belth, keeper of the flame. To Dan Kruger, all respect, the journey continues.

My parents, Don and Cory, worked as chaplains and first responders, including a stint in NYC after 9/11. I thank them for always leading with empathy. Randy, Bob, Jeff, and Donna, I'm honored to be your brother.

My father-in-law, Gregory, and my mother-in-law, Veronique, herself a former journalist, took us into their Los Angeles home as

I reported "Riot Baby." Over the months, Gregory read and championed every draft as the story came together.

My thanks to Carmen—for nourishment and so much more.

Harper and Ondine watched the writing of many of these stories, strips of words cut-and-pasted across various floors and later on screens. I'm grateful to be in your lives. Every day I learn from you.

Cecilia has my heart, and the best editorial chops in the family. Always ready for a caper. A lifetime of stories and love ahead.

Lastly, with deepest respect and thanks to Mike Sager, friend, OG, and co-conspirator, who, by harnessing the means of production, made this book possible.

PERMISSIONS

"Nick Nolte is Racing the Clock to Repair the Damage" was first published in *Esquire*, October 1999. Reprinted with the permission of the author.

"A Deeply Misunderstood Mass Murderer" was first published in *Esquire*, December 1997. Reprinted with the permission of the author.

"An American Family—A True Story of Siblings Who Fell in Love" was first published in *Esquire*, July 1999. Reprinted with the permission of the author.

"Soldiers in the Army of God: The Future of the Armed Abortion Conflict" was first published in *Esquire*, February 1999. Reprinted with the permission of the author.

"A Few Good Nazis" was first published in *Esquire*, April 1996. Reprinted with the permission of the author.

"The Hunter Becomes the Hunted" was first published in *Esquire*, March 2011. Reprinted with the permission of the author.

"Riot Baby" was first published in *Esquire*, May 2002. Reprinted with the permission of the author.

"Into The Heart of Whiteness" was first published in *Esquire*, August 1994. Reprinted with the permission of the author.

"The Right To Bear Sorrow" was first published in *Esquire*, March 1995. Reprinted with the permission of the author.

"At Home with M.O.M." was first published in *Esquire*, July 1995. Reprinted with the permission of the author.

"He Only Comes Out at Night—Billy Bob Thornton" was first published in *Esquire*, December 2000. Reprinted with the permission of the author.

"The Beginning—On Becoming A Father" was first published in *Esquire*, June 1999. Reprinted with the permission of the author.

"Unwed Dad: Marriage is Just a Maybe" was first published in the *New York Times*, June 17, 2001. Reprinted with the permission of the author.

"The Pictures" was first published in *The New Yorker*, June 2, 1997. Reprinted with the permission of the author.

"Edward Teller—Father of the Bomb: What I've Learned" was first published in *Esquire*, January 2002. Reprinted with the permission of the author.

"The Devil & Arthur Miller" was first published in *George*, February 1996. Reprinted with the permission of the author.

"Soul Searching With Francis Crick" was first published in *Omni*, February 1994. Reprinted with the permission of the author.

"Inside South Africa" was first published in *Vanity Fair*, February 1986. Reprinted with the permission of the author.

"Nick Nolte is Racing to Repair the Damage" was reprinted in *The Best American Magazine Writing–2000* (ed. Clay Felker), published by Houghton Mifflin Company; then again in 2003 in *Esquire's Big Book of Great Writing: More Than 70 Years of Celebrated Journalism* (ed. Adrienne Miller), published by Hearst Books.

"The Beginning" was reprinted in 2010 in *Esquire: Fathers and Sons* (ed. David Katz), published by Hearst Books.

"Riot Baby" was reprinted in *The Best American Nonrequired Reading–2003* (ed. Dave Eggers), published by Houghton Mifflin Company.

ABOUT THE AUTHOR

Daniel Voll has written for *Vanity Fair, The New Yorker,* and *Esquire,* where he was a long-time contributing editor. A National Magazine Award finalist, his articles are included in *Esquire's Big Book of Great Writing, Best American NonRequired Reading,* and *Longform's Best War Stories.* His fiction has appeared in *Story, Redbook,* and many literary journals. A Duke graduate, Voll has taught writing and storytelling at UC-Irvine, where he earned his MFA, and in places as varied as Belize and a locked psychiatric unit in Rockford, Illinois. Also a playwright and screenwriter, he has written and produced for television, film, and documentary. Two of his documentaries have been short-listed for the Academy Awards.

ABOUT THE PUBLISHER

The Sager Group was founded in 1984. In 2012 it was chartered as a multimedia content brand, with the intent of empowering those who create art—an umbrella beneath which makers can pursue, and profit from, their craft directly, without gatekeepers. TSG publishes books; ministers to artists and provides modest grants; and produces documentary, feature, and commercial films. By harnessing the means of production, The Sager Group helps artists help themselves. For more information, please see TheSagerGroup.net.

MORE FROM
THE SAGER GROUP

The Stacks Reader Series

The Cheerleaders: A True Story by E. Jean Carroll

An American Family: A True Story by Daniel Voll

Flesh and Blood: A True Story by Peter Richmond

An Accidental Martyr: A True Story by Chip Brown

Death of a Playmate: A True Story by Teresa Carpenter

The Detective: And Other True Stories by Walt Harrington

Soldiers in the Army of God: A True Story by Daniel Voll

Original Gangster: A True Story by Paul Solotaroff

The Dreamer Deceiver: A True Story by Ivan Solotaroff

Mary in the Lavender Pumps: A True Story by Joyce Wadler

The Strange and Mysterious Death of Mrs. Jerry Lee Lewis
by Richard Ben Cramer

General Interest

The Stories We Tell: Classic True Tales
by America's Greatest Women Journalists

New Stories We Tell: True Tales
by America's New Generation of Great Women Journalists

Newswomen: Twenty-five Years of Front-Page Journalism

The Devil & John Holmes: And Other True Stories by Mike Sager

Lifeboat No. 8: Surviving the Titanic by Elizabeth Kaye

Stopping the Road: The Campaign Against a Trans-Sierra Highway
by Jack Fisher

Notes from the Road: A Filmmaker's Journey through American Music
by Robert Mugge

What Makes Sammy Jr. Run?: Classic Celebrity Journalism Volume 1,
edited by Alex Belth

Into the River of Angels: A Novel by George Wolfe

See our entire library at TheSagerGroup.net